THE ETRUSCANS

THE ETRUSCANS

and the survival of Etruria

CHRISTOPHER HAMPTON

'Il passante sentiva come un supplizio
il suo distacco dalle antiche radici.'
—*Eugenio Montale*

LONDON
VICTOR GOLLANCZ LTD
1969

© Christopher Hampton 1969

575 00299 9

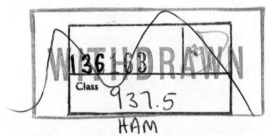
Printed in Great Britain by
The Camelot Press Ltd, London and Southampton

To the people of Italy,
an exile's tribute

CONTENTS

ILLUSTRATIONS

ACKNOWLEDGEMENTS

For permission to include copyright photographs in this book my
thanks are due to the following:

The Villa Giulia for plates 1a, 1b, 2a, 7a and 7b, 8a and 8b, 9b,
10a and 10b, 11, 14a and 14b, 15a and 15b.

Messrs Alinari for plates 2b, 6, 13, 16.

Messrs Anderson for plates 3, 9a.

The British Museum for plates 4, 5, 12.

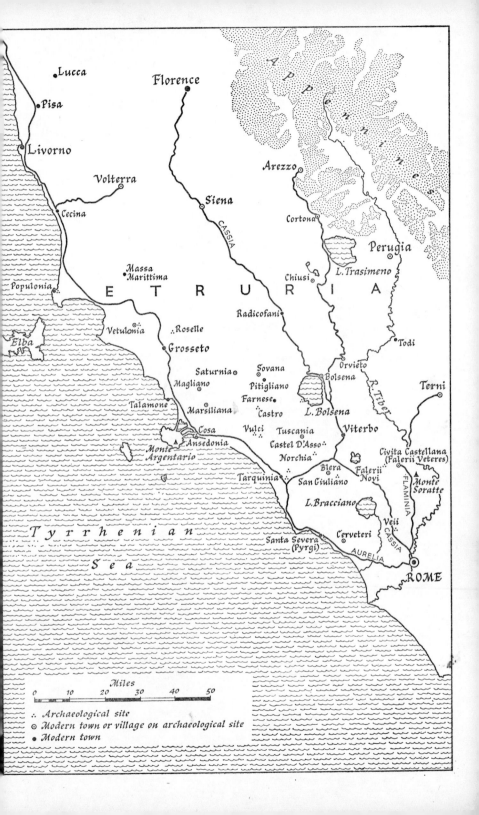

INTRODUCTION

ITALY IS FULL of contrasts, full of dichotomies and contradictions, of echoes and fragments and the hints of continuity. Its roots go back to the prehistoric beginnings of European society; back beyond the "civilizing" political systems of the Romans to the first stirrings of the Mediterranean spirit; to the ancient religions through which man had made "his profound attempt to harmonize himself with nature and hold his own and come to flower in the great seething of life";[1] to the Eastern Mediterranean —the Minoans, the Mycenaeans, the Lydians, the Phoenicians; to Cyprus and Assyria, to Egypt and Greece.

But what is so extraordinary is that in Italy there should have been such a continuous and renewing development out of these roots. From the Etruscans in the North and the Centre and the Greeks in the South to the Romans; from the early Christian Church and the growth of the Mediaeval city-states to the Christian Empire and the Renaissance; from the Risorgimento and the birth of the nation to the modern Italy of post-war technology in the atomic age, there has been a strange and oscillating series of creative explosions. The Italian spirit seems again and again to have been able to renew itself, even out of all the ravagings of foreign invasion. And we are left with a bewildering legacy of creative example and experiment. It is startling enough to find oneself living in a city as flourishing as Rome is after 2,500 years of vicissitude. But Rome is after all only one aspect of the fertility of the Italian spirit. And though it may appear to be the most dominating because it is perhaps the most apparent symbol of this fertility, it is not by any means the most representative or characteristic. Indeed, it can be said that Rome and the worlds it represents is in many respects an exotic and alien growth upon Italy's Mediterranean roots, in spite of the legends associated with its beginnings.

Curiously enough, one of the things that struck me most when

I emerged for the first time from under the great canopy of
Rome's post-war station was that section of the Servian wall,
with its huge squared blocks of yellowish-brown stone, which
the roof's curve actually enframes. At the time, it was simply
among the first of many first and startled glimpses of the splendours of the city, and I did not associate it with that period
immediately before the institution of the Republic when the
Etruscans ruled Rome. But I was able to register the intimacy of
the relation between it and the superb horizontal grey-white lines
of the station; and it has since remained for me a symbol of the
close and deadly relation between the Etruscan and the Roman
worlds.

It was the sense of the significance of Rome and of its contrast
to that other world of the Etruscans, rooted in the soil of Italy,
that gave this book its theme. Rome became the irritant, the
goad, to discovery. For here in Rome the old world and the new
—the old continuing realities of Roman power as they have been
propagated and renewed within the empire of the Church, and
the overgrowth of the modern metropolis, the capital of a newly
secularized nation with its bureaucratic structures and its obsessive
demands—exist in startling and sometimes strangely intermingling contrast. And out there in the Campagna lie the villages,
the towns, the ruins and the fragments, images of a totally non-
Roman world that still persists even in the formulation of its ways
of life; as it still retains, among its enfolding greens, its lipped
rock, its ravines, its sunken valleys, the silent voices of the old
Etruscan spirit, "like the grass of the field and the sprouting of
corn".[2] For though "relentless enemies" had "ruined the cities,
wrecked the temples and crushed the people of Etruria",[3] yet
time has now revealed them to us and brought them back to us as
witnesses to a triumph that belongs to a pre-Roman and a post-
Roman Italy; to a world in fact of the untampered being of man,
and "his striving to get into himself more and more of the gleam-
ing vitality of the cosmos";[4] a world in which life could come to a
natural flowering.

Living as we do today in a world dominated by political
systems in many ways similar to those by which Rome itself, as

Republic and as Empire, triumphed over the ancient world, many of us are conscious of the need to get back to the old organic continuities, to rediscover in ourselves something of that sense of the natural flowering of life which we get from the Etruscans and the Greeks, or even, for that matter, from the men of the Middle Ages and the Renaissance. We need no Hobbes to exhort us, as he did the seventeenth century, to live "in a world that can be measured, weighed and mastered", and "confront it with due audacity".[5] In the twentieth century such a world surrounds us, and every day we are being measured, weighed and mastered by it. For the "vast system of imposture" that Hobbes was attacking has not been subdued. It has simply taken different forms—forms governed by the insistent principles of a materialistic view of the world. We have survived the Industrial Revolution into the Atomic Age, a period of astonishing and almost unbelievable discovery, only to find ourselves exposed to problems, threats and dangers we can hardly cope with, let alone confront. It is not an audacity of measurement we need, but the rediscovery in ourselves of a due respect for the human truths. We need to know that though "geometry is the mother of the sciences", men are the unscientific children of life.

Of course, the inventions of science have greatly enriched humanity. We have "measured, weighed and mastered" so much more than even Hobbes could have conceived possible. Immensities of space and time have shrunk. Continents have become points of transit. A hundred miles is but a two-hour drive. Whereas to the Etruscan, Etruria was a world of physical distances and great variety, to us it is a district, four or five hours from one end to the other. We have partially conquered nature to contain her to our needs. There seems so much to affirm—the amenities and comforts and facilities surround us. This, we say, is progress. We are in control. As for the human being—man, mere man, that "passional phenomenon", that "forked radish"—he can only be controlled and mastered when at last we have taken all the living passion out of him, the sap, the irrational vital sap that makes him so resistant to conformity. And when we've done that, when we've made a robot of him, we can finally establish a triumphant unity, a proper functioning of all the parts of the machine. This is the logic of it. And to what an end, looking a little under the surface at the lost quiet and the lost stillness and the tampered being of man? Looking to where that quiet and that stillness and that being still exist? Between the two there is the gulf of centuries, of worlds. And it is then that one begins to doubt our progress and the optimisms that acclaim it.

In Italy there is the city, an amalgam of these worlds, confused, frenetic, beautiful, unresting, restlessly intent upon the shaping of the future, an accumulation of the struggling of centuries. To the city-dweller and the pilgrim the city is "habitable and reward-ing", a concentration of the social complex in the structure of which we can "read through the eye the variously rich and close human life which the architecture mirrors and honours and provides for";[6] managing to retain something of its splendour, rich with art and architecture; and yet dominated by the mechan-isms and the techniques of the twentieth century, filled with noise and movement signifying the supremacy of abstract principle and the machinery of speculative business.

And then there is the country and its inordinate quiet, its old secret rhythms of change and growth, its villages, its farms, its cultivated silences, its peasants. And here sometimes the contrast can seem total, where with hardship and poverty the old world lives on almost unchanged, linked to the customs of 3,000 years and more in continuity. Here toil is an act, intimately relating a man to his environment. Here work (so long as he has it) is a dimension of his life, to which he bends and breaks; a context which maintains him and contains him, living and dying. And who's to say that this is not as fit for him as the boredom of an office job, the killing tensions of the city, the neurotic prosperity and comfort we would offer him in place of what he has? Any-way, whatever we may think or feel upon this subject, the fact remains that there is a process going on in the modern world which must inevitably affect the integrity and equilibrium of a man's life, and which has no respect for the "peripheries of the individual". This process, with its patterns of violence and dis-cord, its blatant exploitation of sensational events, is insidiously at work on us, seeping through and swamping the felt certainties, the fundamental verities "belonging to our peace".

It is therefore all the more exciting to discover that in Italy one can be a witness to a world the nation has not superseded or absorbed, a world of independent cities, towns and districts that resists conformity; that still retains its human equilibrium, with roots that go back to the Etruscans and the Greeks, and from them through all the great achievements of the Italianate spirit. That this world must disappear (as it disappeared under the unifying impact of Roman power) is perhaps inevitable, given the ruthless conformist ambitions and needs of the modern world. It will be inexorably edged out, crushed, as the Etruscans were. National unity and economic survival are at stake, and the non-conformist is an anarchist. But perhaps it will not disappear for good. Perhaps it will re-emerge in some new form, as the Etruscan spirit re-emerged in Mediaeval and Renaissance art. For the present, however, much of it still remains, and one feels privileged in being able to enrich oneself with it, and learn from its truths. The more so simply *because* it may soon have vanished altogether. For there it lies beside the new—encrusted, crumbling, settled to its ancient contours, riddled with the wearing marks of centuries, extraordinarily beautiful in its scarred and weathered continuity, and resilient still, a pre-industrial and pre-Christian world, a world of pagan sensuousness upon which the twentieth century seems a transitory and superficial imposition. Becalmed and by-passed? Left to moulder slowly into ruin? With bits of it preserved to sate the curiosity of those who could not otherwise conceive of such a world, such quaintness, such useless flourishings of beauty?

There will come a time when much of what we go in search of with such passionate conviction will have sunk into oblivion, receded and shrivelled and fallen, leaving only hints and echoes for the generations of the future to be puzzled by, who will have read perhaps of villages and towns and cities glowing in the eloquence of art. It may even be that only devastated ruins, traces here and there of palaces and churches, frescoes and inscriptions, a desolate abandoned Italy, will remain, lying in the atom-gutted plains among the stumps of ancient cypresses and olives. And if this is so, perhaps they will affect those generations as the ruins of Assyria and Greece and Rome affect us now. And then again perhaps for centuries not, forgotten as the Etruscan world had been forgotten, by people too preoccupied and too intent on building a new world to care; to whom such ruins would be meaningless, a hindrance, best left to rot. If it happens this way it will not be for the first time, nor perhaps for the last. We need only think of the voided hilltops and plateaux where once the Etruscan cities of Tarquinia and Populonia had stood, now choked with fragments, given over to the grass or corn, ploughed up, sown and reaped for centuries; or of great cities like Sakkara, Knossos and Mycenae that lay secret and forgotten in their ruins till the nineteenth-century archaeologists began to dig and to explore.

Which is where I can begin.

THE ETRUSCAN EXPERIENCE

THE ETRUSCANS ARE a long way off in time, buried under centuries of oblivion—a strange elusive race whose language and whose origins are still problematic, even after more than a hundred years of scholarly exploration and research. But if the people as a race and as a civilization have vanished, the roots of their world nevertheless still exist. Only twelve short miles to the north of Rome, the ruins of the city of Veii—whose walls once measured seven miles round—lie below the hamlet of Isola Farnese amid the secretive beauties of the Campagna. Further north, to the left of the Tiber, run the dark Etruscan hills, below whose slopes deep clefts, gorges, ravines and valleys had been formed 5,000 years ago from the periodic eruptions of a string of now extinct volcanoes. And between the hills and the flat Tyrrhenian coastline lies the great Maremma plain, where Cerveteri, Vulci and Tarquinia once flourished among their rich dependencies. Beyond which, beyond Vulci on the borders of Lazio, the papal state of Lazio, stretches Tuscany, or north Etruria as it was before the Roman empire rearranged the broken federation into a dependent province; Tuscany, where the Etruscan spirit, the spirit of the ancient Mediterranean world, seems still to breathe; where many famous towns and cities have their roots in the Etruscan past.

Rome tangibly survives. The cities of Etruria have almost vanished, leaving disinterred and scattered ruins lying secretive amid the folds and clefts of the countryside. If you want to *find* Etruria you have to go in search of it. You have to leave Rome, reluctantly or otherwise, for the brooding silences of the Campagna, and a different kind of world. For the two worlds are quite dissimilar. Rome surrounds you, clamours at you, stuns, pervades. There is so much of it before the eye—it sates the eye. Etruria, the Etruscan Etruria, on the other hand, whispers faintly and intimately at you, and you have to get your eyes and ears accustomed to its half-naturalized beauties before you can get the measure of it—if that is ever possible. The Roman world, in other words, is so much more articulate, so much better documented, so much better known. It is only the voices of silence that speak for the Etruscan world—the forms, the images and symbols to be found in the tombs or in the museums that contain things taken from the tombs; the strange wild beauty of the landscapes in which the tombs have their setting; the architecture and the structure of these tombs, built like cities or carved out of the living rock. For there is little else. None of the cities remain; only the scattered foundations of cities and their walls; a bridge here, an archway there. No literature has come down to us. The Etruscans speak through their art, their humble craftsmen and their architects; their sculptors and goldsmiths and engineers; through their religious living praise of the dead; out of the tombs —almost, one might say, out of the roots of the earth.

For even without its cities and without its literature, the Etruscan world emerges from the shadows with an eloquence and an expressiveness that gives us a profound sense of its greatness and importance as a civilization in pre-Hellenic and pre-Roman Italy. Part of the fascination and the enchantment of the Etruscan experience, if we may call it that, is the gradually deepening awareness one has of getting down to the quick roots of the Italianate world and "the natural flowering of life" which seems to have come from them with the Etruscans. They are part of "the old idea," as Lawrence has it, "of the vitality of the universe . . . evolved long before history begins, and elaborated into a vast religion"[1] which has its expression in the great civilizations of China, India, Egypt and Babylonia, and reaches the Mediterranean shores through Mycenae, Crete, Cyprus, Phoenicia, Greece and Assyria.

So if one goes in search of the Etruscans, one goes not in order to brood morbidly among the ruins of the dead, or to escape into a world of fantasy, but to discover for oneself, if one can, these lost roots of being. In the middle of the twentieth century, stripped of the old fears and mysteries, with new, more lethal and more stultifying absolutes to cope with, one comes to the tombs in that sense, questingly. The experience is not so much a going-back into the past (though it is that too) as a going-down into the dark of being, an attempt to get at the quick of things in terms of hints and echoes.

In the Etruscan hills, among the fluted rust-brown tufo cliffs, above the streams that wind along through the deep ravines, lies the evidence of another kind of truth than that which science has revealed to us, testifying to the existence of a lost world. Useless and invalid in terms of mechanistic progress and the triumphs of materialistic principle. As useless and invalid as a poem. For its rhythms are not the rhythms of a universe dragooned to the Diktat of machines, but of one which—shaped to the organic will, the unreflective impulse, human spontaneity, the old slow rhythms in the blood—turns naturally to poetry and song, and makes of even death a cause for celebration, so that its vital offerings become "an impassioned requiem breathing from the pomps of earth and from the sanctities of the grave".[2]

Even now, very little is known with any certainty about the origins of the Etruscan people. The various theories are still being discussed and disputed by archaeologists, historians and scholars. But they have brought us no conclusive proofs. The Romans were very thorough in their conquest of Etruria. It is said that they aimed at a total absorption of the race and the transformation of its distinctive culture. And it can hardly be denied that they succeeded, or that in the end the Etruscans freely acquiesced in the collapse of their world and the acceptance of the Roman image. That its literature has vanished almost without trace, that its art and its religion so quickly dwindled and withered away was probably the direct consequence of the influence of Rome, delivering the death blow to a declining culture. Even the history was for centuries obscured by the deliberate falsification of Roman propagandists and historians to the "glorious advantage of the Roman state".

Confronted by the living images and symbols of Etruscan art that have come to us out of the long-buried ruins, the picture becomes a little clearer, but without resolving the question-mark. How does one reconcile the cinerary urns of Chiusi with stone sphinxes, Corinthian vases, the early murals at Tarquinia, the Egyptian, Attic and Ionian forms that are characteristic elements in the development of Etruscan art? There is a mass of evidence, but it often takes an idiosyncratic and puzzling form. The sources and influences often seem clear enough, but it is difficult to decide how or when they came into Etruria. Certainly there seems to have been a constant flow of trade, and so much must have come by way of competitors in friendly interchange. And it is certainly true that a great deal that is oriental in the artistic culture of the Etruscans comes later in their history, from the fluctuating influence of Phoenician, Attic and Corinthian arts at a date not before 700 B.C. But these facts, however demonstrable, do not bring us any closer to a solution of the problem of origin. For though the symbolic forms of the very earliest Etruscans are pervaded by a profoundly Eastern sense of the world, they are at the same time strangely intermixed with elements which in some way transform the sources and which give Etruscan art its own distinctive character.

There is an ancient tradition that the Etruscans came to Italy as refugees or colonists from among the Lydians in Western Asia Minor about 1250 B.C. This is supported by certain aspects of their culture, and has its source in Herodotus. Writing in his Histories, about 450 B.C., of a "famine that prevailed throughout Lydia during the reign of Atys, son of Manes", Herodotus states that the famine was so bad and raged for so long that the King decided to take drastic action to ensure the survival of his people. Accordingly he "divided the Lydians into two parts and cast lots". One half was to remain in Lydia, and the other to emigrate. And "over those who were to emigrate he appointed as King his own son, Tyrrhenus". The emigrants, after building and equipping ships at Smyrna, set sail and eventually "reached the land of the Umbrians, where they founded cities, and where to this day they still dwell, calling themselves, after the King's son, Tyrrhenians".[3]

Herodotus went to Italy and may have visited Etruria, which

was then still a flourishing state. But he mentions the Etruscans only incidentally while writing about Lydia, and offers no evidence of their way of life. Indeed, the authority for his account is nowhere verified or verifiable. And though one does not take Herodotus lightly, there are many scholars who believe that the author was simply quoting from legend and hearsay. So that when one reads Strabo, Virgil, Horace and Plutarch, who derived their facts about the Etruscans from the Histories of Herodotus, accepting them as true, we are nowhere nearer to the truth. All that these accounts confirm is the profound respect that later writers had for the "Father of History". As for the role of the Etruscans in Livy's *History of Rome*, this has to be seen in the light of the politics and patriotism of the Roman state, and Livy's records cannot therefore be taken as true. The pity is that no history of the Etruscan people has survived. If we had had Claudius' study, which was said to consist of twenty books, many of the problems that puzzle us might now have been solved. But strangely enough that perished too.[4]

Another account, akin to that of Herodotus, and coming from Strabo, holds that the Etruscans originated from among the Assyrians, or a tribe of them, the Rasena of the city of Rasen on the Tigris.[5] Colonists of the Rasena, it is said, had settled first in Egypt, and later sailed to Italy, bringing with them the great skills of the East, "an oriental love of music, dancing and feasting", and the heritage of a rich and ancient culture.[6]

These accounts began to be seriously questioned in the nineteenth century, when a number of important historians and archaeologists turned their attention to the Etruscans.[7] New theories were put forward, grounded on the conviction that the Etruscans came, not from the Eastern Mediterranean, but either 1. from people who descended from the Alps into the valley of the Po and gradually filtered southwards somewhere around the eleventh to tenth centuries B.C., driving out or absorbing the *terramare* tribes of the marshy plains; or 2. from people already settled in central Italy in the first Iron Age and developing from the fusion of two lesser cultures—the Italo-lacustrian tribes (who disposed of their dead by inhumation) and the terramare tribes, who cremated their dead—with oriental influences coming into Italy through trade and commerce; or 3. from the Villanovans around Bologna and the actual descendants of the terramare tribes.

Nor are these the only theories. But they are sufficient to indicate the mechanics involved. As for the origin and meaning of the Etruscan *language*, this is a problem that has invited as much if not more speculation and contradiction among scholars. The theories are as varied as the ethnological theories; and they are so contradictory and complex as to leave the layman with a feeling that he is dabbling in some kind of esoteric science with its own special rules. But however perplexing they may be, they are also fascinating. If the scholars have spent years on end pursuing abstruse theories of etymology that lead them deeper and deeper into a maze of hieroglyphs, it is a measure of their patience and their zeal, their scholarly conviction, that they still persist. One respects the industry with which they've gone about their task, their prodigious marshalling of fragmentary evidence, the pursuit of each tiny hint, the disinterested, dedicated search for keys and clues. In their explorations the scholars have appealed for comparison (each according to his starting point) to almost all known languages, even to those least likely to produce results. Some have systematically analysed the Etruscan tongue by an "etymological method", and others by a "combinative method" of words and their changing forms within the language itself. Others have tried to link Etruscan to Assyrian, or Lydian, and still others to the Hittites. And there are those who (like the Greek scholar Thomopoulos) believe that the best key for deciphering the ancient idioms of both Asia Minor and Etruria is Albanian. And yet another group hold to the view that Etruscan is not only an Aryan tongue but essentially Italic, and linked in mutual influence if without innate connection to Latin.[8]

This problem of origin is then a vexed and fascinating one, no matter how one approaches it. And the field is still open wide to the arguments of historians and archaeologists. In time, it may be that one or other of the existing theories will prove to be correct; that some piece of overwhelming evidence will come to light to resolve the issue. But maybe not. Maybe the origins of this people are so complex as to need a combination of all these theories to account for them. Maybe as a people they evolved out of a fusion of races—the terramare tribes, the Villanovans, the Lydians, the Phoenicians, the tribes from the North. It is hardly possible to deny that there were indeed people living in Etruria long before the historical accounts begin; or that when or if another race came from over the sea to conquer them they would have gone to form the culture that we know of as Etruscan. Certainly the culture could not suddenly have come into being fully formed, however highly cultivated the invaders. By the laws of social and organic growth it would have emerged gradually, painfully, obscurely, out of complex roots; the stresses, oppositions, conflicts that create form and order—a long record of abortive attempt and struggle and failure imperceptibly clarifying out of darkness and obscurity to produce a balanced and cohesive world.

But as to how and when and why the elements combined are not questions I can attempt to answer. Nor is it my purpose to answer them. They require the scholar's training, his patience with minutiae, the dust of fact, the will to dedicate oneself, as Elia Lattes did, to a theory. I am, however, well aware that without the scholars the Etruscan world would have been largely shut to us. It is they, after all, who have made so many discoveries possible. And if I seem to be content with giving mere outlines of some of their theories, that is because it is not my purpose to theorize over the Etruscans. It is enough to say that the question of where they came from and why they chose to settle in that area between the Arno and the Tiber which became Etruria is still not settled; and that when or if it does eventually come to a settlement, it will not invalidate the image that we already have of the mature civilization itself.

That this image is incomplete, fragmented, complex and obscure; that it does not give us anything approaching a coherent picture of Etruscan society and culture, is another matter. Here it is a question of imaginative conjecture and exploration of the living forms, a question of the scholarship of imagination, as well as of a scholar's findings. Here the facts and images and forms exist before our eyes. They are an invitation to the senses to attempt to break across the barriers of time and silence and to find there, in the voices that speak *out* of silence, the vital spirit of a world. And the gaps that leave us puzzling over the unanswered questions of Etruscan civilization (gaps that include the almost total disappearance of their written language) only serve to emphasize the positive and profoundly eloquent nature of the images that remain.

These, the scanty ruins of great cities dotted about Etruria, the tomb-cities with their architectural façades and carved reliefs that came to light almost intact after 2,000 years during the last century at Cerveteri, Tarquinia, Chiusi, Orvieto, Norchia, Castel D'Asso and many other places; the arches at Perugia and Volterra; old walls that still exist round Arezzo, Cortona and Volterra, the great curved bridge at Vulci, and another at Blera linking two parts of the necropolis; the terracotta, tufo and bronze sculpture to be found in the museums; those marvellous votive figures and carved implements and household articles and jewellery scattered in their thousands throughout Europe together with the rich treasures of Etruscan, Attic, Corinthian and Ionian pottery found in the tombs; these constitute our startling legacy from this vanished civilization, a legacy that awaits each new discoverer, and is still there to excite and challenge the imagination.

This art, the architecture, these rich treasures, presuppose the existence then of a highly developed culture, confident and complex, and very closely organized around its religious life into city-states linked by a common vision and a common purpose. It would have been a very different kind of culture from that of Rome at its height, or of twentieth-century Europe. The signs that we find carved or painted, embossed or incised on stone, terracotta, bronze, gold and silver, indeed on every kind of material and all manner of objects in early Etruscan art, are all symbols of worship and of ceremonies whose allegorical significance takes us back to the very dawn of civilization. There is in them that cosmic sense of the vitality of the universe and of man as a worshipper bowing before the great forces of nature that is characteristic of all early religions and that is somewhere at the root of the Etruscan vision of life. The Lucumon or Prince, together with the augurs and other nobles of the priestly caste made themselves the guardians of this vision, the sacred laws of the Etruscan Discipline. They communicated these laws to the people and nourished this vision in them by symbolic act and by example, and governed accordingly no doubt, as leaders must, in the full knowledge that it is impossible and even destructive to attempt to explain the laws of statecraft and religion to those who have not spent long years learning their secrets. They would have know that "the cosmic ideas" cannot be imparted, except to a few. The people, as Lawrence has written in Etruscan Places, can never "be more than a little aware. . . . Give them symbols, ritual and gesture. . . . The actual knowledge must be guarded from them, lest knowing the formulae, without undergoing at all the experience that corresponds, they . . . become insolent and impious. . . . The esoteric knowledge will always be esoteric, since knowledge is an experience, not a formula." And so, as Lawrence puts it, "the clue to the Etruscan life was the Lucumo, the religious prince. Beyond him were the priests and warriors. Then came the people and the slaves," who "felt the symbols and danced the sacred dances", and who "were always kept *in touch*, physically, with the mysteries".[9]

One has this sense of a people possessed of a joyous positive thrusting vitality, a people rooted in the physical world and breathing its mystery in spontaneous act. What one sees (in the tombs, on the vases and cinerary urns, in the sculpture) reflects a race whose energy and will and whose spirit springs with the uncorrupted impulse of life. There is brutality and crudity and warlike ambition, all those signs of masculine virility, but also and with this, a sense of unselfconscious joy, an intimacy and tenderness that go far beyond the crudities of the surface. "To the Etruscan," Lawrence has written, "all was alive; the whole universe lived; and the business of man was himself to live amid it all."[10] And especially is this sense of confidence and continuity, of conviction and vitality, reflected in the tombs, and the Etruscan attitude towards death.

The balance of these essential characteristics, of this intimate religious feeling for life, this confidence in a "happy immortality"; the relationships between the various strata of society—between the Lucumones, the priests and the people; between men and women, city and home, war and peace, death and life—must have been a very delicate one. The civilization endured for a few centuries, making itself the dominating power in Italy somewhere around 700 B.C., and maintaining its position for at least another 300 years. What is so surprising about this is not that from the fifth century onward it began to collapse, but that in the end it collapsed so completely as to leave almost no traces behind. Within 200 years of the Roman conquest its language, its religion, and its distinctive culture had been virtually elminated, and its ethos, except in the obscurest senses in which it can be said to have influenced and acted upon the Roman character, had been transformed. One might hazard the suggestion that the Etruscan spirit has continued to play an essential part in shaping the Italian character, particularly in Tuscany; that its rich and idiosyncratic culture must have influenced "the slow, complex and many channelled process which culminated, centuries afterwards and on other soil, for a brief stretch of time, in the perfect union of Italian and Greek in the great Romans: Cicero, Lucretius and Virgil". One might say that even now the spirit of the Etruscans still lingers on in Tuscany, despite all the centuries of change and transformation, reappearing in the peculiar intensities of Giotto's art and in much else, earlier and later, as in other unanalysable ways. Also, "it is generally admitted", according to Aldo Modona, "that the Etruscan language continued to exist for several centuries" after the time of Augustus, "if not as a spoken idiom, at any rate in the same way as Sanskrit exists today. Lucretius speaks of *carmina thyrrena* which were read in inverted order, and he speaks of them as of a thing well known and used in his own day. Three hundred years later the haruspices (or diviners) attached to the armies of Julian the Apostate read their ritual books no less well than those of the time of Cicero, although there are those who believe that they must have made use of Latin translations."[11]

But the fact remains that as a race the Etruscans had to all intents and purposes ceased to exist by the early years of the Empire, sunk into permanent and total eclipse beneath the bright pragmatic materialist sun of the Roman world, and its genius for organizing and indoctrinating and convincing its subject peoples of its superior principles, its innate right to command, to lead and control.

We may put it that the Etruscan civilization had fulfilled its "destiny", spent itself, and that another, of a very different kind and in an earlier stage of its life had taken over. That is *one* way at least of putting it. We may say further that the achievement of the Etruscans was to have crystallized in their political institutions, their attitude to life, their way of thinking, their culture and their art, the old Mediterranean spirit; and that without this achievement Rome and the Greco-Roman culture could not have triumphed in the ways in which it did. It may be true anyway that the Etruscans had more or less completed the natural span of a culture prophesied by the Augurs on the basis of the mystic number twelve by the time it was in the process of being systematically and pitilessly destroyed. Even Rome lasted no longer as a culture, though with so vast an Empire, organized with such zeal for self-preservation, its influence has been so much greater.

It is more than probable then that the seeds for the Etruscan culture had already begun to take root in Italy as far back as 1200 B.C., growing slowly, painfully, developing out of long experiment, perhaps in the intermingling of native tribes with foreign peoples from the North and from the South and East. But by the seventh century it had almost certainly become the dominant power in Central Italy, and had begun to find mature expression as a culture—in politics, religion, art and architecture, and in all those interrelated skills and disciplines that give cohesion and a sense of common purpose to a people scattered across large areas.

From this point onward till the Romans revolted against their kings, the Etruscan world was continually expanding. Moving outward from Etruria, the civilization appears to have spread southwards and northwards and across the Apennines to cover a vast region which by the middle of the sixth century included the peoples of Umbria, Latium, Emilia, Liguria, Lombardy and even parts of Campania. But it was of course in Etruria itself that the civilization reached its greatest splendour, and achieved its maturest, its most organic and original forms, as the ruins of its cities and the works of art that have been found among them are there to testify, 2,500 years later.

At its height it even dominated Rome, which was then perhaps no more (despite Livy's claims) than a minor city among many, and was no doubt immensely strengthened and vitalized by the rule of its Etruscan kings in the century between 623 and 510. During that period "the Romans had made their city one of the largest in Italy", having learnt to utilize Etruscan skills and methods in building arches and temples and palaces, in draining the land, navigating the sea and refining their political institutions. It would not be unreasonable to suggest, as Robert Graves has done, that the Etruscans had conquered and captured Rome and remained in control of the city till they were expelled by the revolt of the people.[12] This is certainly not the picture Livy gives us, but then it is not difficult to detect in his *History* "a political and patriotic bias" which sought to play off and play down the Etruscan role in the making of the Roman state. "The same national pride," as Mary Cameron put it long ago, "which made Romans claim descent from gods and heroes and refuse to acknowledge any more probable ancestry, also led them to put back into the shadowy past institutions and customs which only came into existence when the development of the Roman state was already far advanced."[13] It is anyhow more than likely that for the first two and a half centuries of her existence Rome was virtually an Etruscan city, and part of the Etruscan world. Unfortunately though, however plausible this sounds, it remains conjectural, and the legends that surround the early history, a Roman image of the Roman world, still cling. One can only say that the confidence, the vitality, the positive thrusting energy, the sense of well-being and joy reflected from the murals at Tarquinia and from almost any Etruscan work of art between the seventh and the fifth centuries are an incontrovertible evidence of Etruscan certainty and command and mastery of their way of life, the flowering of creative will; and that all this must undoubtedly have had its influence upon Rome.

Yet with the successful revolt of the Romans in 510 B.C., the breaking of Etruscan sea-power by the Sicilian Greeks at Cumae in 474 B.C., and the coming of the Gauls from the North, the Etruscans were weakened, checked, contained, their confidence shaken, their supremacy challenged and threatened. Forced back into Etruria, they were put on to the defensive. And though in 500 they were still a great and powerful nation, for them the fateful turning point had come. They had stumbled, they had begun to falter; doubt had entered into the Etruscan soul. From this point on they were fighting for survival—although it was to be more than a century before the strain would tell; and then the decline became rapid, bitter, convulsive, precipitous, and finally engulfing.

Rome—perhaps more responsible for this decline than any other power that threatened the Etruscans—attacked them soon after its revolt with a vehement and merciless persistency that never let up, in spite of the fact that she had other enemies to contend with, till they had been destroyed, obliterated. She had emerged in 496 out of the Battle of Lake Regillus (a historic battle for supremacy between the Latins and the Romans) as a new and restive enemy at the head of the Latin League. And she was very soon declaring war on the city of Veii. The ten-year conflict that followed between the Veientines and the Romans, though ending in 475 with a forty-year treaty of peace, in effect marked the beginning of the death struggle of the Etruscan people. They had embarked on their increasingly desperate and losing battle for survival. Veii, for instance, was twice more subdued (in 425 and 406) before being finally wiped out; and in the intervals of peace that were observed between Rome and the Etruscan League, Rome was all the time strengthening herself, in wars with the Sabines, the Aequi, the Volsci, preparing herself both territorially, internally and in the concentration of her resources, for mastery.

Though the fourth century was to witness an apparent artistic renaissance based upon a powerful Hellenistic influence, by 400 B.C. doubt and confusion have begun to affect and to undermine the Etruscan vision of life. This is very clearly and everywhere reflected in their art from the end of the century onwards—in the sudden appearance in the tomb paintings and on vases of contorted figures, figures from the black underworld, the figures of devils and monsters, of Charun with his hammer, of Tuchulcha and others, hideous, with beak-like noses and serpents writhing on their limbs, their eyes shining with a sinister light in their bluish faces, staring out of the dark. What is the significance of this radical change of image, this contradiction to the joyous, life-giving and light-inhabiting creatures of the earlier painting, "that old confidence in a happy immortality",[14] if not a symptom of collapse, decline, of terror and despair? Though J. D. Beazley in his book on Etruscan vase-painting, demonstrates that this need not necessarily be so—that the change may be simply one of "taste"—he can only demonstrate this by ignoring the facts, few as they are. Such a radical "change of taste" must itself be a symptom of *something*. It is not to be seriously suggested that the devils began to appear because people expressed a demand for devils. Of what are they the symptom then if not some profound transformation in the psychology of the Etruscans? The "terrors" symbolized on the vases and in the tombs may all indeed be "terrors of transit" as Beazley calls them, but then all terrors are transitory—they rise up out of the unconscious and vanish back into their own dark. So this cannot explain away the sudden threatening arrival of these creatures from the dark, the unknown, the amorphous world beyond the light. It would seem reasonable to assume that they are the expression of doubt and instability, loss of that conviction and faith in the physical world, the world of dance and form and light, which the Etruscans once held unquestioningly.[14]

Anyway, less than a hundred years after the first struggle with Rome, in 397, Veii had been finally devastated, abandoned to its fate by the other cities of the Etruscan League. Following quickly upon which the nearby towns of Capena (in 395) and Falerii (in 394) were attacked. And at almost the same time the Gauls were invading Etruria from the North, and a powerful Syracusan navy was sacking the flourishing cities along the coast to further weaken

Above: 1a VILLANOVAN HUT URN, IN CLAY. Eighth to seventh centuries. From Veii. Found at sites throughout Etruria.
Below: 1b VILLANOVAN BRONZE GROUP—sword, ossuary and flask. Eighth century. From the Cavalupo necropolis at Vulci. The ossuary has a shield-shaped lid (*p. 185*).

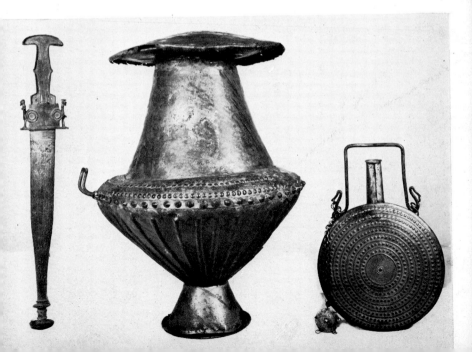

2a VILLANOVAN CINERARY
URN. Eighth to seventh centuries. From Veii. Such urns
are representative of the pre-
Etruscan culture at all Etruscan city sites, often covered
with a lid or helmet in clay
or bronze.

2b HUT URN IN BRONZE. Seventh century. From Falerii Veteres. Studded sheet
bronze with struts on the roof representing wooden cross-beams, as in Plate 1a.

Etruscan power. It was an offensive on several fronts that the Etruscans were having to face, and with the growing power and assertiveness of Rome (harried but strengthened by war) they found themselves less and less able to keep their defences intact. Though a war between Tarquinia and Rome ended in 351 with a treaty of non-aggression, Caere was nevertheless forced in the same year to submit to Roman domination, and detached from the League. And when in 311 at the end of the Treaty, the Etruscans re-established the League and turned to the offensive against Sutrium in a belated attempt to ward off the formidable power of Rome, the Romans at once invaded central and eastern Etruria, and defeated their enemies at Perugia. This battle was followed by yet another treaty with a number of Etruscan cities, though not with Tarquinia, which was forced in 308 to cede parts of its territory to landless Romans and conclude a separate treaty. Finally, with defeats at Volterra in 298 and at Sentinum in 295, and the yielding to Roman colonists in 290 of Vulcian territory, followed by a new submission on the part of Caere and the expulsion of the Volsinians from their city, Etruria was now virtually open to the Romans, its spirit broken to resistance. So that all the Romans had to do was to walk in and take control.[15]

Which is exactly what they proceeded to do. By the end of the third century the whole of Etruria was under Roman domination, with the Etruscans submitting peaceably and passively, yielding initiative and will, forced into servile subjection. No doubt soon after 250 B.C., rich patricians moved into the cities to begin the process of converting the people to Roman ways, and no doubt many Etruscans were taken from their homes to become slaves to these patricians or to others in Rome itself. And no doubt too the Princes and noble families of Etruria would gradually have been drawn to Rome either for protection or in pursuit of the attractions of the expanding city. And as the power of Rome increased, and its materialistic ethos spread and deepened, so the Etruscan cities would have languished and declined till they and their culture had ceased to exist, the whole complex structure of the society withering away, sapless above dead roots, collapsing into servile dependence and apathy—a process no doubt hastened by the devastating presence in Etruria from 215–204 of the Carthaginian armies under Hannibal that virtually stripped the land of its produce, leaving waste and chaos in their wake.

It would be wrong of course to attribute the Etruscan collapse exclusively to the Romans. The Gauls, the Sicilian Greeks and the Carthaginians also played their part in bringing it about. Nor would these external enemies have been the only cause. Recurrent epidemics of malaria played havoc it is said with the peoples living in the coastal plains of Etruria where, due to the chaos and confusion of war, the laboriously created system of irrigation and drainage broke down and the waters formed into stagnant pools and turned rich land into marsh. (Even up till sixty years ago the Maremma was full of malarial swamp and marsh as it is said to have been in the years after Rome had crushed the Etruscans; though now it is fertile again as it must have been in the age of Tarquinia and Caere.) And there must have been some degree of dissidence and disorder within the Etruscan state itself, in the relations between the various cities of the League; weaknesses and flaws perhaps inherent in the very structure of the society. For indeed, it seems that authority and power, the whole responsibility for the organic working of the state, was concentrated in the hands of a small group of nobles—the kings and priests and dignitaries whose intimate knowledge and insight into the mysteries of statecraft it was that held Etruria together, and gave unity to its scattered peoples, guiding them and speaking for them in the secret disciplines of the Etruscan religion.

But all the same the Romans were probably the most merciless, and certainly they were the most ambitious, of the Etruscans' enemies. And they were probably the greatest single factor among all those which brought about the collapse of the Etruscan world. The Romans *had* to subdue them in order to become the masters of Italy. And this is what in fact they did—by war, by occupation, by conversion, and by savage suppression. A belated rising in 196, for example, was swiftly and brutally crushed. Then, in the early years of the first century B.C., the Etruscans were involved in the civil strife that convulsed Rome and her territories under the terrorizing reigns of Marius and Sulla. When several Etruscan cities went against Sulla by sheltering the colleagues and followers of Marius, Sulla's punishment was to place permanent military colonies in them and to institute a reign of terror in which many people were slaughtered, as a means of bringing about the rapid extinction of the Etruscan nation, regardless of its demonstrated loyalties. The period is "thought to have caused the death of about half a million Romans and Italians", with whom, in the words of F. R. Cowell, "perished the best and most active citizens of Italy".[16] Nor was even this the end for the Etruscans. In 40 B.C. Octavius Caesar, the famed Augustus, was to destroy Perugia for having had the audacity to protect Lucius Antonius (Marc Antony's brother).[17] As an act of barbarism this was not perhaps of any particular note, being only one among many other and similarly murderous reprisals; but it may be said to mark the final moment in the record of Etruscan history. For after this the Etruscans become indistinguishable from the Italians, and their territory is merged by the Emperor Augustus into the Seventh Region of Italy as an integral part of the Roman Empire.

It is significant that the later period of Etruscan decline should also have coincided with a gradual and increasing corruption within the Roman Republic itself. The story of this, as Cowell puts it, "provides in a relatively simple form an excellent illustration of the complex and disastrous interaction between private interests narrowly conceived and political privileges irresponsibly exploited".[18] Which is, to say the least, a mild way of putting it. But Cowell directs himself to a gradual exposure of the bankruptcy of the Roman State—that unpalatable record of dictatorship and lust for power, corruption on the grandest scale, civil war, indiscriminate massacre and the mass use of slavery. When Cicero himself, the great Republican, was murdered for denouncing Marc Antony and the corrupt leadership of Rome, "his head and hands were cut off and sent back to Rome for Antony and his wife to gloat over". And the ensuing slaughter of "300 senators and 2,000 *equites*, doomed by Antony's proscription lists" in one of the most disastrous and barbaric crimes of Roman history,[19] was a final convulsive act in the life of the Republic.

But, as Cicero has testified, the Republic had been heading for such disaster and such collapse long before the establishment of the Empire.[20] And above all perhaps in its exploitation of the slave market. Not only did the slaves deprive thousands of "independent craftsmen and manufacturers of work", but the rich became richer, lazier, more complacent, more corrupt, the poor became poorer, and the organic links between the levels of society loosened, frayed and broke. Slaves, maintained "in Rome and in large towns as evidence of the wealth of their owners", became "a sheer drag on the productive energies of the Republic", weakening the whole structure of relationships, and injecting into them dangerous discontents.[21]

If it is true, as Cato had said, that the backbone of Rome had been the small farmers, the independent peasant smallholders,[22] then this backbone had already been broken and the marrow sucked out of it a good while before the final collapse of Etruria. The Etruscans themselves must have been among those who went to swell the ranks of the slave labourers—spiritless, dejected, without will or purpose, those hundreds of thousands of auctioned men who could never have been expected to give a vital thrusting impulse to a society that treated them like pack-animals; who would work grudgingly, shamed, humiliated, harbouring resentment and hatred and murder in their hearts against their flabby overlords. "We may take it as a . . . law," Lawrence writes, "that the very deepest quick of a man's nature is his own pride and self-respect." And we may also take it that if under insult he "may be patient for years and years", yet in the end he will break out into violence and murder, or band together with other malcontents to create civil disorder.[23] Which is what happened. "Riots and open revolt became more frequent and from 139 to 71 B.C. a series of armed risings by rebellious slaves were put down with great difficulty and at the cost of much loss of life."[24] One even finds oneself being surprised that Rome was able to maintain control. The fact that she could do so implies a greater discipline among certain sections of Roman society than would have been suspected; and that not everyone in Rome had grown indolent upon riches.

And yet, in spite of the brilliant and astonishing achievements of the Empire, particularly under Augustus, who established a general peace lasting many years and encouraged an atmosphere in which the great Augustan writers could thrive at ease, the rot had already begun to set in before the breakdown of the Republic, leaving history with a record of crime and corruption, of irrational indulgence and madness, of perversion and irresponsibility such as we find difficult to reconcile to the genuine principles of reason and enlightenment, of civil law and order, of civility and justice that went into the making of the Roman state. That record and those principles existed side by side as antitheses in the momentum of power. But so completely had Rome (by the time of the emperors) mastered the art of organizing her resources and subjecting to positive support her conquered peoples that for more than 300 years of the Christian era she could remain supreme as "mistress of the world", in spite of disease and perversion and abuse at the centre.

But the dichotomy was there, the dissonance, the internal division, eating away at the structure, slowly rotting the foundations laid with such care, such painstaking labour and sweat of the spirit by the early citizens of Rome. These early Romans, "a stolid, matter-of-fact and puritanical people, intensely loyal to their family, their state and their gods, willingly accepting such authority with perfect discipline"[25] formed a community that would not have tolerated the selfish, lazy, irresponsible and avaricious rich of Cicero's time. But then such men, the parasites of society, leeched to it and sapping it of its creative energies, are always the product and the consequence of expansion and power and wealth and increasing complexity. It is inconceivable that Rome could ever have made herself the mistress of Italy with "fish-breeders" for leaders.[26] These men had been spawned out of triumph, feeding on the riches of the state, born to abundance and ease, and softened, corrupted, sickened by it.

So it was not to be expected that the Etruscans, in the last two or three centuries of their existence as a people, dominated by the power of Rome and totally submissive, could have long resisted the softening process, that yielding of integrity and will to the corrupted standards and values of their Roman masters. "When the flower of the nation had perished," Mary Cameron observes, "it is easy to understand how those who survived fell into degrading subjection. The masses became mere servile hirelings working for alien masters. Those among the upper classes who bowed their necks to the yoke and were allowed to retain a shadow of their former prosperity lived on in ignoble obscurity, deprived of political importance. Having seen the centres of their artistic and intellectual life ruined and destroyed, they degenerated into those obese and lazy Etruscans spoken of with contempt by Roman writers."[27]

In the Romanized murals at Tarquinia, as in countless sarcophagi and vases from every part, one can see the effect of this softening, this yielding, upon the characteristic Etruscan spirit. The figures become stiff, unliving, flabby, fat, indulgent. They no longer have that energy, that vitality, that strange idiosyncratic vividness of form by which earlier the Etruscans had given symbolic expression to their beliefs. They have become literal. They present us with portraits of people, things, dead facts, without conviction and without joy. The old confidence, all the magic and the mystery of the Etruscan art representing joyous communion between the living and the dead, have gone. And we are left with fat pedantic patricians, a materialistic record, dead as a list.

And so the Etruscans vanished. A world had stuttered into silence, conquered, crushed, sinking back into the earth, withering like a dead flower, its people turned into dependants of the Roman state and fashioned into citizens of Rome. Looking for them, for a glimpse of their distinctive world, we must turn away from these last stutterings of art; turn back in time, to the centuries of Etruscan mastery, where the fascination of a life-enhancing discipline is mirrored in the tombs, in bronze and terracotta, gold and tufo. And it is from twentieth-century Rome, twenty-five centuries away, we must begin our search; leaving the capital, going out into the dark Etruscan hills, the plains, the valleys of cleft green where hidden folds of earth expose their wounds of rock; into the deep ravines of fluted tufo near the lips of which the ruins lie. Now that I have briefly sketched the history, it is my purpose to describe what I have seen and found in journeys throughout Tuscany and Lazio, of the Etruscan world in its true setting.

The ruins, the fragments, the scattered stones of vanished cities, tombs and walls and arches—these are an essential part of the experience. But so also is the country which contains them, secret and remote and intimate, revealing itself moment by moment in its unpredictable and startling contrasts, each turning a discovery, and everywhere pervaded by suggestions, echoes, hints and traces of the ancient world. For as Lawrence has said, even "the ceaseless industry of naked human hands and winter-shod feet, and slow-stepping soft-eyed oxen does not devastate a country, does not denude it, does not lay it bare, does not uncover its nakedness, does not drive away either Pan or his children".[28] It is contained and containing, in spite of progress, in spite of change and devastation; and it retains today the stilled and secretive eloquence of its past, the past of the Etruscan world. And if it is mostly in the museums that one finds the evidence, nevertheless many of these museums—and some of them the most interesting—are themselves to be found in the heart of Etruria. Here the gravity and confidence, the vividness and joy, of the Etruscans, that celebration of the secret roots of being, can be rediscovered and relived. But always in conjunction with their settings, the deserted ruins, the spirit that breathes in the earth; and at the most elemental and organic level, in the tombs, the carved and pillared tombs for instance at Cerveteri, or at Norchia and Blera and Orvieto, and the painted tombs of Chiusi, Orvieto and Tarquinia. Above all at Tarquinia, where the dancing figures have a beauty in them "as of life which has not finished", reflecting "a peculiar large carelessness . . . very human and non-moral", "dancing a dance with the elixir of life" in them; men and women full of life and therefore full of possibilities, "quite serene, and dancing as a very fountain of motion and of life",[29] in contrast and in balance.

And so it is to these things, and the exploration of them, that we turn, expectantly, in fascination; not to the dead but to the living, to the life-enhancing spirit that is in the Etruscan vision of life.

TARQUINIA: THE VOICES OF SILENCE

NINETY-TWO KILOMETRES out of Rome lies the great bared plateau of the acropolis of the Etruscan city of Tarquinii, inland from the sea on the Maremma plain. It looks across its valley at the gaunt thrusting towers of the present-day town, known till the last century as Corneto and built on a high ridge of land where the tombs of the necropolis are concentrated in their thousands.

This is in many ways the most exciting of the great Etruscan sites, for nowhere else in Etruria is one likely to find quite such a rich harvest of images. Not only does the town itself boast a museum with an eloquent collection of objects from the tombs stretching through eight or nine rooms of a great mediaeval palace; there is also the sombre magnificence of the setting; and there are the tombs themselves and their paintings. And it is above all perhaps these paintings that distinguish Tarquinia— more than sixty of them having survived 2,500 years of change and decay. Beneath the ground they keep their silence. Here a people declares itself through the mythic veil of art, moving in silence to the rhythms of music and the dance, caught in the act of life. Here, the impact of a living impulse recurs, inexplicably maintained and renewed in a celebration of community and spontaneity offered to the dead.

But first of all there is the setting. One comes to it from Rome along the Via Clodia, through the Campagna, past Bracciano, Manziana and Orioli, moving deep into old Etruria (a country of dark hills, veined with tiny streams and hidden lava clefts) to cross the frontier into Tarquinian territory at Veiano on the River Mignone. A little further on, beyond Barbarano Romano, the landscape opens out to give sweeping views of heath and cleft and valley dominated by the stony slopes of Monte Romano. And here, after turning seaward through the flowing contours of this Maremma landscape, one catches one's first glimpse of Tarquinia's roofs and towers and the bare flattened hill of the Etruscan acropolis inland from the town, quivering perhaps in the haze of mid-morning. Then, round two or three curves in the road, the Roman aqueduct swings into sight, half-buried in the corn, running straight across a dip between two hills, and beside it is the dusty track that leads to the acropolis.

This track dips down in a long curving ribbon through a hollow, going up along a contour of the hill to bring one out onto the open plateau. Here on this vast flattish hilltop, given over to the rich green silences of the corn, it may at first seem difficult to accept that there had ever been a city. But then you notice the stones lying scattered about all over the hill among the blades of young corn, piled into mounds and lines where the farmer has ploughed and sown. They are the blocks of masonry from vanished walls—great pitted squares and rectangles in tufo and sandstone. And among the furrows wherever you step lie the fragments of clay pot, brick and stone and column, the shattered remnants of a city's world; indifferently turned by the plough, year by year broken up, ground into the soil—these vestiges bring a remote reality very close.

Climbing a slight rise crowned by the stumpy ruin of a Roman building, one looks across the hilltop. There are dips and hollows, but the main impression is of an area artificially flattened, on an incline rising gradually to the edge of the hill nearest the modern Tarquinia. It is a strangely moving sight, for although the ground must have been tilled and ploughed and sown and reaped for centuries it still manages to retain something of the shape given to it by the city—of what had once been a great capital of Etruria, originating probably as far back as the ninth century B.C., and intimately bound up with the traditions, laws and religion of the Etruscans. Even to reflect upon the possible events of the seventh and sixth centuries before Christ when, at the height of Etruscan power and influence, Tarquinia was probably the dominating centre of culture, is to invest the place with significance. For here the Etruscan vision came to its maturest expression, having absorbed and assimilated all the diverse pre-Etruscan elements

that were its roots and brought them to a vivid and articulate
flowering. Here, tradition has it that the boy Tagus (a son of
Jupiter?) sprang from the furrow while Tarchun the founder was
marking out the limits of the city with a bronze plough, and gave
his laws to the land.[1] And out of these laws came the rule of the
Lucumones, who were to become kings of Rome, and the priests
who with them were to make themselves the guardians and the
spokesmen of the Etruscan religion. The legends may have no
foundation in fact, but "they show that in the dim ages when
tradition was forming, Tarquinii was a centre from which
organized law and art was given forth, and whose great men were
leaders and rulers of the surrounding peoples".[2]

Walking among the fragmented remains of this world, one
finds oneself thinking in terms of the inevitable decline and
collapse of great nations. Of how, after 500 B.C., the decline of
Tarquinii itself, as of all Etruria, began. Of how, slowly but
surely, as the deadly struggle with Rome deepened, Tarquinia's
power and authority, and with it no doubt the power and the
confidence of the Etruscan people, began to weaken. Of how, as
battle followed battle and treaty followed treaty, Tarquinia
would gradually have been drawn further and further along the
path towards defeat and submission. And of how finally, in 308,
the people had no choice but to bow to the Romans and accept
the laws of an alien world. And yet how strange it is to reflect
that Tarquinia should nevertheless have remained on its ancient
site for centuries after this. True, one can accept that it would
have continued to flourish for a time, even as a Roman dependency. And we know that in 90 B.C. its people were conceded
the citizenship of Rome. But with the metropolis so close, and
with the image of Roman success and power dominating the
whole of central Italy, Tarquinia could not long have maintained
its place as a great city. It had served its purpose, and now that
the Etruscans had yielded to the triumphant machinery of Roman
civilization, so in almost every sense significant to its continuing
vitality, must Tarquinia too have yielded. What if, as late as the
second century A.D., it did still have left to it a last fleeting moment
of distinction when under the Antonine emperors it was noted

for its beauty and the beauty of its setting? Cities don't collapse overnight, unless they are destroyed, and it is hardly surprising that such an important place as Tarquinia should have continued to function. But by this time it would have had little more than a shadowy resemblance to the city it had been 700 years before. And in the centuries that followed, little by little reduced and reduced, settling deeper into obscurity and neglect, visited by famine and poverty and war, it would no doubt have gradually sunk into a condition of complete decay, its inhabitants lingering on and dwindling year by year among the ruins. It was finally abandoned in the early Middle Ages for the neighbouring town of Corneto—which was itself an ancient fortified area— and its remains left to settle into the earth and to vanish beneath an advancing riot of grass and bramble and entwining root.[3]

On a lower spur where the hillside has obviously been re- inforced to support the walls a few great blocks of tufo are still in place, rising up among others that have fallen away. From here one can look down into another valley, furthest away from Tarquinia, above which and all along the hillslope of which the walls had obviously once stretched. And further up towards the *arx* of the city, on the northern side beyond a stone farm hut, lie the exposed foundations of one of the three Etruscan temples discovered here. The ground-plan is very clear—a large rectangle divided into three parts and facing out over the valley, the front wall rising six or seven layers high out of the hillside, its huge stone blocks merging into the contours and emerging out of them like old resistant roots, the truncated roots of a great tree. On my first visit I clambered about among the stones, stood dwarfed below them, and at one moment just checked myself from falling down through a wide dark well-hole, unprotected and very deep. On the edge of this hole I peered down, and imagined myself lying there, trapped in the earthy dark. Then I stepped away, retreating from possibility into the actual moment of an April morning, across the mossed grey stones, with a sudden stabbing sense of the privilege of being alive—caught and held within the exact present, momentarily without past or future, like a man who casts no shadow. And at once it was as if I had stepped outside time to sense, in the air and under my feet, the atmosphere of this lost city where it had collapsed, its roots dying trapped in the dark earth—taut in the silence, unheard, ungraspable, forever vanquished. And above these roots we walk, unhearing, unknowing, and in the end uncaring. And yet there was surely something, I thought, we could answer to. Surely something remains that could make us turn a moment and stop and listen and see and recognize; some pulse of being that has not quite stopped beating, that belongs to Italy, to the people of Italy, and to Europe, and to each of us?

So one can say that even though this city has almost completely vanished, its spirit still remains to fertilize Italy and the Italians. "Behind the Middle Ages," as one fascinated writer, Mary Cameron, has put it:

> behind the terrible days of the breaking up of the Roman Empire, behind that Empire, with its horrors and its glories, comes the original root and stock of European civilization. Without it, Roman culture is only half explained, Roman power is a yoke, under which the nations bent in an outward uniformity, their natural evolution checked and diverted. Buried deep in the ruins of a dead past, germs lay dormant, ready to spring up and fructify when the time came, acting like yeast in the slowly reviving intellectual and civil life of the ages that have been called Dark, and filtering back into the life-blood of Europe.[4]

This is a heritage, an inheritance that belongs to us, even to those of us who come from the cold "barbarian" North. And it is not simply a remote and intangible heritage, a heritage of echoes, of the echoes that linger among desolated ruins. It has its tangible forms, its languages, voices that speak out of the silence in the shape of the dancing figures and the animals of the tombs, celebrating the act and the feast of life, intent upon their ritual salutations to the world of living beings. And so one turns to those light-inhabiting creatures of the Tarquinia tombs, finding in them an affirming impulse that draws us into a kind of intimate communion with all these hints and echoes of the Etruscan spirit.

There are all those other survivals too—the vases, the votive figures, the bronzes, the jewellery, the sculptures in stone—to bring this spirit closer. But it is to the tombs after all that one goes for its deepest expression. For here the Etruscan spirit triumphs, in an art achieved out of the spontaneous wish to delight and with a rapt sense of participation in the things of the living world. What the Etruscan painters lack in sophistication and refinement they more than compensate with their joyous energy and vitality, their celebration of the gifts of being.

As Lawrence has said of them: "They were like children: but they had the force, the power and the sensual knowledge of true adults. . . ."[5] From the salutations of the Augurs in the Tomb of the Augurs, to the high-stepping horses in so many of the tombs; from the feast-scenes with their tenderly linked couples to "the bits of 'pornografico'" in the Tomb of the Bulls, you feel the truth of this. Even these pornographic bits, as Lawrence affirms, "have the same naïve wonder in them as the rest, the same archaic innocence, accepting life, knowing all about it, and *feeling* the meaning, which is like a stone fallen into consciousness, sinking, its ripples ebbing out and out, to the extremes. The little pictures have," in effect, "a symbolic meaning, quite distinct from a *moral* meaning—or an immoral."[5] If the man-faced bull calmly accepts the man copulating with a woman who is lying on another man's back, and charges with lowered horns at the two men venting their lusts on each other, this "is not judgement. It is the sway of passional action and reaction: the action and reaction of the father of milk."[5]

The experience of the tombs is elemental and liberating. Here there seems no need of complex intellectual attitudes. No explanations are to be sought, no theories paraded. Rome and its yoking materialism, its rhetoric, its calculated and spiritless power, its ostentatious displays of wealth, its imaginative bankruptcy, are far away. Time has no place, as a record of fact. Temporal events have become symbolic. The moment is eternal, ritualistic, ceremonial. Until, that is, you come to the later tombs, when already the Etruscan spirit has begun to shrink and wither into itself, to fumble and get lost in the darkness of defeat, to yield up its vision of things.

In the great tombs, right through from the early archaic Tomb of the Bulls (dated by Arturo Stenico and others to the beginning of the second half of the sixth century B.C.) to the tombs of the fifth century, life seems to flow naturally in the figures and through the scenes. One feels that "behind all the dancing was a vision, and even a science of life, a conception of the universe and man's place in the universe which made men live to the depth of their capacity".[6] There is this repeated celebration of the dance, of sexual joy, of the delight of living and of contact. And the symbolic images which decorate the tombs—the curves and rippling lines, the circlets and flowers and leaves, the leaping dolphin and sea-horses, the birds and leopards and lions and bulls—are an intensification of this impulse, done with swift unhesitant conviction, just as men might speak the language they were born to speak. Even the occasional errors of outline that occur are rather like the momentary hesitations and wrong directions that people take when they are speaking passionately. Or as Stendhal puts it: "The man who is dominated by a deep feeling seizes at random the clearest, the most simple expression, and often it gives a double meaning. . . . It does not occur to [him] . . . to adorn an idea with a piquant turn of phrase; he thinks not at all of others."[7] And so it is with these paintings; they are done with a "childlike" intentness of feeling, a passionate absorption that enacts and presents the forms, without comment and without reflection.

Leaving aside for the moment those paintings which belong to the period of Etruscan decline, one may say, on reliable authority, that Etruscan tomb-painting falls into three distinguishing periods. Beginning with the few paintings that remain from the seventh century, the first period is defined by the impact upon it of Corinthian art, and the art of the Attic black-figure vase. This lasts till about the middle of the sixth century. Then from the middle to the end of the century come a series of paintings in

which the Ionian style predominates (though there are elements
of this present even earlier). And finally, after a period of transition, the influence of the Attic red-figure vase and its elegant
forms prevails.

Of the first, the earliest Archaic period, there are no examples
among the Tarquinian tombs, and very little anywhere, though
the Tomb of the Bulls, painted around the middle of the sixth
century, is not much later. The British Museum possesses the
famous *Boccanera* slabs, taken from a tomb at Caere; the Louvre
another set of Caere slabs; and until a few years ago the seventh-
century paintings in the Campana Tomb at Veii could still be
seen, though they have now partially vanished. But to the second
and most triumphantly expressive period belong the Tomb of the
Bulls, the Tomb of the Augurs, the Tomb of the Lionesses, the
Tomb of the Inscriptions, the Tomb of the Dead, the Tomb of
Hunting and Fishing; of the Olympiads, and the Bacchantes; of
the Baron and of the Chariots—all of which are to be found at
Tarquinia.

The last is a culmination of this half-century of development,
as it is also a transitional work in which the influence of the Greek
red-figure vases can be felt. And from it all of a sudden this
influence, and the impact of the triumph of Classical Greece,
becomes predominant, in a period of great vivacity and brilliance
to which the famous Tombs of the Leopard, the Triclinio or
Feast, and the Funeral Bed belong, as well as three or four others
which, however, bring the painting of Tarquinia to the edge of
the precipice down which the Etruscan world was so soon and
so rapidly to fall.

One carries away with one from the tombs indelible images. If,
as has been well said, "energy is eternal delight",[8] then here we
have it visually before us, life and song and music and action
trapped in forms that enable us to be ourselves partakers. This
is one great privilege that art gives us—the sense that we are
part of the recurring festival of life, with the sap rising and coming
again to flower. Though Sir Kenneth Clark, in his book *The Nude*,
dismisses the Etruscan forms with almost contemptuous indifference in four lines about Romanized tomb-figures and a curt

dismissive note about "inherent naturalism"[9] and without a single mention of the figures in these tombs at Tarquinia, his indifference seems to me a fault and his omissions glare out from the book. He does not trouble to allude to the Etruscans even in his admirable chapters on Energy and Ecstasy. They seem not to be worth more than his brief note—"owing"—for him—"three-quarters of their art to Greece".[9]

But for many of us, or for some at least, the Etruscan paintings have an originality, an immediacy, an idiosyncratic and mysterious quality, a "potency and beauty",[10] that is quite their own, arising from a profoundly symbolic vision of the things of life. To be sure, they are not laboured over, smoothed and refined for the sake of the "aesthetic effect". They are not subtle in the sense that Praxiteles is subtle. They are not in fact consciously after effect at all; there is no *dwelling* upon detail. Those anonymous painters wanted swiftly to communicate the intensity of their conviction. Indeed, they had to be swift, in the nature of the conditions—colour was laid on to the wet stucco and dried with it, allowing for no second thoughts which do not leave their mark. And it is in the very swiftness of its execution that their work has its impact—at least for those who have not refined their sensibility away to the point at which they cease to be in contact with the spontaneous impulses of art. "In the tombs," Lawrence writes, "we see it: throes of wonder and vivid feeling throbbing over death." Energy, ecstasy, joy; the sense of awe at the "mystery of the journey out of life and into death".[11]

We see it in the earliest Tarquinian tomb, the *Tomb of the Bulls*, with its symbolic central scene depicting a naked man approaching a fountain on a blue-maned high-necked horse while behind the fountain another man hides, armoured, waiting, as if to attack. These figures represent Achilles awaiting Troilus as he moves calmly and peaceably on his way. They are clearly inspired by Greek vase-painting, and the style blends certain Corinthian and Attic elements with an already pervading Ionian influence in a curiously vivid way. But they are peculiarly un-Greek in feeling. They seem to have come out of the old East, through the cultures of Crete and Cyprus and Mycenae, from the Hittites and the Phoenicians. And the most extraordinary thing about the tomb is the profusion of haunting symbols and formalized plant and tree patterns that surround the scene—very strange and haunting, a landscape of the spirit in reds and creams. One notices that strange symbolic palm-tree, for instance, like a great sun-flower between Troilus and the fountain; the pomegranate border; and the odd plant that thrusts itself up under Troilus' horse. Then there is one tree, leafless, that has hung upon it a green circlet symbolic of the female power. And also of course there are the two bulls and the graphic sexual play that they react to; and above them heraldic winged lions, a horse and rider and a zebra-headed lion. And there are two scarves of office (sacrificial fillets) draped between the trees, carelessly, and almost without regard to design. The effect of the whole is indeed a characteristic immediacy and swiftness that takes no heed even of mistakes in execution, where the first sketching of the legs of Troilus' horse remains quite visible. But one does not look here for suave sophisticated art, conscious and rationalized—there are those who, precisely because it lacks this, would no doubt refuse to even *consider* it as art. What one sees here, and what haunts and charms the senses, is "a simple uninitiated vision of the people . . . the symbols pregnant with emotion"[12]—a vision presented with unsceptical conviction, direct and elemental, totally unobscured by second thoughts or portentous underlinings.

Near this tomb on the necropolis hill is the *Tomb of the Augurs*, where the solemn, intent farewell to the dead of the two priests standing on either side of the doorway on the far wall expresses the grief and homage of a people. Here there is gravity but no morbidity. The sense of hieratic ritual, the symbolic nature of the gestures, and the economy of presentation, give the two figures a kind of monumental and tragic intensity of feeling. Their stillness is in total contrast to the activities on the two side walls— the gesturing arbitrators of the contest, the servant carrying the chair, the massive nude wrestlers themselves, the masked figure (or *phersu*) on one side inciting the dog and on the other leaping away as if pursued; the hooded man entangled with the dog; and the birds that hover or fly between. These scenes belong to the world of light and of action, and certainly their vigour moves in a different direction, away from stillness and grief and tragedy; except that on the right wall immediately next to the central scene a black-cowled servant girl sits curled on the ground in an attitude of sorrow, and the standing bearded figure beside her turns back with a gesture towards the priests as if himself paying homage as he leaves the dead. The links exist. Between the un-moving priests and the "exuberant representation of vitality and of movement"[13] depicted on the side walls there is an organic relation—the organic relation of life and its exhilarate energy to death and the stillness of death; of life continuing in the midst of death; and the journey of life towards death.

In the almost contemporary *Tomb of the Lionesses*, all this is there—the delight, the vigour, the solemnity, and a sense of mystical and sensuous community, here symbolic of the sexual roots, the renewal of life. The two heavy-uddered spotted beasts on the pediment of the far wall have their place as the heraldic guardians of the dead. They are long-bodied, with long tails and flickering tongues—creatures out of the dusk, not really lionesses at all. Below them stands a great krater with an emblematic green circlet draped around the neck. And on either side of this stands a musician—one playing a zither, the other a double flute. Then, to the right, come a pair of dancers, each leaping towards the other, knees lifted, smiling, joyously intent—the woman with her castanets, the dark-skinned man with his wine-jug. In contrast to whom, the lone female dancer to the left is doing a slow gliding classical dance, her blue-ribbed cloak swinging as she moves.

On the two side walls, between columns of the Tuscan style, are painted four monumental male figures, reclining relaxed, as if at a funeral banquet, listening and watching. They do not have their women with them, perhaps because this may be the tomb of a woman; but each holds up in his right hand an offering, his vital gesture to the complement. One—the best preserved—holds up an egg, the ovary of life. Another raises an almost obliterated drinking cup. A third has a sprig of laurel in his hand, while the fourth offers a green wreathed circlet, like that on the krater, symbolic of entry, community and issue, the female source. And at the feet of one of the men a tiny nude flute player gestures to his master.

Below runs a frieze of sliced, open pomegranates, blue and green by turns inside the serrated rind, echoing the udders of the lionesses; and these alternate with an opening lotus flower. And finally, below again, dolphin are seen leaping towards the curling waves, with birds between them in unerring flight. Everything, in fact, seems under the rapt spell of music, a music that flows along the outlines of the forms, quickening and slowing as the eye moves from dolphin to dancer and dancer to dancer, from heraldic lioness to each dark-skinned man on his couch; from dolphin to dolphin and bird to bird.

The dolphins and the birds play their vital part in others of the tombs, but nowhere with more vivacity or more acuteness of observation than in the *Tomb of Hunting and Fishing*. These frescoes are unique not only among the paintings of Tarquinia but also among the art of the entire classical period, primarily because here man is no more than an element in the scenes depicted. He does not dominate, he does not rule. He moves among the fishes and the birds. He climbs the rocks, he dives straight and swift towards the sea, he rows *upon* the sea and fishes from it, he stands tensed with his catapult upon the rocks. He has become an element in the physical world, and is contained and mastered by space, remaining at the same time vividly alive within it. The elemental forces of nature, the earth, the sea and the sky, give him his place, he has his being even as the birds have theirs. Here the whole universe is alive. In the clear air the birds are rising and scattering in swift sure flight, blue as the tunics of the men and red as their skin, and the men are below them or among them, as the diver is with them in space; and the dolphins leap or dive. "It is all," as Lawrence said of this tomb, "small and gay and quick with life, spontaneous as only young life can be. . . . Not impressive or grand . . . but . . . with just a sense of the quick ripple of life. . . ."[14] As "life-enhancing" indeed as anything that art has to offer.

The *Tomb of the Baron* has been dated a decade or so later than the Tomb of Hunting and Fishing, at the height of the Ionian

influence, coming at a critical period in the development of
Tarquinian painting, and of Etruscan art in general, when the
Attic red-figure vases were beginning to affect the forms, since
it was painted somewhere close to 510 B.C. The cross-currents it
thus betrays give the tomb an intimate and glowing atmosphere,
hushed and solemn, that is quite its own. The figures of horses and
people, so vividly presented and so richly coloured, seem to move
or to poise without sound—not as if they were a long way off, but
as if they had entered an atmosphere suffused with a softening
calm, as on a summer evening when the sun has set. It is full of
the grave mystery of salutation, of recognition and contact.
Though the little blond flute-player so intently pipes, his notes
seem almost too soft, too elusive to hear. And yet you *can* just
hear them in the moist evening air. It is as if everyone were on
the point of movement, stilled in the moment, their energy taut
and contained. There is direction of gesture, as of movement.
One can see that the horses—black and red, reined in lightly by
their riders, light, high-necked, high-stepping—are moving
towards the boy with the bearded man and the woman who
offers her salutation to them. But they move ceremonially,
between heraldic trees and the circlets hanging from the frieze,
under the leaping dolphin and the hippocampi.

The tomb is small and low and compact. It is the intimacy that
counts. In their glowing dark the dead would have lain there
haunted by the whispering of flute-notes, haunted, caressed and
reconciled against time's slow defilement and collapse. No
shadows, no ghosts, no terrorizing demons, no threatening darkness. Only the radiance and warmth of living things carried into
and beyond the stillness of death—the idea of life, continuity, love,
a vital yet unpretentious sense of Being and of the persistence of
flesh—"alive and shining in the dusk of contact".[15]

But when you have come out into the sunlight and taken
the dusty track away from this part of the Necropolis towards
Tarquinia, and to a path that leads under the aqueduct to the
third-century *Tomb of the Shields*, you leave the trapped magic of
that joyous vision of death for quite another world. Suddenly
it is all changed. Something radical has happened, the magic is

gone. Almost three centuries have passed. Suddenly, in this large four-roomed cavern, house-like in its form, you are faced with darkness and shadow and gloom. It may be that *something* of the old thrill is left, even so, as you go down the flight of steps, and especially when you enter the inner room of the shields; but it is dissipated by the tone of cold disenchantment that dominates. After the smallness and intimacy, the gaiety and colour of the older tombs, one finds the very largeness cold and empty, too full of shadow. A winged angel, half-obliterated, hovers on one wall, casting a strange depressive mood over the central room, a vague deathly greyness. And as one picks out other figures, one is somehow disappointed. The life seems to have gone out of them. They do not glow any more, they have no being of their own. They are illustrations, figures in painted scenes. The emotional and religious symbolism has all but disappeared. Only its outlines, its conventions, remain. The banquet that the couple are indulging on the right wall in front of the room of the fourteen shields, may be richly and minutely descriptive; but it is only a banquet, a little dinner-party taking place between two people. The clarity and minuteness of the detail has no emotional or vital relation to anything but what is actually going on. You will find observation of detail in the banqueting scenes of the Tomb of the Leopard, as in many of the other great tombs. But there it is always subjected to a dominating symbolic vision, by which every object and every creature becomes subtly interrelated and fused into an emotional unity—made to play its part in presenting and enacting belief, joy, delight, the identity of flesh and spirit, body and soul, fact and symbol.

In the Tomb of the Shields one is conscious of some disastrous change having taken place in the Etruscan soul; of some destructive calamity having occurred. And when one thinks of the date of this tomb, the end of the third century B.C., it is hardly surprising. By then the Etruscans had been virtually defeated by the Romans after struggling to keep themselves intact against successive (and sometimes simultaneous) wars with Gaul and Rome and Carthage; and Tarquinia itself had yielded to Roman rule, existing as a subject state since 308. By then doubt and defeat had entered the soul, and the old confidence, the old elemental sense of joy and vitality, of intactness and integrity, had been destroyed. Now the figures are portraits of a particular family called Velcha clinging to the vestiges of their communal and cultural heritage; individuals isolated in their petty aristocratic pride in a world which has collapsed around them.

No wonder that when you go to visit the interlinked third- and second-century *Tombs of Orcus and Polyphemus* (which lie under the modern cemetery a little way back up the track towards the far end of the ancient necropolis) you find yourself moving through a huge gloomy cavern inhabited by devils such as the grotesque beak-nosed Charun, with his huge heavy wings, and those Greco-Roman warriors and sages who act as understudies in the presentation of Greek myths. Doubt, collapse, terror, gloom, darkness, and an empty gesturing to the outlines of the old truths have taken over. The "wonderfully suggestive edge" that Lawrence talks about in relation to the presentation of the essentially Etruscan vision, that "flowing contour" which depicts "living things surging from their own centre to their own surface"[16] has almost completely vanished. Vestiges only remain, hints and echoes. To be sure, the famous much anthologized head of a woman in full profile on the right wall of the Orcus tomb at once attracts. And it *is* rather a delicate and charming piece of work, with something left of the Etruscan clarity and directness. A little too overtly delicate perhaps, and just a little too specific, to convince. The Tarquinians have by now bowed their heads and acquiesced in the triumph of materialism—so that all they are left with now is reflection and shadow and darkness, a languid echoing of Hellenistic models, their spirit faltering disembodied in the dark, deprived of will and conviction.

These tombs have their great value and their interest for us not as art but as a record of historical and psychological change. They form a significant human document, far more telling than words, relating to the fate of a people. Whereas before, everything, even the element of the grotesque that is in some of the earliest examples of Etruscan art (such as the Gorgon heads that formed Antefixes to the façades of temples), was "a symbolic bowing before the great forces of nature", now it degenerates into meaningless caricature. The bestial obese figure of Polyphemus, with his huge ear and his teeth bared in the long black slit of his mouth, the one monstrous nightmare eye in the process of being gouged out by Ulysses' thick pointed club; the bald nudity of a young winged demon and his languid wingless companion; the melancholy staring eyes of Greek heroes; all these images tell their tale. And perhaps most significant and telling of all, between the sages Tiresias and Agamemnon, one suddenly notices a number of little black figures climbing and swinging about on the leaves of a tall plant, loosed in space, shrunken, tiny limbo creatures, representing the spirits of men. Is this what it comes to in the end, one asks, rubbing one's eyes and looking closer? These little insect-creatures seem to demonstrate once and for all the completeness of the transformation that has taken place in the Etruscan spirit. The soul—that once danced in the full daylight of the upper world, vivid with the instinct of life, delighting in the festive moment, a vigorous and human presence—has become a mean small black anonymous insect; a little black smudge flickering about between the effigies of heroes.

And so, when Sir Kenneth Clark, in that dismissive and derogatory tone, talks of the Etruscan tomb-figure displaying "his stomach with a complacency which would have shocked a Greek profoundly",[17] he is talking about tomb-figures belonging to the centuries of Etruscan decadence and collapse, when Rome had already impressed its imperious and spiritless image upon the nation. And by his total omission of any reference to other and earlier Etruscan forms, he leaves the unfortunate impression that this is all in fact there is to the Etruscans. But they will not be passed over in such a way, referred to briefly and contemptuously in relation to their formulation of the nude during a period when the spirit of Etruscan art was already more or less spent. One needs only to think of the little diving man in the *Tomb of Hunting and Fishing*, or the wrestlers in the *Tomb of the Augurs*, or the naked Troilus in the *Tomb of the Bulls*. But there are many other examples, among those thousands of small votive figures for instance, that are scattered throughout the museums of the world, and are to be found especially at the Villa Giulia in Rome. And as for the tomb-figures themselves, one could mention the Cerveteri sarcophagus of the Couple as an example of the great resources of Etruscan art at its best. Admittedly the Couple are not nude, but they do not display their stomachs and there's no fatness, and the bodies are moulded with a tenderly expressive and plastic skill which gives this work a high place among the art of the ancient world. It has something of the mysterious tenderness and intimacy that is in the smile of the Veii Apollo, which is also in the Villa Giulia, together with that vitality and confidence common to all Etruscan art of the sixth century B.C. Though "Roman poets of the Augustan era" may have applied to the tomb-figures the epithet *pingues et obesi Etrusci*, as Sir Kenneth observes,[18] they would certainly not have seen either the painted tombs or any of the works of the centuries of Etruscan command. And if they had seen them they probably wouldn't have cared for them, taking into account the tastes of the period. But the reclining figures in the *Tomb of the Lionesses* are anyway anything but obese—neither fat nor indulgent nor even touched with a trace of the slumped complacency characteristic of so many Volterran ash-chests and Tuscanian sarcophagi. There is nothing of the slug or the sloth about them. They are vivid and strong and calm, and under them the dolphin leap. They, in common with so many of the figures in the tombs, have about them the vigorous simplicity that the figures in Giotto's Assisi and Padua frescoes have—symbolic intensity, the sense of contact, a corporeal and tactile presence, energy and interior weight.

The conspiracy of silence or of contempt which was started by the Romans and has until recently kept the Etruscans almost out of history and art, except for the brief dismissive note, is now perhaps being broken. And it is these qualities I have mentioned that will make the Etruscans "a source of highest aesthetic delight for a period at least as long as decipherable traces of (their) handi-work remain",[19] as Berenson said of Giotto. High claims perhaps; but, in common with Giotto paintings, they make their "powerful appeal to our tactile imagination, thereby compelling us, as do all things that stimulate the sense of touch, to take their existence for granted. And it is only when we can take for granted the existence of the object painted"—as we do in the tombs—"that it can begin to give us pleasure that is genuinely artistic."[20]

This is not, of course, to suggest that Berenson would himself have been drawn to the tombs—though he does write enthusiastically of "genuinely archaic art". "Such art," he says, "is necessarily the product of the striving for form and movement. . . . It may exaggerate any one tendency to the extreme of caricature, as indeed it frequently does: but through its presentation of form, or of movement, or of both, it never fails of being life-enhancing."[21] Nor do I wish to imply that the Etruscan artists had anything like the skill, the conscious intellect or the capacity of Giotto—indeed theirs was in some sense "only the simple uninitiated vision of the people". What I do imply is that Giotto, as an artist, had this vision, and displayed it in his very articulation of the Christian symbolism; and that the irresistibly infectious spirit that is in Etruscan art comes to flower again in Giotto, as it came to flower in others of the great Tuscan artists of Mediaeval and Renaissance Italy, and in the architecture of the cities that had sprung up again out of the roots of Etruscan cities at Orvieto, Perugia, Arezzo, Cortona, Firenze, Volterra, Chiusi and Tuscania—those roots lying dormant in the earth and in the blood of the people of Etruria; and perhaps not even yet exhausted.

TARQUINIA AND ITS MUSEUM

SITTING OVER LUNCH at a trattoria which overlooked the sea-gate of Tarquinia and the flat plain that stretches down to Porto Clementino and the sea, I found myself trying to visualize the town as Lawrence had seen it thirty-five years ago. He had sat "at the tin tables of the cafe above the gate watching the peasants coming in the evening from the fields".[1] But that was probably on the opposite side, where the Piazza is larger and more open, and where there is a corner bar, which may have been the one he refers to, with tables outside close to the wall. But thirty-five years is a long time, and since his visit there has been a war, and Italy has vigorously accepted "the age of technology" and the "miracle". Would Lawrence, I wondered, have found the town much changed? Today the streets and squares are choked with cars and scooters and small three-wheeler transport vehicles, that seem constantly to be moving in and out of the gate below. No longer do the peasants "drift in" through that gate, as Lawrence put it; they ride noisily in. And there will be no "Dazio", or town customs man, to ask them questions "if they carry bundles", or to prod "the pack on the ass". That little performance has now become part of the mythology of the Mussolini era, and it seems already to have assumed something of the flavour of a legend. Outside the wall there are now two petrol stations and a large parking area for cars and buses, and people come in from far and wide to be taken round the tombs.

Even as I ate my lunch I could see where, down beside the gun-grey walls of the Palazzo Vitelleschi, a fleet of six cars had gathered, with the official from the Museum ready to climb in beside the driver of the first. People no longer walk to the tombs, as Lawrence and his guide had done. Prosperity has brought its comforts, and can whisk you off almost to the very spot itself. "Walk?" we say. "But it would take us half an hour to get to the *first* of the tombs!" And as for the tombs themselves, a group of visitors will spend as long descending the steps to them and coming up again as it takes to look at the paintings. Two or three minutes is enough, it seems. You peer round, make a few remarks, the guide talks incomprehensibly about some detail or another, and then you are up again in the air, perhaps with relief, who knows.

All this, of course, touches little more than the surface of things. Here at Tarquinia many pasts persist—interactive, multiple, weaved into the texture of the life of the town. Behind the façade, much no doubt is left of what Lawrence had perceived, the continuities of the peasant world with its roots stretching back through all the vicissitudes of Italy's besetting history. And no doubt even centuries ago the peasants would have come in from the fields at dusk—after "working the land", as Lawrence put it, "with that careful, almost passionate attention the Italian still gives to the soil"[2]—in much the same way as they do today, despite cars and motor-bikes. The present Tarquinia, the town itself, is an amalgam, a haphazard growth in brick and stone and mortar, of that history. It has even absorbed remains from the Etruscan city, abandoned on that other hill beyond, and wherever you walk there are the signs, the apparent and implicit signs, of history and change.

It is only since 1872 that the town has been known as Tarquinia. For at least 1,300 years before that, since A.D. 504 and the earliest surviving records, it was called Corneto. And from the records we can assume that it was once a place of some importance. In 1056, for instance, the city joined with Tuscania in defying the Church at the instigation of Robert Guisgard, in the first of many rebellious actions. Less than a century later it was sacked for taking the part of the Antipope Anacletus. And twice, in 1169 and in 1203, it came into conflict with Viterbo. Frederick II occupied the city in 1270, and five years later it was once more sacked, no doubt for some new act of defiance, by the Imperial troops. During the fourteenth century, the century of its highest development, many powerful princes stayed there, either on their way to or from Rome. At that time, it had a population of

35,000, more than fifty churches, and seven hospitals. And it was
important enough, even in 1492, for Alexander VI to seek refuge
there from the plague, and later for Julius II and Leo X, staying
at the Palazzo Vitelleschi, to grace it more than once with their
presence.[3] After which it gradually declined, its monuments
lapsing into neglect, its people decimated by disease, and especially
by the ferocious attacks of malaria that were a curse to the
district until the early years of this century, when the Maremma
was drained. So that now the mediaeval city—with its many
towers, its churches and its houses—lingers on as a record in stone
of a former splendour, in melancholy reflection, gaunt against the
sky. Not that Tarquinia's history is at an end. People live there
with vigour, and it will go on quietly shaping itself out of the past.

Being on the hill of the necropolis, the site is unlikely to have
been inhabited until after the collapse of the ancient city. But all
the same it has its own links with the Etruscan past. One has the
sense of roots entangled untraceably; of vanished events and
moments assuming a mythical and imaginative reality—all of
which one finds oneself coming into an obscure identity with.
It is not that the Tarquinian past in itself can be made to live
again. It lives on only perhaps in so far as we are able to make it
live through facts and to reach back into ourselves, to where the
symbols and images and events of our own lives lie, and a sort of
correspondence, an imaginative transference, can take place.
"Corneto can have charms for few," was George Dennis's verdict
a hundred years ago.[4] But though the peculiar intimacy, the
melancholy quiet of the place, are not perhaps of the kind to
excite the curiosity of many, they give it a special charm that
adds in fact to the experience of Etruscan Tarquinia a sense of
density and depth, a physical and historical continuity.

The Palazzo Vitelleschi aptly demonstrates this. It has a superb
colonnaded courtyard with open upper galleries and gothic
arches; and a great gaunt cube of a tower rises from one corner,
built of squared blocks that lock together closely, testifying to the
skill of mediaeval craftsmen and the continuity of a craft mastered
centuries before by the Etruscan masons. And most important of
all it houses the collection of Etruscan antiquities.

In the courtyard, first, are a number of sarcophagi in furred grey nenfro, a stone of the district. The rough-hewn reclining figures lie staring up, half-collapsed upon the coffin-lids, in attitudes of plaintive appeal—wide-faced, the eyes far apart, the energy and vividness of limb gone slack, the stomachs swelling. But even though these figures belong to the centuries of Etruscan defeat and the dominance of Rome, they still have something of an aura about them. They are massive, calm, severe. They accept their fate, perhaps complacently, but with an odd kind of child-like equanimity. And they aren't all totally collapsed into slothful indifference with fat stomachs. They may have little of the eloquence of the earlier Etruscan forms, but they still sometimes retain a touch of the symbolic mystery, even in their poses. It was still in the blood, after all, and one can sense it in the carving, in the very idiosyncrasy of the forms, however blurred and slackened, however backward-looking. The *Phiale* or *Patera*, a disk with a raised centre, which, for instance, one sees in the hands of the male effigies, is no mere object, but an ancient symbol of the creative roots, the source of fertility, "the indivisible god, containing within himself the germ of cosmic life".[5] It still carries something of the symbolic power, however negligently and carelessly held. Indeed, there is one sarcophagus here which emphasizes this in a particularly touching way. A thin, long-necked, whippet-like dog is depicted resting his head upon the *patera* where the man holds it against his thigh. Here dog and *patera* and man are in intimate contact; and though the dog seems literally to be mourning his master and is perhaps *too* literal to carry much symbolic weight, he nevertheless takes his place in the scheme of things as an image for the instinctual natural energy of life—a reduction perhaps, linked passively to death, yet still a part of the indivisible universe.

The carving on this sarcophagus, of soldiers in battle, is in the Hellenistic style, for it belongs to the third century B.C., but the effect for all its clumsiness is of the shadowy ritual of another, pre-Hellenic age. It seems to look back to it, even through the weary gestures of the fighters, even in the portrayal of exhaustion, weariness, collapse—in the despair for instance of the old man leaning on his spear, hardly able to stand upright. And on other sarcophagi the carving brings back vividly the old rapt world of symbolic forms. In one sunlit corner of the courtyard, again, there is a relief of two curling sea-horses heraldically facing each other—muscular and rippling; and another of two winged rampant beasts on either side of a large *phiale*. Then there is the famous *Sarcophagus of the Magnate*, which, though rather late and Romanized, still has a characteristic Etruscan liveliness about it. One of its reliefs, depicting the battle of the Centaurs and the Lapiths, reveals the late Etruscan obsession with demons, where two Lapiths are being tormented by winged genii, one of whom has serpents twined round his arm, and the other a sickle and a torch, as in the Orcus tomb and on many of the vases. The polychrome colours in which the sarcophagus is painted are wonderfully preserved, and there is a long inscription engraved in red letters around the cornice. We are here a long way from the symbolic ceremonial of the tombs perhaps, but the piece has its impact all the same. There is at once a heavy attempt to portray a mythology of vivid forms, and a sense of plaintive longing as if for the gaiety and carelessness of the old vanished mystery. Indeed the great interest of so many of these late sarcophagi lies in the consistency of their attempt to keep intact the collapsing values of the Etruscan world; and they cannot help but betray the resignation and the weariness or the shoulder-shrugging complacency that comes upon a people whose world is falling to pieces around them. Still it may be said that the positions of the figures are more or less the same as that of the man in the Tomb of the Lionesses or of the sixth-century Cerveteri sarcophagus of the Couple. But all the tautness and vitality, all the marvellous hieratic dignity has gone, and we are left with pathos and fatalism, the passivity of the day-dreamer dreaming out his vanquished life.

The cemeteries which extend along the heights around the site of the ancient city have yielded a vast quantity of beautiful things over the last 150 years. Much inevitably has gone, bought and sold upon the market, scattered far and wide, to end up in museums and private collections as far apart as America and

Russia. But it is reassuring to know that so much of Tarquinia's art should have remained to enrich the place itself; and it is exciting to hear that new discoveries can be made even today, after a century and a half of continuous excavation. Among the most sensational finds of recent years for instance (by C. M. Lerici, with the help of electronic devices) was the 1959 discovery of the sixth-century Tomb of the Olympiads.[6] The only pity is that the tombs should have to be left empty; that they should all have to be deprived of their contents. But people are unfortunately not to be trusted. Given the inadequate means available for maintenance and protection, and the alarming successes of the tomb-robbers (who are finding the Etruscans more profitable than ever) it would not be possible to risk leaving things behind a mere locked door. So the next best thing is to have a fine museum on the spot, arranged in such a way as to act as a setting to the tombs and an eloquent commentary upon them. Which is exactly the function and the achievement of the Tarquinia Museum. Coming from the Tomb of the Baron, for instance, with the impact of those glowing colours and forms still fresh, one finds oneself suddenly confronted by the lovely cot-like sarcophagus in terracotta which is to be found in one of the lower rooms. This, with its high-necked long-tailed horses, its dividing plant-forms, its dark nude men caught within their flowing contours, has the same quick poetry as that marvellous little tomb, done with a minimum of fuss. The experience of the tombs is confirmed and given perspective, richness, depth, and we are back in the world "before Christ and the logos", with nature accepted as "the mystical spring of strength and of life",[7] the regenerating source.

There is much else in the Palazzo Vitelleschi to confirm this view—the odd curves of plain black bucchero, those early eighth- and seventh-century funerary urns with their constantly varied geometric patterns; the superb proto-corinthian hydras of the seventh century, richly decorated with processions of formalized animals and patterns of closely interwoven circles; the sixth-century Attic black-figure amphorae and hydras with their nimble athletes, their bacchic scenes and scenes of battles and their symbolic animals, enacting homage to the elemental forces which they symbolize. And even when one comes to the Greek and Etruscan red-figure vases of the fifth and fourth centuries, elegiac and lucid, the magic is still there, in spite of rationalism. It may be that the purely Etruscan pieces do not have the delicacy or the precision of the Attic; that in comparison they seem crude and awkwardly executed; but they have all the same a characteristic liveliness, a curious careless energy.

And in one sense comparisons are not what count here. If the Attic pieces stand out for their sheer quality, we are not less interested in the Etruscan pieces, where the manner even of painting similar scenes is quite distinct. What counts here is that the various styles and periods, the diversity of forms, give us a complementary sense of the Etruscan delight in fine things, and a comprehensive view of the growth and decline of a culture. And when the Etruscan paints the heroes and tragic figures of Greek myth, even as late as the fourth century, he paints them unreflectively and carelessly but with a kind of spontaneous conviction. There is one showcase, for instance, which exhibits nine purely Etruscan painted vases, with silhouetted figures of swiftly running athletes, with male and female dancers, their hands and feet lifted, their bodies turned or extended in the delight of movement; there is even a silenus alertly making for a woman. These bear out the unpredictable, one might almost say "fauve", beauty of Etruscan art as against the suave and sometimes monotonous virtuosities of the Attic black-figure pieces which appear in all the museums in such profusion. Granted the Attic Greeks had brought the technique of vase-painting to a point of high refinement; yet they lack the kind of quirks and audacities that give the Etruscan pieces their special charm and particularity. Etruscan art, even in decline, never gets refined away to the point of impersonality, but remains vividly (and waywardly) singular. One turns from a fourth-century amphora perhaps to the two large bucchero hydras of the sixth century, embossed with processions of ornamental figures above a band of grimacing gorgon shield faces; and from these to the great winged horses close by in honeyed terracotta with traces of colour remaining, taken from a temple of the acropolis. These fourth-century horses,

3 GOLD BRACELET AND FIBULA. Seventh century. From the Regolini–Galassi Tomb at Cerveteri. The figures are embossed on sheet gold with geometric motifs and outlines in granulated filigree (*pp. 165–6*).

4 VOTIVE FIGURE (FEMALE) IN TERRACOTTA. Seventh century. From Cerveteri. One of the earliest examples of Etruscan sculpture. Found with two others, one male, one female, and a gold clasp (*p. 168*).

have the grace and poise, the sensuous animation of Greek models; but there is a stylization about the forms which makes one think of the horses in the Tomb of the Baron and the head of the sixth-century horse in the Tomb of the Bulls, with its oddly stylized blue mane. The logic of proportion may be Greek, but it has the Etruscan vivacity.

Tarquinia was of course among the first of the cities of Etruria, and there are some beautiful pieces even from as far back as the ninth and eighth centuries, from the so-called Villanovan period. Indeed, Tarquinia has been found to be particularly rich in the well-tombs that produced those superb bronze and impasto cinerary urns with upturned bowls for lids, which exist in such abundance in the Florence Archaeological Museum. These and the objects in bronze and in gold often found buried with them are not peculiar to Tarquinia. Nor are they called Villanovan for any other reason than that it was at the cemetery of Villanova outside Bologna that the first examples were discovered. Some nineteenth-century theorists, on the strength of these Bolognese finds and others beyond the recognized limits of Etruria, put forward theories that the early tribes that settled in Italy had come down from the north from Germany. But these were later called into doubt by the overwhelming evidence that came to light from all over Etruria to demonstrate that this Villanovan culture was equally as active during the same period and even earlier at places as far apart as Veii, Vetulonia, Bizenzio and Tarquinia. And with the discoveries at Vetulonia, made as late as 1880, and at Populonia, unknown till the first decades of the twentieth century, these theories were clearly contradicted, leaving the question of origin still open to examination.

Here at Tarquinia there are some superb examples, and one large cinerary urn in particular holds the eye with its incised geometric patterns and the studded, crested bronze helmet that covers it. There are many bronze implements and ornaments too—spearheads, knives, forks, cups, pins, brooches, pendants, rings, and great shields studded and embossed with zig-zags and meanders, and other objects in gold or amber or bone. These things are often minutely worked, into many and varied patterns

C

and forms. No matter how small the object or how mean, it has lavished on it the minute attention of the craftsman, and is invested by his skill with a mysterious human significance. One needs only to look at the plain black impasto vase with its long three-branched neck and tense extended lip (found among other pieces from a seventh-century tomb) to sense the impact of the form, its vital phallic thrust. Or at the greyish-brown ribbed jug in the same case with its neck rising to a raised lip that follows out the curve of the handle. Even such apparent simplicity has its charge of meaning, its conviction, the peculiarly unclassical quality and power of the Etruscans.

Indeed, everything tends to illuminate and to confirm the experience of the tombs. And when you discover that the museum actually contains five of the most famous and most endangered of the tomb paintings themselves, the link between museum and tombs is brought as close as it can ever be. The paintings were cut away from the rock, wall by wall, and reassembled in a great long room on an upper floor of the Palace. The operation must have been delicate in the extreme, but was carried out with great success, leaving the frescoes almost unharmed. It may seem a questionable thing to deprive the paintings of their proper setting, of the unique atmosphere created around them by those little underground chambers. But then one could say the same of most museum pieces—which are bound to lose something of their meaning by being abstracted from their surroundings. And we have to accept that if these frescoes had been left in place much longer, they would have vanished for ever from the walls, their colours fading, the stucco crumbling away under the action of the damp. This was how the *Campana Tomb* at Veii vanished, and how the condition of the *Tomb of Hunting and Fishing* is day by day deteriorating. You can even see the beads of moisture forming on the rock and seeping through to loosen and dislodge and flake away the coloured surfaces. So either the frescoes were to be left to their fate, or cut away from the rock and housed in places where they could have some protection. And though the purists may be all for leaving them, as things are Tarquinia will be the fortunate possessors for at least a foreseeable future of five of the paintings and perhaps more as time goes on and the authorities find time and capital to do the necessary work on others.

The earliest of these tombs, which has been dated to the end of the sixth century—contemporary, that is, with the Tomb of the Baron, the beautiful but almost ruined Tomb of the Dead Man, and the Cardarelli Tomb—is also one of the latest to be discovered. It was found in 1959, the year before the last Rome Olympiad; and by a strange coincidence, all the figures on the side walls of the tomb happened to be athletes engaged in strenuous contest. Hence its name: the *Tomb of the Olympiads*.

Let us look at this tomb in detail. On the end wall, opposite the entrance, you will see a shut door, half obliterated, painted to symbolize the entrance to a sepulchre. This door stands between a man and woman, who dance before it a kind of propitiatory ritual dance, distinct from the games. But on the left wall the competition is in full swing. Here, four charioteers are engaged in the thrust and flurry of contest, tensed to the urgency of the race, their muscles flexed, their bodies intent upon the thrill of headlong movement. The last of the drivers has lost control and is about to fall, and this incident adds a sense of anxiety and striving to the race, making victory or defeat seem vitally to matter. But it is the way in which the hair of riders and horses is blown back from their foreheads; the way the men are tensed forward, their muscles tautly in play; the whole intent and flow of the design, that gives the scene its vivacity. These men, one feels, are in triumphant celebration of their dead. Triumphantly, precipitately, in the sheer joy of motion they ride. And on the opposite wall, where three runners move, arms outflung as if in the course of a hard- and fast-fought hundred metres, the energy and tension and the vivacity are concentrated even more into the muscular details of arms and torsos. Those vivid profiled Ionian heads, the fleet nude bodies, move towards the end wall, away from another figure who, with his arms thrust back behind him, seems about to make a jump; and a fifth, with discus in hand, who stands balanced for his throw. And then, at the end of this wall, much disfigured (a shadowy figure) appears the *phersu* or masked joker—he who in the Tomb of the Augurs (with which this tomb has affinities both in its theme of enacted sport and its symbolic door) presides over the combat with the dog. Perhaps he personifies or parodies the negative threatening forces of the unknown dark, as the *gorgon* or the *maenad* heads from the pediments of temples. But he is on the verge of the action and he cannot disturb it. Nor is he seriously intended to. He exists as a kind of watcher, and perhaps sometimes as an entertainer, who prances about between races, grimacing and clowning.[8]

"Everyone," George Dennis wrote in the 1840s, "must be struck by the inappropriateness of such scenes to a sepulchre"; adding that "happily for us . . . our view is not bounded by a paradise of mere sensual gratification."[9] But to at least one observer, the scenes of these early tombs seem, on the contrary, profoundly appropriate; every bit as appropriate and as just, one might say, as those conceived on the "high vantage-ground of Christianity",[9] as Dennis puts it—if not more so, since it is life rather than death which is celebrated here; life and its potentiality as life, rather than the dark intangibilities beyond life. It was not "a glorified existence" the Etruscans sought to represent, but a joyous salutation, a gesture from the living world, an offering of intent and vital being to the dead. Their "active religious idea", in Lawrence's words, "was that man, by vivid attention and subtlety, could draw more life into himself". For them, as for the whole of the ancient world, there were no personal gods. "It was the living cosmos itself . . . which was divine",[10] and the figures of the tombs are symbolic of this vital principle, celebrating the mystery and the delight of death and life, even as these athletes do.

Dennis never saw the tomb of course, but he did see the more or less contemporary *Tomb of the Dead Man*, and from his description of it, you get some sense of the contrast (as he saw it) between the scene of mourning—where a young woman leans towards the dead man "in the act of drawing his hood over his eyes"—and the scenes (as they once were) on the other walls, where four naked men dance "in Bacchanalian frenzy", one playing a flute, two others offering up drinking cups, the fourth holding a circlet in his hand. To Dennis they seemed "unconscious of, or indifferent to, the mournful scene adjoining".[11] But this is to judge from

Christian standards, by which we reverence our dead with silence and gloom and solemn prayer; and it is only in the light of such a judgement that these dancers are likely to be seen as "incongruous and inappropriate".

The figures in the Tomb of the Dead Man (even in Dennis's time "torn into fragments and almost destroyed") have now all but vanished. But enough of them remains to prove that they are very similar to the figures on the Olympiad tomb. One notices, for instance, the striking similarity between the bearded man on the end wall of the former, and that of the last of the three runners in the latter. These profiles, with their intent staring eyes, their long rounded noses and curious ornamental forelocks, are very distinctive and idiosyncratic and Etruscan—and if at the same time they have their reference to Ionian forms, that is simply to affirm the closeness of the links between the ancient Hellenic cultures of the Mediterranean world. Competent authorities (Moretti, Stenico, Pallottino and others) place these tombs somewhere between 530 and 520—a few years earlier, that is, than the Tomb of the Baron, in which the influence of the Attic red-figure vases imported into Etruria at that time marks a decided shift of direction and of style.

In the *Tomb of the Chariots* (delle Bighe), the second of the five frescoes in the Museum, which has been dated to around 490 B.C., there is at once a feeling of transition, of culmination, of change. For the first time the decoration is divided into two parallel friezes. The lower and larger of the two depicts figures stylized in the archaic manner, banqueting and dancing on a red ground. But in the upper and smaller frieze (which is no more than a foot high) the numerous athletes, riders and charioteers, seen against a creamy background, are closely linked to the forms on Attic red-figure vases. These contrasts of style seem clearly to indicate that Etruscan art had reached a crucial stage in its development—which is hardly to be wondered at; for even at this very moment were the cultural and artistic bonds which had linked the whole of the Mediterranean world beginning to be undermined and loosened. The old "cosmic vision", the "ancient idea of kings . . . who are gods by vividness", of those who had "lived, ultimately, by the subjective control of the great natural powers",[12] was dying. The archaic world, in other words, was being superseded. And although the triumphant logic of the classical Greek ideal was to have a positive influence upon the Etruscans for about a century afterwards, this was very soon to be confused and sapped by the debilitating influence of Rome. For Rome, one remembers, had already (in the fifth century) started on her journey towards conquest and supremacy.

The Bighe Tomb, however, reflects nothing of this, except implicitly, as a record of the transition between one world and another, between the old archaic world and the emerging ethos of classical Greece. For it is still quite unmistakably Etruscan in its character. The naked athletes of the upper frieze have an immediacy, a freedom and careless exuberance that links them closely to the dancers and celebrants of earlier tombs. They are perhaps more studied, more decorative and therefore less profoundly symbolic than those flying athletes of the Olympiad Tomb. Yet—riding, jumping, wrestling, pole-vaulting, throwing the javelin or the discus, preparing their chariots or the swift high-necked horses (painted in red, blue or white) for racing, they exist in their moment of quick being like children. And even the spectators seen grouped under tents, on stands or platforms at the corners of the walls, seem to be taking part.

This is a richly decorated tomb. For besides the innumerable athletes of the upper frieze, there are the three pairs of males of the lower, reclining on their couches in the characteristic pose, making their symbolic offerings. And on the right wall—both female and male, the women dressed in tunic and chlamys, the men almost naked—are the dancers. Among whom, one in particular stands out—a girl, invested with the delicate feline grace of an enchantress, playing the double flute, dressed in a long white robe with a red mantle, and wearing on her head a red and white conical hat. Then, on the pediment of the far wall, a reclining male figure—garlanded, naked to the waist, head turned to the centre, hand raised in offering—for the first time takes the place of the heraldic beasts, each side of the central scrollwork beam support, where a large krater stands between two naked servers. But the animals have not gone. How could they be left out? Two panthers and a pair of geese heraldically adorn the pediment above the doorway. Nor is even this all; for the beam of the ceiling itself is decorated with large spoked discs like suns, the symbolic *patera*; and on either side the slopes of the ceiling are rich with a chequer-work of squares in red and cream.

This tomb is of unique interest, then, in referring both to the archaic forms of the earlier tombs, and to the immaculate figures on Greeks vases, which were to herald the artistic triumphs of classical and Hellenistic Greece. It marks, in other words, a turning point. Twenty years later, when the famous *Tomb of the Triclinium* (or Feast) was painted, the transition from one style to another, from one world and one way of seeing and feeling things to another, had been made. The archaic simplicity and vigour, the swift almost careless articulation, the symbolic intensity, no longer dominate. One may say that the peculiarities that so distinguish the forms of Etruscan painting are no less apparent here than in the earlier tombs. But they have been transformed by the impact of the Greek world upon the painter's sensibility.

Indeed, it is the very fluency and elegance of the painting that makes the Tomb of the Triclinio perhaps the most famous of all the tombs at Tarquinia. It was painted a few years after the equally famous *Tomb of the Leopards* (not in the Museum) which, both in composition and in treatment, it resembles. But what a difference there is in the art of the painting! The painter of the Triclinio tomb shows himself to be a master, in possession of an artistic culture at once refined and experimental, with a command of form and of line that is quite clearly neither improvised nor approximate. This indeed is one of the distinctive features of the work. It is considered, sophisticated, conscious, and far superior in execution and in expressive intent to the Tomb of the Leopards. Notwithstanding the vigour, the charm and the gaiety of the latter, with its striding musicians, its feasters, and the pair of magnificent heraldic leopards that adorn the pediment above the banqueting scene, it remains a trifle stereotyped, belonging in spirit to the old archaic world and its immediacy while at the same time having yielded something of the old symbolic intensity, since in style it is decorative and lyrical. Whereas the painter of the Triclinio tomb magnificently resolves the problem, moving with certainty and precision and reconciling the deep-rooted values of the Etruscan culture with a new freedom of expression.

The elegance and poetry, the sense of fluid and harmonious movement, the conviviality that pervades the whole tomb, and the brilliance of the colours, quite ravish the senses. No wonder Dennis was a little shocked, for it was this tomb that brought forth his diatribe on the theme of inappropriateness.[13] And yet there is such tenderness, such gravity in the presentation of the dancing and the feasting, and such vivacity, that one surely cannot remain indifferent to or unaware of the ceremonial religious intent of the scenes. They are surely expressive of something more than "the highest sensual enjoyment". For one thing, a strange ennobling fluency and calm, a subtle hieratic grace, dominates and contains even the most apparently abandoned of the dancing women on the side walls. These figures are not engaged in any indulgent bacchanalian frenzy. They seem on the contrary to be poised in the act of honouring their dead within the high flowering of their vivacity. Everywhere, there is the sense of community, of contact, of joyous emotion; in the swing of the richly bordered garments worn by the women; in the curves of the limbs where they are to be seen through the transparent skirts or tunics; in the stylization of the folds of mantles and tunics; in the gestures and the intent profiles; in the closeness of the contact between the three pairs of men and women (the third but for the man much ruined by damp) reclining in the midst of their banquet attended by their servants; in the cat and the fowl that move beneath the tables; or the trees that form a delicate tracery linking dancer to dancer, and the exotic birds that balance on the branches. And how lightly and with what rapt quiet the two musicians move, caught in the mystic trance of song.

These are not the creatures of a gloomy prohibitive religion, "a system of spiritual tyranny" rendering Etruria, as Dennis has it, "inferior to Greece". If Etruria was inferior to Greece, it was certainly not in religious principle. She may have proved herself in course of time inferior to Rome as a nation of warriors and killers (as the English were to the Normans); but Dennis has to admit that it was her religion that "bound its votaries in fetters, if not of entire harmony, at least of peace". "Those civil contests," he observes, "which were the disgrace of Greece, which retarded her civilization, and ultimately proved her destruction, seem to have been unknown in Etruria."[14] Surely the application of the pejorative "inferiority" depends on what you mean by it. A "spiritual tyranny", if that is what it was, that manages without cruelty or constant repression to keep the peace between its people, is a tyranny one ought to be able to applaud. It certainly does not deserve to be called "inferior"—except that in embracing the arts of peace it leaves itself exposed to those superior races that thrive by nature on the arts of war. I find it difficult, anyway, to understand how Dennis can write about the "gloomy, unbending, imperious character"[14] of the Etruscan religion, and then go on to describe the scenes of "joy and festivity" that he finds in the tombs. Perhaps he means to imply that the tombs have little reference to the religion. But this would be manifestly absurd. For even the Tomb of the Triclinio, apparently so dedicated to the pleasures of godless living, is permeated with a ceremonial religious view of life, and its spirit is one of tenderness and reverence for its beings, held within their moment of ecstatic spontaneity before the gates of death, as "the life-bringers and the death-guides".

The two other tombs in the Museum are almost as impressive, embodying their own particular themes of celebration, the one named after the great ship painted on its left-hand wall, the other after the empty cushion-piled funeral bed that occupies the far wall. But it is not with these that I would wish to bring this chapter to a close, but with a brief look at two other tombs among the many that lie scattered about the necropolis. The Cardarelli Tomb (named after the poet Vincenzo Cardarelli, born at Tarquinia) and the Tomb of the Bacchante, are not often visited because of their condition, but they demonstrate with particular intensity the peculiarly Etruscan qualities. It is probable that they were both done by the same painter, for stylistically they have much in common. They have been dated to between 520 and 510—earlier, that is, than the Tomb of the Baron, perhaps a little later than the Tomb of Hunting and Fishing, and more or less contemporary with the Tomb of the Olympiads.

The *Cardarelli Tomb*, like so many others, is a joyous festival of dance and music. In all, there are thirteen human figures on the walls of the tomb, each offering his gift to the dead before the red and cream studded door on the far wall, each referring to the fertility and vigour of the living world. Even the studs in the door have their significance. They take the form of little cream circles with flame-red centres, reflecting the circleted discs that decorate the central beam and the circlet offered by one of the male figures, as the symbol of fecundity. On the pediment above the door, each side of a red and white scroll, a strange spotted gazelle rears up, its front legs splayed out, pursued heraldically by a red-bodied lion with one paw raised—perhaps to strike, in the act of trapping the gazelle before sinking its teeth into the hind-quarters.

To the right of the door a man in a diamond-patterned tunic plays the double flute, an amphora on the ground in front of him. To the left a krater stands before a lyre-player, who is now half-defaced by damp. The music whispers on in homage to the dead, tenuously, outside the great red door. Yet on the left side-wall a woman dances, in sheer delight of movement, in flowing robes, her arms spread out, moving to the rhythms of this music or another music—perhaps of the servant flautist on the other side of the plant that divides the wall in two. This woman (hair covered by a beautiful conical headdress or *tutulus*) is flanked by a female slave with a drinking cup raised in one hand and a mirror in the other, and another slave with a fan. Then comes the flautist, turned to face her, smaller than she but taller than the slave and therefore of higher rank. And behind *him*, a full-sized nude male stands poised, his left arm raised in swift ecstatic greeting, offering up a kylix, a circlet draped over the forearm, the right arm flung back above the head with hand crooked in that strange hieratic gesture which is almost mime, and the head tilted exultantly in wordless salutation.

On the right wall next to the flute player, a nude male lifts his knees in the gaiety of dance while a little slave behind him plays the lyre. These two are divided from the others by a tall decorative plant—beyond which stand a slave with a wine-jar and another naked male in the act of tipping a kylix towards him to drink. The plant has a red belt thrown carelessly across its formalized lower branches.

Finally, on each side of the entrance doorway, a nude wrestler stands, big-limbed, big-bellied, leaning a little backward. Each faces the other, as if calculating an attack, in the virile spirit of competition and of play.

There is a flute player of course in the *Tomb of the Bacchante*, and all but two of the figures are depicted in swift ecstatic movement—hence the name of the tomb. But this is certainly no ordinary bacchanale. It is a ceremony, a homage to the dead, again symbolic of community and contact. The room is tiny, little more than half the size of the Cardarelli tomb, but the figures in it nevertheless seem large, full-bodied. They do not stay flat against the walls, they glow at you, inhabiting space. The heraldic gazelles and lions on the pediment, and the encircled discs and leaves that decorate the central beam repeat almost exactly the pattern of the other tomb. But here there is no door. Instead, a sharp-leaved plant thrusts up; and each scene is separated by a similar plant; also little circlets of leaves hang from the eleven-banded frieze.

The most conspicuous of the figures is the couple on the right-hand side of the far wall. A dark-skinned man with grizzled beard has put his arm around the shoulder of an elegantly-dressed young woman—fair-skinned, according to the convention. They are both in motion, walking together, intimately in contact. He—striding, thickly built—gazes at her in positive and masculine delight; and she has turned her head to smile back up at him a swift impulsive smile the radiance of which is accentuated as much by the outflung arms as by the tilt of the head and the *tutulus* that covers her hair.

The painting, only a little marred by damp and age, is done freely, and the outlines demonstrate an undeliberated childlike assurance, the forms having been clearly visualized beforehand by the artist. It is the *freedom* of the execution that is childlike; for the vivacity, the tenderness, the sexual charm and the intent gaiety of these lovers is profoundly adult. They are images of celebration. They have the glow and the mystery of affirmation about them. They belong to the world, and characteristically it is their vividness they offer in homage to the dead.

And what are we to say about the other figures? The lyre-player, dancing, his instrument reversed, who occupies the left-hand side of the end wall? (One is here reminded of the competition between Apollo and Marsyas, when Apollo sang hymns to the gods with a reversed lyre to demonstrate his superiority.[15]) Or the nude flute-player and the man with the raised drinking cup of the right-hand wall? Or the group of dancers on the left? There is certainly an air of abandon and gaiety about them. But this is not the abandon and gaiety of drunkenness, but rather of praise. These people raise their arms and leap and turn in praise. They seem caught up in the trance of life, inhabiting the light, and moving through it vividly, as the lovers do.

And what, finally, is most remarkable about this and so many other tombs at Tarquinia, is that there are no warriors, no scenes of deadly combat or of cruelty. War, that killing struggle, is far away. The dead are feted, entertained, in gravity and joy. This is their privilege. The living do not drool or whine, or strut. They dance; they play; they smile. They see their dead in terms of light and music. And the highest honour they can think of is to offer them, these dead, the pleasures of community, of love and amity and friendly competition. And the quavering phrases of the double flute seem to hover in the air, a signal to the dancers and their lifted knees, their curved-back hands that trace the patterns of the music.

This is one of the most striking and disarming characteristics of the Etruscans—in so far as we see them through the remnants of their world. It is a strange fact: that they should have demonstrated so pronounced a bias toward the arts of life and of peace; that so few of their scenes should have been dedicated to the celebration of martial triumph and of war. Nowhere before the fifth century does one find men idolized as destroyers or conquering heroes, as armed warriors. In fact it is only on the late, and Romanized, ash-chests and sarcophagi of Volterra, Chiusi and Tuscania that you find any pictures of battles; and these—however vigorous—often portray the weariness and pathos of war. And the obsessive contorted forms of the winged genii that come then, come only to cast heavy and monstrous shadows across the living world, as symbols of insecurity and defeat. And what warlike figures there are in the tombs seem frozen into passivity, to have lost their capacity to move, to have become mere effigies, voided of life. How different from the dancers of the Cardarelli Tomb or the Tomb of the Feast, where the figures move quick with life and the triumph of life, even to the edge of silence and death, and beyond.

And so one comes up out of the tombs, into sunlight, on to the open green. And there before one are the hills, and there, again, is the voided plateau of the ancient city. And it is hard to credit that the images one carries with one could possibly refer to a people so remote, a culture quite so extinct or quite so buried as the temporal world would suggest. As one walks across the green ridge, with Tarquinia lying ahead and the sea glistening suave in the western distance, the Etruscans nevertheless seem very close, and very much alive, in spite of the temporal fate that submerged them. They survive here like voices, glowing off the walls of their subterranean tombs, dancing their delight in life, and with something of the essence in them of the vigour of life—as if in the certainty that the values they celebrated could survive even death; as indeed (at least until now) they have.

4

TARQUINIA: HOMAGE TO THE DEAD

ONE GOOD FRIDAY evening, after a day spent inland around Lake Bolsena, I made my way back in the dusk to Tarquinia, where I had taken a room for the night. The town lay winking in a cluster of lights on the hill, and by the time I'd reached the sea-gate, a thin fine rain was falling. I was the more surprised, therefore, to find the town crowded with people. For a moment or two I wondered even what they were doing out in the streets. It was as if I'd stumbled unprepared and uninformed upon some private celebration. It had all but slipped my mind what day this was. I stood watching the people moving about in lively groups all up the long main street, and mingled with them as they drifted towards the Piazza. In the dark and under the lights knots of people stirred and swayed and broke apart and formed again, appearing out of doorways and side-streets, arriving on scooters or in cars, peering down from windows. It was a noisy, excited gathering, the kind one might have expected to see at a wedding. There were the young men, dark-skinned in their starched white shirts and dark suits; the older men, stiffer, less at ease, their collars too tight, their suits too formal; the girls parading up and down in couples; the women shepherding children as they talked; the fathers and grandfathers standing in doorways with babies (dressed as if for christening) in their arms; and the watchers leaning from their windows like spectators at a play; and here and there among the crowd, little girls flitted about in tinsel wings. There were the sudden encounters and explosive greetings, the smiles and shoutings of friends. And everywhere an infectious sense of expectancy, as though some great event were soon to be enacted.

As of course it was. And I had wandered in like an unsuspecting pagan, a casual visitor from another world, to mingle with the crowd and to watch with them where in the darkness of the street beyond the upper end of the Piazza, groups of people could be obscurely glimpsed preparing for it. Yes, of course, these people had gathered here to pay their homage to the dead Christ. But that procession forming in the darkness, and the intent expectancy of the crowds, gave a special tone to the proceedings. Christ was soon to be paraded through the streets, but was that all? It seemed to me that at the same time some other and more ancient ritual was about to be celebrated.

Anyway, up there in the dark the flurry of amorphous activity at last began to crystallize, to harden and to form. And suddenly the lights went up, and one caught glimpses of exotic swaying canopies, a cross, a blue-robed effigy, a gilded sun, all sorts of indefinable emblems being raised aloft, and the men of the band in peaked caps raising their instruments. At which the crowd went quiet, pushing intently forward to form a wall of figures on either side of a wide lane; and a moment later the procession had begun, stirring and emerging under the rain to the sombre if theatrical sounds of a Verdi funeral march.

It was a queer, naïve, ambiguous and strangely moving spectacle, this. Alarming almost. Exotic and garish and solemn and morbid and hypnotic. Implicit with local superstition. I was an observer, a stranger, an alien presence here; a sceptic. And I had no use for idols or idolatry. But it was impossible, all the same, not to be affected by the shudder of awe that transformed these laughing people into worshippers. What difference was there in essence between the Etruscan bowing to the godhead in the dying sun and them—these people taut before the image of the dead Christ? This ritual worship of the dead, the pagan celebration persisting in the imagery of Christian ritual, was not to be dismissed with a shrug of superior detachment.

Three young men in brown headed the procession. They walked very slowly, one of them staggering under the weight of a huge pine cross. They were followed by lines of silent little girls in ankle-length blue, hands joined in prayer. Then came a life-size wax effigy of Christ seated before a golden baroque sun, bound, with bloodied knees, his carriage borne by six bearers in white. After which, three blue-robed hooded figures followed, bound together by heavy ankle-chains, the middle one bearing another cross of massive size. A murmur now passed through the crowd. Some crossed themselves. There was a sudden fixing stillness of attention. Suddenly, the smiles had vanished, and looking round upon those faces I could see no sign of disbelief. The symbol had triumphed over the charade.

But it was the long draped funeral bed, with the Christ lying full-length on it in the agony of tormented death, that seemed most to affect the onlookers. The body lay under a white lace coverlet lifted at the edges by four winged cherubs; and as it swayed by even the murmur ceased. Here and there a hand flickered out to touch the coverlet. Men bowed their heads. Women dipped and crossed themselves. The image had become invested with the weight and mystery of faith. It mattered little that it should look garish and sensational and maudlin and contrived. It symbolized a state, a mystery, the mystery of the journey into darkness, personifying triumph over the void, the old deep fear of death, a rhetoric that could satisfy and reassure, at least for the moment. Although death might have its natural place in these people's lives, as part of the pattern of life itself, now it must be isolated, borne aloft, exposed and worshipped like a fetish in the streets. Indeed this *was* a kind of fetish—worshipped, as the dictionary has it, "for its magical powers . . . a principle irrationally reverenced".

In the light, unnoticed rain, to the melancholy sound of the band further up the street, the dead Christ passed. Behind him came a seated rococo Madonna, lamenting before a golden sun, hands clasped, eyes turned upwards, eyebrows knitted to express her grief. And she in turn was followed by the large empurpled figure of the cardinal-bishop of Corneto, lifting his hand in blessing at the head of a train of young girls, each mournfully and whitely carrying an image. One held above her head a scroll; another walked with a pale wax nail-punctured hand against her cheek; another, tall and grave, had a small cross pressed to her lips. There was the ladder, too, the spear, the sponge, the crown of thorns, a coil of rope, the nails, each emblem carried with reverential care. The people watched in silence as these lovely

long-robed girls, like solemn vestals, glided silently by. They
were followed up by more lines of little jostling angel-girls and
angelic little boys. And at the tail of the procession came a group
of shuffling ancients, stiffly dressed, their leathery faces shut with
concentration. Then the lane closed in behind, and one could hear
the band proceeding somewhere half downhill through the town.
So that many in the crowd began to drift in the direction of the
sea-gate and to take up positions in the square before the Palazzo
Vitelleschi, where eventually the band emerged from out of a
narrow street before the great crosses and the swaying canopies
to turn uphill again and back to where they'd started off.

It was a chastening end to the day, a sealing of it, this exotic
ceremonial, this half-pagan salutation to the dead, this fetishist
survival of pre-Christian custom. It was difficult to think of the
Etruscans in the presence of these images, these idols decked out
in the finery of doll's-house queens and kings. And yet one had a
sense among the people of quick submissiveness and belief,
characteristic of a spirit that has vanished from the modern world
—a spirit linked to myth and folklore, to ancient rituals which are
of the people and their immemorial roots. Maybe there is nothing
that could link these present-day Tarquinians to the people of
Etruria; yet this ceremony to the dead god who will rise again
has its roots in the myths of the pre-Christian world, as we all
know—in the festival of Dionysus, for example. Here was Christ,
a Dionysus re-created, symbolizing godhead and fertility, however transformed. As all over the ancient world men had sacrificed
and paid their homage to renewal, the new life of the earth, the
renewal of life at the turn of the season, the miraculous enacting
forms of nature, so they did now. What could have been more
natural than that Christianity should have taken over such a basic
ritual to express its creed?

Many of us, perhaps justifiably, would assume that such cere-
monials ought to be dispensed with. We might argue (in keeping
with our materialistic concepts) that they are to be deplored as
retrogressive and irrational; that they reflect the "nacreous haze
of superstition"[1] which keeps people in a state of grovelling
submission to false gods. In the light of reason and the great

discoveries of science, how could it be otherwise? Which puts the people of Tarquinia into an unflattering position. We might call them backward, that is, ignorant and bigoted and steeped in superstition. But then how does one account for their delight, their quick sense of a community? As the gullible delight of children? If so, then their ignorance, if that is what it is, has its compensations, and enables certain special kinds of knowledge (knowledge of community, of contact, for example) to survive.

It may *be* that science has the answers, and that people who indulge in symptomatic flourishes to the old controlling fears, of life and punishment and death, will have to be dissuaded, gently weaned from them. But suppose in weaning people to "doubt" and "truth" it should deprive the "common breed" of their unscientific sense of how to live and what to live for, stripping them of their illusions? Will they come into a new and deeper sense of their community, a better understanding of the rhythms of their lives? One does not know. But certainly you cannot deprive a people of their ancient, perhaps hidebound, customs, without offering them something comparable in return, some-thing other than doubt and truth or than the machines which are its products. When the ceremonies of innocence are done with, and the great unknowns have been put in their place, together with the people who have cashed in on *fear* of the unknown, then perhaps humanity will be freed of all that awes and haunts it—as the Tarquinians of their own Spring ritual, with its tinsel and its rhetoric and its fetishist survivals.

But freed into what? Still the deliberating human consciousness, for all its brilliant products, seems but a fumbling attempt before the vastness of the universe, and the effortless unself-regarding beauty of its forms. Noting, for instance, the black and orange markings on the back of nothing more significant than a beetle, or the perfect balance and precision of the little flower found upon the hills and roadsides round Tarquinia, with its long straight stem, its horizontal spiky leaves, and the five flat pale-blue petals of its flower, one thinks of the symmetries of art reflecting the symmetries of nature; of man's own creative instinct when it is least laboured and least analytic; of praise and acceptance and conviction and community. And remembering Tarquinia's Good Friday procession, one thinks of the hieratic farewells to the dead of the Augurs in the tombs—celebrating the great journey from the light into the dark, and the promise of renewal and of continuity lying quiet in the dark as it closed round. In this sense, life and death are part of the controlling energy of the universe, the feared unknown, and there can be no freeing of people from that. So, for the Tarquinians, there was life and its gifts. Men came, acknowledging their fortune, awed by it, and went, haunted, "into the dark, into the night, into the obscure dark night of death and renewal".

5

TUSCANIA

Tuscania lies about fifteen kilometres inland from Tarquinia. You come upon the town without warning round a bend, since it is sunk down slightly in the plain, and the road ends in a square outside one of the mediaeval gateways, where four roads meet. The walls of reddish tufo, blackened in the rain, rise in great squared blocks, with towers placed at intervals between this gateway and the next one further down. Outside the walls, on a rise at the far end of one avenue, the façade of an ancient church, stripped almost bare but with its rose window still intact, faces down towards the square. There is an air of decayed importance about the place. Tuscania was once a city—"la fiera e ribelle Toscanella medievale",[1] it has been called; a city of the Middle Ages, long since shrinking back, arrested in its growth by fever and misfortune, like Corneto. But though now no more than a small town or a large village, Tuscania nevertheless has a special claim to distinction; for it is a town where the cultures of Etruria and Rome and the Middle Ages come into intimate and visually expressive contact; where the evidence of an artistic and historical continuity exists for us, bringing the place another, quieter, kind of fame. Inside the walls, it is much perhaps like other Central Italian towns. There are the narrow streets, the old crumbling stone houses side by side with others cheaply built to fill up gaps; the shops, the bars, haphazard little squares. And there is hardly any gesturing; the place keeps unobtrusively to itself, and continues quietly to thrive. Greater Europe and America have not yet, one feels, discovered it, and maybe never will. But then you come across a large square at the far end, with a parapet overlooking the ravine below and the town behind. And here you find yourself approaching a row of reclining figures which appear to sprout from the parapet, taken from the sarcophagi in which the late tombs of Tuscania abound. These heavy, wide-faced

creatures, like those in the Museum at Tarquinia, stare out or
upward under the sky, hieratic, big-boned and careless in their
slumped poses, embedded in the wall as if rooted there, lying
calm and impassive against the background of crazy roofs and
walls the square looks back on. Out in the open with the wet of
the rain upon them and the light shadowing the rough blurred
surfaces of stone, their monumental sluggard calm seems doubly
expressive.

But these figures are mere hints of what Tuscania has to offer—
defining its roots, the span of its history. Though already the
mediaeval walls themselves, still intact, have referred us to the
rebellious Toscanella that had more than once aligned itself
against the Papacy, you have to go out and down a little way
below the town, now rising high above you, to get the full
impact of the place. It is the symbolic splendour of the eighth-
century fortress-basilica of San Pietro on the crown of its hill, and
of the ninth-century basilica of Santa Maria Maggiore directly in
line below it on the same hill, that give Tuscania its distinction.
The two churches lie apart, isolated among the green tilled slopes.
And the impact is the greater because of the unexpectedness of
the position. With their façades flowering upward from porticoes
encrusted with figures and elaborate geometric patterns to the
great disc-like marigold windows, these churches are among the
most extraordinary monuments to be found in Central Italy,
precisely because they are such rare examples of the blending of
the early Roman basilican style with the styles of Romanesque
and Carolingian Europe. The influence is from the North of Italy
in the mainstreams which flow on one side from the Byzantine
East (as you see it for instance in San Zeno at Verona) and on the
other from Lombardy and France.[2] The façades are rich and
floriate in a way that is quite alien to the spirit of Roman architecture, though the form of the interiors indeed reflects the
proximity of the metropolis.

But more extraordinary even than the existence, in such close
proximity, of these two Christian churches, is the intimacy of
their relationship to the Tuscania of the Etruscans, and of that
Tuscania to the Roman town into which it was transformed.

Indeed, when you reach the top of San Pietro's hill to stand in the grassy shade of its nave wall, you can see below you the flowering circle of Santa Maria's window, and a little to its right, on a slight hill beyond the road, a stretch of ancient wall in reddish tufo, cut square and belonging to the Etruscan city of the fifth century B.C.; immediately below which lie the reticulated brick ruins of a Roman bath from the Augustan period. Nor is this all. The very hill on which San Pietro stands was once the acropolis of the Etruscan city. Which makes it probable that the basilica itself, together with its double towers, its palace, its grassy courtyard. was raised upon ancient foundations. There is even evidence for this in the section of massive wall that is visible beneath the presbytery. This hill, too, commands the landscape around it— formed of deep gorges and dark, shrub-covered valleys which drop away on either side. Opposite, in full view across the other side of the adjacent valley, for instance, lies the vast necropolis of *Pian di Mola*, and on the other side of the acropolis there are more rock-tombs, including the *Grotta della Regina*, which is a spacious chamber supported by two massive columns, with a labyrinthine passage around it that almost encircles the tomb. The acropolis in fact stands at the centre of a vast area riddled with tombs. Twelve different localities have been identified and excavated, ranging from the earliest pre-Etruscan period to the centuries of Romanized decadence. Moreover, in explicit recognition of the intimacy of the relationship between the successive cultures of Tuscania, a small Etruscan museum has recently been housed in the palace that forms one side of the Piazza in front of the basilica of San Pietro.

All these interrelations, all the references and echoes that are brought into play by the images and symbols of three cultures, give one a strange illusory sense of the ultimate reconciliation of historical time; of the supersession of time; of the profound correspondences and links that exist between worlds apparently separated by a thousand years; of one symbolic language growing out of another. One accepts the distinctions and differences. One is perfectly well aware that in fact neither of the two churches could possibly have been conceived outside the context of Christian Europe and the complex developments of style and of form that it fertilized. Nevertheless, between the symbolic forms of Etruscan art and the fabulous animals, the griffins and dogs and bulls and winged lions that decorate the façade of San Pietro or the marvellous nenfro carving on the portals of Santa Maria Maggiore, there is no contradiction, only a profound sense of continuity and confirmation and correspondence.

How did this miraculous concentration, this unique flowering that spans three cultures, come about, here on this soil, in the depths of the Maremma? Certainly Tuscania would have been fertilized and challenged by the near-by presence in the Etruscan age of the cities of Vulci and Tarquinia. And equally as certainly the Romans would have been impressed and themselves stimulated by a centre as fertile and productive as the necropoli prove Tuscania to have been. But how does one explain the sudden effortless flowering of the Mediaeval city, after centuries of decadence and obscurity, in an architecture as significant as that of Santa Maria and San Pietro? Perhaps it was the proximity of Viterbo, larger and more important at the time; except that Viterbo cannot boast two such churches. Or perhaps the influence of the early popes, or of men on whom the ancient buildings of the town exerted some kind of compulsive attraction. Whatever the reason, now they seem to dwarf the town, and they refer us back to a time when Tuscania must have been a place of considerable importance—for you do not build such shrines in backwaters.

Looking up at the richly encrusted carvings that surround the window on the upper façade of San Pietro, one is at once struck by the images represented there. They have a vivid ceremonial pagan appeal. It is the mystery of the natural world, its diversity, its energy, its fecundity, they celebrate. The window itself, linked to the *patera* in symbolism, is a composite image of the sun, of the flowering earth under the sun, of the logic, the geometry, and the symmetry of nature and its inexhaustible inventiveness. And inside the square which frames it are eight sculptured forms—the one in the top right-hand corner (of an angel) being the only overtly Christian figure, the most striking being the pair of dragons and the pair of dogs, one on each side, that are depicted running down the verticals. The dragons have the look of the Etruscan sea-horses and sea-monsters and other winged beasts found in the tombs and on sarcophagi, heraldic symbols of natural energy, curling, flowing, vividly formalized. And one has already seen a similar dog to these on the sarcophagus at Tarquinia. Here, each dragon is in pursuit, but each dog is just ahead, leaping, bounding along. The dog on the left is placed just above a winged lion with its paw holding an open book—the apocalyptic lion, that is, of St Mark. And the other has almost reached a similar image, this time of the winged bull of the apocalypse; while opposite the angel at the top is a sleek but heavy-pawed griffin (or griffin-phoenix) with its wings open.

The outer columns are supported by two bulls, like caryatids, their hooves planted firmly on carved corinthian-styled bases. They thrust head and shoulders forward in the queerly vital Etruscan way in which the crouching lions at Chiusi and from Vulci thrust their half-obliterated heads forward. These columns in turn frame the rich decorative motifs that surround the three-columned window-arches on either side of the great sun wheel. The motifs of the left-hand carvings are very Roman in style, with medallion heads and shoulders framed by elaborate floral patterns and leaves. A man-headed sheep occupies the top medallion and the whole design apparently depicts the pastoral Christly world of virtue. Below it is a bearded Samson-figure, nude except for a cape, who tenses himself, knees bent, under a great weight that presses down from above—yet with confidence and assertion, almost with ecstasy. But the scene on the right-hand side of the window is in startling contrast to the other. What are we to make of it? What does it symbolize? The underworld? The floriate universe of the devil? The godless natural world itself? Some diabolical trinity? That figure at the bottom with a serpent twined round his arms, fluently bearded, the solemn contorted face shown threefold, eyes mystically shut and the intentness of a god, is surely an exotic creature, even in this teeming universe of beasts. A symbol, then, of the life-giving source, out of whose three heads the curling vine grows, creating within each curl a strange symbolic progeny? Both source and flower, however, for his

multiple head appears again at the top, the crown or culmination
of the curling pattern of this "tree of life". Does he represent
some savage and satanic caricature of the garden of Eden? The
corrupting tree of knowledge, the forbidden fruit? Perhaps. Yet
here, a sensuous non-Christian imagery takes its place beside the
other beasts in this exotic flowering stone, referring ambiguously
back to the old pre-Christian world, man's worship of the creative
forces of the universe, the vitality of the cosmos.[3]

The interior is divided into three naves by short thick columns
and immense arches that rest upon capitals carved into curious
variants of Ionic and Corinthian. It is a triumph of the Mediaeval
spirit; and the basilican form, as we remember it from the
Hellenistic prototypes and its Roman examples, takes on a new
meaning. Classical regularity has vanished, and in its place you
have the rugged asymmetry and eccentricity that is a denial of the
classical principles of order and proportion, and an assumption of
the mystical illogic of feeling, of the aspirant human spirit—
diverse and unconformable. Here faith, or feeling if you like, the
human sense of the particularity of things, takes precedence over
reason. It is an impulse of praise that dominates, of celebration
rather than of serene contemplation—as it did in the Etruscan
world and in the Christianity of Northern Europe. And in the
crypt, above all, the mystical dark of faith commands, where you
move among the close gathering slender columns—twenty-eight
of them—in the half-light.

Inside Santa Maria, which is as impressive, there is a fresco of
the Universal Judgement. It has Christ enclosed within the Eastern
symbol of the rainbow, as he is found in Mediaeval Rome, the
Rome of the Greeks. Here the figures are rigid, hieratic, solemnly
composed, a schematic music of the spirit. It is an austere symbolic
mediaeval concept, this crowded judgement scene, painted about
the middle of the fourteenth century, in the wake of Giotto, and
with something of the intensity of Giotto. But what most strikes
one is the monstrous grinning nude devil on the right, larger
even than the Christ; for in the position of his arms and torso, he
clearly echoes the pose of the diabolic sun-god on the front of
San Pietro, except that his black-bearded head is a grotesque

cartoon-head and has nothing of the dignity and impassivity of that other head, whether god or devil or both. Here, where he leers, pot-bellied, open-legged, he is a bald convention of denial, of the evil blood, the black sap of the pendant genital root. There on San Pietro, in the sun, he remains an ambiguous and potent symbol. Here he revels, corrupt, indulgent, in his place in hell. There he silently presides, a god himself, a creature of the light.

The façade of Santa Maria is itself much more subdued and much less ambiguous than that of San Pietro. It has its lions and its gargoyle heads and its lovely rounded porticoes, and the main doorway is richer and earlier than the Lombard doorway of San Pietro, which, with its abstract Cosmatesque mosaics, must have replaced the original one. But the Madonna and her cocooned child above this central door, and the solemn figures of the guardian saints who stand in effigy on either side of it against the Carolingian fretted stonework (which reminds one instantly of the sixth-century B.C. plaques from tombs at Tarquinia) represent the spirit's triumph, its renunciation of the world. The two saints, Peter and Paul, with their eyes shut, invite us to no world of sensuous delight, but seem themselves intently fixed upon a visionary inner world, beyond the flesh and beyond death. They have indeed the calm and the resolution of death about them. Yet all the same there is a quickness, an unclassical Etruscan quickness in the rugged shaping of the forms and in the very textures of the stone, as in the nenfro sculptures on the two side porches. Here, Mediaeval Italy exists as it is impossible to see it anywhere in Rome—caught under the spell of faith, symbolized with peculiar intensity, at a meeting-point, as a unique fusing, of the spirit of contrasting worlds.

One comes upon such eccentricities in the lovely little Etruscan museum attached to San Pietro. But here there is no renunciation, no thrusting under of the flesh. Even the most noticeable pieces, that collection of specifically Tuscanian tomb-figures in nenfro and terracotta, are of the earth, embedded, rooted, and particular. They are all of the period of melancholy decadence—complacent, slumped, the vital tension gone, the spirit slack. Yet sometimes half the body seems to sit alertly upright—detached from its lower

half perhaps, from the genital root, lacking the flow of being and
as if truncated, paralysed, sexually broken, but at least with
something left, some internal echo of the vanished quick. The
faces are of individuals done by local artisans, modelled sometimes
with a startling force; complacent faces, the faces, it is true, of fat
landlords, indulgent, literal, uncomprehending and indifferent,
given in; but positive in their acceptance of the sensual and grati-
fying world. One female face of the first century B.C. wistfully
dreams; and on another of the same period there is a kind of
hostile defiance. But the men have almost all of them the look of
creatures fattened on the corruptions of the Imperial court. It is
as if the artist had set out to make embittered caricatures of men,
for these portraits, whatever else they may be, are not flattering.

The collection of pottery is small, for the museum was only
instituted here in 1961, and for two centuries before this there had
been sporadic excavations on the part of both private and official
speculators and collectors. During the last century, especially,
when there was little check upon the activities of enthusiasts,
the tombs were explored and rifled, stripped of their contents. At
the time for instance when George Dennis was writing his book,
in the 1840s, there was much traffic between the local excavators
in Tuscania and officials from foreign countries buying for
private or public bidders. A sarcophagus bought for England,
"unless of extraordinary beauty", as Dennis put it, would
"average less than £20, including freight and land-carriage . . .
according to Signor Campanari's computation, who has shipped
a whole museum to this country".[4] A great mass of material
from the cemeteries that surround the town has therefore been
carried away from Tuscania to lie obscurely and inorganically in
museums and private collections throughout the world, denied
their context in the place of their origin—you have to go to
Florence to see things in bulk, and there you will find such
powerful pieces as the huge sixth-century lion in nenfro which
once guarded the entrance to a tomb. But there are still many
tombs in the area which have never been excavated, and in the
last few years some very interesting pieces have been brought to
light to enrich the local museum.

Even at the moment the collection has its own special intimacy, laid out upon the two floors of the lovely mediaeval building which houses it. On the ground floor are the stone sarcophagi. But the long room above, with its balcony overlooking *Pian di Mola* and the gorge beyond, is large enough to take with ease eleven terracotta tomb-figures and a number of showcases for the pottery. And here the pieces range from the seventh-century to the latest Etrusco-Roman period. Great gaps exist of course, under the circumstances. The museum contains no Villanovan pieces, though there is no doubt that the culture of Tuscania (however subsidiary) goes as far back as this and even farther. Not only have numerous fragments of seventh-century biconic cinerary urns been discovered on the *Colle San Pietro*, but the very position of Tuscania between Vulci and Tarquinia and Bizenzio, where Villanovan pieces of all kinds have been found, would indicate that Tuscania was in the midst of an intensely productive area. Notably absent also from the museum, but for one or two small cups, are the painted Attic vases found elsewhere in such profusion. Which is a good thing in one sense. For the museum is the more free to put on show and to show off to advantage, the seventh-century and sixth-century Corinthian pieces, and the impasto and bucchero ware gathered from the tombs. Notable among these are a grey ribbed beaker with curving handle and raised lip similar to the one at Tarquinia; a red, ribbed impasto urn that swells out in a high-chested curve from its punctuated base; a lime and black two-handled Corinthian cup painted with exotic birds; and a Corinthian wine-jug or *olpe* with bands of processional animals and symbolic flower patterns in yellow and brown.[5] One examines these and other pieces with minute attention. They deserve it. They have the vividness of things that have come out of a natural feeling and love for swelling sensuous shapes, done with joy, each piece a unique and particular form that has its intimate reference to the human world for which it was produced, and the daily needs of that world.

One may go down afterwards into the valley below the Pian di Mola necropolis and venture into the great gorge that continues on from it; but this takes time, and the tombs cannot be properly explored unless one is prepared to set aside a good part of the day to them. These Etruscan places are not disposed for the flying visit. They demand time and energy and physical involvement, tenacity and will. For they often lie deep among the riot of the greened rock-slopes of these volcanic landscapes, here and throughout Lazio, in triumphant solitude. And the little villages that lie close to the tombs are *part* of the experience—ancient survivals suddenly emerging out of the enfolding clefts, and almost always poised at the edge of a steep volcanic cliff on one side of a ravine.

THE TARQUINIAN NECROPOLIS: NORCHIA, CASTEL D'ASSO, SAN GIULIANO, BLERA

THE TERRITORY OF Tarquinia, bordered on the one side by the Mignone River, and on the other by the Fiora, by Caere and Vulci, is rich in Etruscan remains—some no more than fragments and allusions, a bit of wall here, a group of tombs there; some lying sunk in the earth still awaiting discovery; others stretching away on all sides like cities, as they were conceived. But they do not draw attention to themselves. They lie half hidden amid the silences of rock and bush and broken cliff-slope, stripped perhaps of all movables but still retaining the impact of their architectural forms, where the streams glint and quiver along their beds. And so one has to go in search of them.

First, then, and in many ways the most impressive of the four sites to be defined, is *Norchia*. It lies in a flat valley formed probably from a subsidence of the plain and protected by its surrounding cliffs of tufo. A central area of land that had not subsided divides the valley at its further end into two narrowing glens or fissures; and it is here, according to the Etruscan custom, that the remains of the city lie, defined by the ruins of a Lombard church and other fragments from an abandoned Mediaeval village, with the tombs all around upon the adjacent slopes.

As part of the territory of Tarquinia, Norchia was probably of no more than secondary importance politically and culturally. But judging from the evidence of the tombs alone, it must have been a rich and thriving town with a civic pride and dignity of its own. These tombs display an architecture of great interest and variety, cut from the rock in the form of houses and temples and dating from the seventh century into the time of the Roman conquest. Many of them, especially the earlier ones, have an impressive formal beauty, monumental and austere, which at once indicates a highly developed culture and the characteristic Etruscan tenderness and sense of ceremony. As one sees them today in their secluded valley, they make their impact with an eloquence and a conviction that is only deepened by the natural beauty of the setting. They speak of the solemnity of Etruscan belief, of that austere delight in shaping the landscape to their needs, and that sense of ceremonial care and respect, which is so marked a feature of the Etruscan attitude to life.

Norchia offers no sign to the casual passer-by, even when moving close to it along the Tuscania road. One sees only the wide plain stretching away to distant hills beyond the spiky winter brushwood or the rioting flowers of spring. An unobtrusive little road below Vetralla leads to a farm ten kilometres inland, and from there to the necropolis itself, lying secluded in its valley 60 feet or more below, where a stream winds between the tufo, turning out of sight through wooded clefts to where, a mile away, the walls rise.

A path skirts the farm and moves down close beneath the cliff, cut from the rock. This was probably once part of a planned approach to the necropolis. For accompanying it in the lipped tufo that hangs above are the faint traces of long straight grooved lines, carved to give the effect of architectural mass. There are even indications—where the cliff seems to hang out over the path—that it may at one time have been arcaded with columns, though now the rock has been broken into and prised away by the insidious roots, the subtle stealth of centuries of change.

Down in the sheltered bowl itself, the valley suddenly opens out round a spur of rock to reveal, all at once, a sweeping face of cliff where the tufo runs 200 feet or more, cut sheer and formed into huge architectural blocks representing temples, with the deep grooved lines of cornice mouldings running sure and clear from temple to temple in long horizontal bands. It is a veritable "amphitheatre of tombs", as Dennis exclaims,[1] noting the shape of the setting—a kind of visual fulfilment of the natural forms, where rock flowers and the spirit of ancient man becomes an intimate expression of the roots which nourished him, symbols of community, and a tangible witness to the vanished truths of the Etruscan world. For these architectural façades are facts. They still retain their *presence* and something of their significance, giving us the power to feel (if not to think) our way towards those truths, and to guess at them, even if we cannot know them, even though they be dismissed with a shrug by those accustomed to the persuasion of more clamorous and more documentary voices.

To be sure, nature seems to be hard enough at work in its own way obliterating the signs. It has been said (by Lenoir, in 1832) "that the slope from the base of the tombs to the banks of the stream was cut into steps";[2] but no traces of these remain. One great block of tufo from the façade lies heavily among the grass at the bottom of the cliff, its deep scored lines uppermost, evidently torn away at some time by infiltrating roots of trees, and leaving a great pinkish gap above. But apart from this the links are almost unbroken, and culminate at the far end, just before the whole façade breaks off into a veritable chaos of rock and shrub, in the most striking symbol of all. For here the rock has been carved into the form of two pediments, one of which is still complete, though of the other only half remains from another subsidence. (The vanished pediment, which had fallen into the valley below, was taken to Viterbo, where it can now be seen.) In the triangles of these pediments symbolic groups have been carved, where the figures are still recognizably defined. They seem to depict battle scenes, for one can make out a man with a raised sword, another lifting up a comrade, another on his knees, and yet another flourishing a shield. But the tufo, crumbling away under the nibbling effect of lichen and of exposure to more than 2,000 years of weather, has blurred and melted all the features and the detailed moulding of the figures so that they seem little more than faceless effigies. But they nevertheless cling to their condition, and encrust the pediment like strange indecipherable hieroglyphs—probably representing an Etruscan adaptation of a Greek myth, since it is clear that these two pediments are later than the adjoining façades.

Beneath them are the vestiges of dentilled cornicework and ornamentation, and jutting down from the overhang of the

5 THE POLLEDRARA KORE. Seventh to early sixth centuries. From a tomb in the Polledrara necropolis at Vulci. Carved in gypsum (*p. 187*).

6 CANOPIC URN. Seventh to sixth centuries. From Chiusi. Among the most strikingly original of the Canopic urns produced at Chiusi in the seventh and sixth centuries (*p. 212*).

pediment the stump of a column remains, together with the traces of the capitals and bases of three others. In addition, the pediments "terminate on each side", as Dennis observed, "in a volute, within which is a grim, grinning face with prominent teeth, a Gorgon's head, a common sepulchral decoration among the Etruscans". And "over two of the three remaining volutes is . . . a lioness",[3] symbolic guardian of the sepulchre, of which there are many striking examples to be found in Etruria.

Underneath these pediments, within the portico, on the reddish surface of the wall, protected a little by the overhang, are the faint remains of ancient colouring and the mouldering vestiges of mural reliefs. You can just make them out from below. But to get a clearer view of them, it is necessary to climb up the cliff slope till you are standing close to the wall. It is not a difficult climb, and it ends at the ledge that once supported the columns of these façades, and which runs along the whole length of the cliff below the sculptured verticals of wall. Here the crumbling reliefs of a large round shield, a mace, the outstretched wings of a Charun figure (the winged genius of death from later Etruscan mythology), a helmeted head with a sword above it raised by what had once been an arm, and a full-length figure blurred and smoothed of all particularity, indicate a scene rather similar to those in the Typhon Tomb at Tarquinia. From which one can infer the dates of these reliefs to be perhaps roughly equivalent— no earlier, that is, than the third century, though the archi- tectural structures themselves upon which the figures were carved are two or three centuries older, the whole complex, with its bold horizontal cornices, suggesting a much more austere and ancient form of building, Egyptian or Phoenician rather than Greek in style.

Desolated by weathers and the spoliations of tomb-seekers, fading year by year, merging into the background of the calcined rock, these figures yet still leave their traces of a world for us to recognize, set in their pediment. And from them the more durable forms of the other tombs stretch away along the cliff-face, imitating the façades of temples—plain-faced, their deep grooved mouldings shadowed and their angles sharp and clear-cut in the

D

sun. Walking along beneath them one comes to gaps separating one tomb from another, where the rock has been cut away to form steep flights of steps that lead on to the open ploughland and platforms above, to places where the most ancient pit and trench tombs once lay.

Below the walls again, perhaps ten feet below, are the narrow entrances to the tombs, going deep into the heart of the cliff. You peer down and in; you may even want to *go* in, squeezing your way through the doorway, as I did. But there is nothing much inside—a roughly shaped chamber with beamed ceiling perhaps and hacked-out walls. Nothing but emptiness, dank emptiness, the desolate emptiness of abandoned places. It is not like this out in the open. There the forms blend and intermingle. But inside there are only the hacked walls and the stone couches for the dead; all else gone—the dead themselves, their bones, their dust, and all the ornaments and offerings that lay with them, all gone, snatched away or swept away, leaving a few fragments maybe, a few bones, but nothing that could ever be of value, either to the world at large or to the buyer from potential robbers.

From here one can see the ruins of wall and church rising at the crest of their rocky spur, where the valley splits into glens and the river forks off out of sight between the cliffs round a shoulder of rock. In the valley, two narrow slatted bridges lead to gradually rising ground below the cliffs of the acropolis, where a long low grotto tomb lies, cut from the rock and pillared. It is large and gloomy, and has become worn and blackened from long use as a shelter for cattle and cattlemen and implements. But from here one gets a first sight, in the cliffs immediately opposite, of the reddish architectonic forms of temple-façades that rise terraced in groups on the upper rock. They leap out at the eye—glowing one beyond another among the brown spiked branches, their sharp-angled walls jutting out from the background or glimpsed through shrubbery. These are much earlier than the tombs in the amphitheatre and resemble those to be seen at Castel D'Asso, which are of the seventh and sixth centuries. With their crisply defined horizontal cornice mouldings, their windows and door-ways outlined in relief on the façades, and their right-angled positions on the cliff, they make a powerful impact. The door-ways, for instance, narrower above than below, and in some cases having panels recessed one within the other and rectangular lintels pointed at the lower edges, indicate a Doric influence; and the actual structure of the edifice—its walls retreating from the base to the summit and including the massive horizontal cornices—is markedly Egyptian in character. Nor is this all, for Modestow and others have noted the resemblance of these tombs to tombs seen in Lydia, Caria, Phrygia and Lycia, also carved out of the rock.

There are twice as many here as are to be found at Castel D'Asso, ranged on both sides of the acropolis, and one notes peculiar variations of detail from tomb to tomb—one having a window above the door (both false of course, for the entrance to the chamber is below), another only a window, a third a door without recess, a fourth with a simpler narrower cornice, and all of them displaying mouldings of at least six differing patterns. And there is one isolated monument, high up and all but inacces-sible on the hill in front of the acropolis, that is recessed into the cliff, and has in fact three recesses—each "7 feet wide and $2\frac{1}{2}$ feet deep" and "seven feet in height"—"separated," as Dennis defines it, "by prominent pilasters rounded in front like half-columns, and having curious fluted capitals".[4]

On the acropolis itself lie the ruins of the Lombard church, placed at the junction where perhaps the ancient *arx* once was. There are no traces of Etruscan wall—the remains belong to walls of the mediaeval village of Norchia—or Orcle as it was called in the ninth century, according to an epistle of Leo IV[5]—which was abandoned because of malaria in the fifteenth century. Judging from the area of this height, the ancient town would seem to have been smaller and less important than the number and magnificence of its tombs indicate. But there is now no telling, for beyond the vestiges of an ancient gateway cut through the cliff, and another on the opposite side with signs of a road, nothing remains. What does remain, and what the sensitive visitor will carry away with him, is the lyrical desolated beauty of the place, and the astonish-ing presence of those stone sepulchres that emerge out of and merge into the landscape as the authentic if unchronicled witness to the spirit of the Etruscans.

Castel D'Asso may lack the range and variety—of architecture and landscape—that distinguish Norchia, but it has other attractions which compensate. Like Norchia, it is in a secluded valley almost on its own—a site, as Dennis pointed out more than a hundred years ago, "bearing at every step indisputable traces of bygone civilization, scarcely six miles from the great thoroughfare of Italy (the Cassia) and from Viterbo, the largest city in all the district".[6] Like Norchia, too, its acropolis carries the remains of mediaeval habitation—though in this case only of the castle after which it takes its local name, Castellaccio. And like the tombs that lie closest to the acropolis at Norchia, the style of the monuments at Castel D'Asso testifies to their high antiquity. The place, in other words, is an essential part of the Etruscan experience, and not to be missed on any account. For even if one has been to Norchia, one is not likely to get any real impression of what gives Castel D'Asso its peculiar atmosphere until one has seen it. For one thing the colour and the texture of the rock is different; and the relationship of tombs to landscape is of quite a different character. And though there are fewer tombs here than at Norchia, they lie concentratedly together, with their ornamentation and their inscriptions forming a composite image, and their façades rising high above one, sometimes even to a height of 30 feet.

The necropolis lies about eight kilometres south-west of Viterbo across the plain, and not much more from Norchia itself. Outside the mediaeval walls of Viterbo a lane runs uphill, and then moves for perhaps a mile between walls of reddish tufo, becoming a dark, gloomy, tunnel-like passage topped by shrubbery, till it emerges on to the plain. It then continues more or less straight through the fields, giving an occasional distant view of the towers of Tuscania, to end at a farmyard on the edge of the ancient acropolis, with its ruined tower ahead among the trees. Here one makes a steep descent into the valley, a great flat open base through which the Rio Arcione runs. And at once one notes that as usual the tombs lie on the side facing the acropolis, high up and set back in the cliffs. They seem almost inaccessible from a distance, and even more so from immediately below. But there are paths, partially stepped, among the outcrops of rock that take one up to a sort of platform from where the twelve or thirteen tombs range along the cliff-face, hewn from the rock—vertical temple-façades of the earliest and severest style, an architecture impressively defined by its wealth of detailed carving.

The very first of the tombs is of particular interest, for it rises to a height of 30 feet or more, with the double-grooved mouldings of its flat roof dropping in a curve to the cornice of the main façade, on which is carved the relief outline of a door with pointed Doric lintel, and below which lies an open vaulted chamber with its inner wall receding from the façade, where another false door stands immediately above the actual entrance to the tomb. When Dennis was there a hundred years ago, this sepulchre contained "eight or ten sarcophagi in nenfro—simple, massive and archaic in character";[7] but there are none now, only the dark abandoned silence of the rough-hewn chamber itself. Many of the tombs on this cliff-face have a form similar to this one, though not so large. And almost all of them are separated from one another either by being recessed or placed forward, or by means of a detaching space between, as at Norchia, sometimes with steps leading up to the plain. The lower of the moulded doors, the one above the entrance, often has a niche in the centre, probably to hold an urn or a cippus inscribed with the family name.

The sepulchre itself, when it is not blocked up by earth or fallen rock, has a shelving approach cut through the rock into steps, and the doorway narrows to the top and is often curved. But inside there is no attempt to give any decorative shape to the room, whether large or small. Just as at Norchia, all finesse is reserved for the façades, though some of the rooms do have ledges or benches of rock for the sarcophagi, and others sunken pits ranged on each side of a narrow passage, where the coffins were placed. And in one tomb, the sunken coffin pits radiate from a central point like the spokes of a wheel, no doubt to symbolize the sacred circle of fertility and immortality.

These terraced façades look out over the wide valley to the acropolis, where the castle tower rises out of the trees. Then the cliff turns sharply in to a narrow glen, on the other side of which there are one or two more tombs, while up the glen itself they lie facing each other on both sides, with a path running between them like a street between houses. It is from the top of this glen (where there are the remains of ancient roads cut into the rock, one leading off in the direction of Tuscania) that another track, the one used by Dennis,[8] approaches Castel D'Asso; and from here the form of the necropolis is that of a street lined with temple-houses that turn off to right and left along the cliff-face overlooking the valley.

Because of their exposed position (even though enclosed in a secluded valley) the funerary ornaments of the tombs—the vases, necklaces, brooches and implements they would once have contained—were probably rifled very early, even in Roman times, so that there is no evidence of them in the museums. But in the plain immediately above the cliffs there are others, left undiscovered by the robbers of successive ages, which when excavated yielded many pieces of great interest—bronze mirrors "with figures and inscriptions, tripods, vases, large studs representing lions' heads, besides articles of gold and jewellery, scarabei, etc., with painted vases, some of great beauty and archaic Greek design",[9] especially two black-figure amphorae, now in the Viterbo museum.

The tombs with inscriptions are mostly in the narrow glen, one of them at the right-angle of its entrance on the left, the others further up, though there are some vestiges in the cliffs of the great valley. The letters are carved deep into the surface above the false doors on the façades, and can be made out even from a distance, being four or five inches in height. One that I saw I recognized as the tomb Dennis had described, which is extraordinary in itself considering the length of time that has elapsed since he was there. Part of its cornice has fallen. And "on the fragment yet standing," he says, "you read ECASU", in Etruscan of course; "and on the prostrate mass is the rest of the inscription, INESL. TITNIE", so that the inscription, containing sixteen letters, read from right to left, would seem to be reasonably intact. Curiously enough, it recurs on other tombs—one in the cliffs of the valley retaining only the letters INESL, another, read by Orioli on a fallen piece that has now vanished, the fragmentary ". . . UTHIN . . . SL . . ." And, according to Dennis, it has been found on other sites as well as this.[10] The pity is that these inscriptions are fast vanishing. Though we may say that those remaining have managed to last out for more than 2,500 years, there are nevertheless fewer now than there were a mere *hundred* years ago. And nothing can stop the slow obliterating process that is at work upon them and upon the tombs.

Much still remains, however. And the fascination of these tombs is the concentrated impact of their architecture, blending with the earth and rock and stamping upon it an eloquent symbolic language of praise. Imagining "the effect such a scene is calculated to produce upon a sensitive mind, especially on those to whom an Etruscan necropolis is a novel spectacle",[11] as Dennis puts it, one recommends Castel D'Asso without reservation. More valuable, however, is the record it offers to add to the documents we have of the sparsely documented history of this people. Though it cannot give us specific details of the changing pattern of a civilization, it nevertheless gestures to the underlying values which gave that civilization its vigorous place in the world as one of the great makers of Italy, speaking silently, remote and half-obliterated yet with a strange compelling eloquence out of the silence of landscape.

The necropolis of *San Giuliano*, which lies little more than twenty kilometres from Castel D'Asso and less from Norchia, does not suffer by comparison. Not only does it contain tombs of every kind, both isolated and in groups, from the earliest period to the latest, including some with temple façades such as are to be found at both of the other sites, but it has a setting almost equally as impressive—wilder, more intimate, and if anything more secluded. As one comes to expect, it is this, and the actual placings of the tombs, that give the Etruscan settings their particular tone and atmosphere; and therefore San Giuliano is not to be confused

with either Norchia or Castel D'Asso. The necropolis is further
distinguished from the other two by the fact that it lies quite
close to an area still inhabited, the small village of Barbarano
Romano, itself placed like an acropolis on the tip of a cliff that
splits into glens on either side.

The view of the village, as you pass by the great rust-brown
rounded towers of its entrance gateway and cross the new bridge
that spans the ravine, is startling enough. It is all there, rising in
the rusts of tufo from a cliff pitted with caverns. And should you
choose to enter the village itself, a shortish walk through its
poverty-stricken main street, past the unkempt crumbling walls
of its houses, will bring you very quickly to an open place at the
far end where the cliff falls away to overlook a deep glen, itself
riddled with tombs. It is another of those astonishing sights in
which the landscapes of Lazio abound—not a little qualified here
by the smell that comes from just beyond the wall, which is
apparently the local rubbish dump, and from the worn tufo
compounds to one side, where you can see pigs wallowing.
Strange to note that these latter, these walled animal pens, are
also carved from the rock, and that there is evidence that they
are very old. They look in fact like the foundations of abandoned
buildings—tombs perhaps or even houses—and some lie empty
further down the cliff, the scarred signs of former habitation
below the level of the lowest stones of the village.

To get a closer look at the cliffside seen from the bridge, you
have to go down through a stepped alley that descends through
an archway partially carved from the tufo and at least 20 feet long.
This comes out nearly half-way down to the bottom of the ravine,
with the cliff and the village walls rising high above. Here you
can see that all the caves are blurred and worn away at the edges,
many of them in use as sheds for pigs and chickens and farm
implements, hacked roughly out to serve the needs of the villagers.
Some of them, however, lie half-way up the cliffside, almost
inaccessible, with the remains of stairways leading up to them, and
faint signs of carving scarred on the lintels. Obviously these were
tombs once. If so, their function has now been so transformed as
to rob them of all significance. And where the path goes down

to the bottom of the cliff, there is an air of sinister decay, smelly and rotten, so that looking up towards the village the whole reddish-rust mass of the rock itself seems on the point of sub-sidence or collapse; and one leaves the place with relief, more than ordinarily aware of the defiling processes of history and time.

But the necropolis of San Giuliano is not here. If there was anything Etruscan here, it was probably some kind of extension of the area of the ancient settlement. For San Giuliano lies buried away in a half-forgotten valley two kilometres off, and can only be finally got to on foot. The path to it lies at the top of a cutting, hidden from view by bushes and a high bank of earth. As at Castel D'Asso it moves steeply downward among the wintered trees into a deep secluded valley. On the way, one catches sudden glimpses through the branches of reddish cliffs on the other side, glowing in the sunlight, with the dark rectangular openings of tombs cut into them. And the track drops away among the sapling glades until it splits into two and dips to a stony stream bed, which one crosses on to soft green pasture slopes immediately below the cliffs.

Coming out into the open, one emerges into a taut expectant quiet such as it is possible to find only perhaps in such intimate hidden places as this. For immediately one has that sense of having stepped into a world of trapped presences, a place intan-gibly possessed with the spirit of a vanished race. Or so at least it seems. On one side the reddish cliffs rise high and flaking from a tangle of undergrowth, pierced at intervals by the cave-black doorways of tombs. On the other side the valley is closed off by a sheer thrust of tufo rising up in a massive natural wall. And straight ahead the valley widens out to fork away on either side of another vertical of red rock crowned by grass and shrub, through which peer squared blocks of ancient wall—defining the characteristic position of the city area and its relation to the necropolis.

Moving down towards this wall along a path beneath the cliff, one looks in upon the rifled silences of the tombs, noting the slanted ceilings with their heavy central beams, and the stone-pillowed beds—emptied, hollow, echoing, blackened. Most are roughly carved on the outside, their doorways narrowing to the top, unornamented. One of them, long and low, its entrance half-obscured by bramble, has a ceiling of elaborate transverse beams, and internal niches which must once have held the insignia of its occupants. Another, fallen away from the cliff, lies half-buried in the grass, with the carving of its ceiling still definable. There are seven or eight here in all, none of them particularly distinguished externally; and one is just about to ask oneself where the others are when, a little beyond them, the cliff gives way to a wooded grassy ridge immediately across from the acropolis. From the top of this ridge, one finds oneself looking through a mesh of leafless branches into another valley sunk even lower in the landscape, and across it to steep cliffed slopes that rise up on the other side. And there below is the necropolis—merging into the rocky hill-slopes and out of them, tombs half-obscured by dense shrubbery, sharply defined by the black shadows of their doorways or by the sunlight upon their Doric lintel mouldings. And at once the eye picks out the projecting right-angled walls of what looks from a distance like a great greyish-red stone temple, quite low down, defined dramatically against the hillslope into which it is set by the three stepped layers of massive architrave that crown it, each divided by deep horizontal cornice grooves; and the traces of windows and doorways that decorate the 30-foot façade.

Moving closer, one lets one's eye wander up and across the muscular formations of these cliff-slopes to the great cavern-like rectangles of two tombs high up on a spur to the right and the row of doorways immediately below them; to the terraced verticals of rock that echo the form of the temple-tomb itself, and back again to that arresting form. And as one gets closer to it one sees beyond, high up on the same hillside, another massive right-angled temple-wall, yellow with lichen, corniced, roofed with stepped blocks. While all around the carved doorways of tombs, some of them with traces of lintel mouldings above, as at Norchia and Castel D'Asso, begin to appear among the tangled undergrowth. What seems from a distance a mass of tumbling vegetation and rock surrounding the architecture of the great temple tomb yields with every step some new façade, some new half-buried architectural detail. All at once, one is stepping in upon a world belonging to the roots of history, a world in which man had celebrated his momentary existence under the sway of the natural world, bowing to it, part of its intent fecundity. It is indeed exciting to look across at that half-emergent temple-palace, and to walk to it through the trees and stand beneath the massive angled walls that thrust 20 feet up out of the cliff. Its impact is of the grave monumental beauty of the Eastern Mediterranean, of Crete and Mycenae, the Lydians, the Hittites, the Sumerians. The stilled energy and the simplicity of the form links it to the underlying continuities symbolized for instance in the scattered fragments of great cities all around the Mediterranean. It seems to belong here, rooted in the landscape as the natural rock is, part of the incessant ceremonial of the earth. And even though, when you go in through one of the two doorways cut low into the façade, you find constriction and darkness and the rough-hacked walls of primitive rooms, this is somehow no contradiction. The dark, the damp and the emptiness predominate, but you are moving in among the roots, that meeting-place of life and death.

And if "one does not feel oppressed" in a place like this, that is perhaps *because* the tombs seem so naturally to define the continuities of the landscape. There is simplicity, directness and spontaneity in the shaping of these little rooms and the carvings that decorate their façades. It is the decadent and morbid, the mechanical and pretentious that oppress. These reassure. They put their spell upon you, the spell of the young indwelling spirit of a people, strong with the strength and certainty of youth. Here, death is no neurotic obsession; it has its part to play in the cyclic pattern of life, and is defined in terms of continuity, the potent forces of life that in these old religions man bows down to and is part of.

Here, you would have found no inversions, no Calvinist denials, no dichotomy between man, religion and the natural world, no "mood unknown to Nature", no "lax adult appeal to sense", as Jack Clemo, the savaged Christian poet, puts it, masochistically reaching out to the "taste of blood, Anguish that makes each tip-frame a gibbet";[12] but an appeal through all the senses to the gravity and joyousness in things, the sexual energy of life. The scourgings of the outraged Puritan seeking to prevent or to reduce the infiltration of the living sap (as sin or as temptation) into the bodiless realm of spirit, seem an alien intrusion here. This is the world before Christ and the Logos. It is life that triumphs. For the Etruscans, the dead are part of the continuity of life, reflecting it, physical, particular, belonging to the earth. Even in Christian terms it was "the rite of the love-feast and the Eucharist" that "preceded the gospels and determined their form".[13] Which is what the Puritan forgets, of course. He sees only the stripped tree of the cross and the agony of the tormented spirit in the flesh; the flesh imprisoning and contaminating, and the pagan earth denying God. Having learnt only too well to feel disgust for the sexual potency of his roots, he must cut himself off from the earth as the ancient world knew it and scourge himself with denial. But not these people. For them, one feels, there was no division, and therefore no contradiction, between the internal world and the world of the roots of things.

The necropolis at *Blera*, four or five miles north-west of Barbarano along the Via Clodia is, like San Giuliano, close to a village. But in this case the links are more intimate and organic, for Blera itself lies at one end of the mile-long ridge that contained the Etruscan necropolis, and that drops at the other to an ancient bridge where four glens meet and the necropolis begins.

The setting is magnificent, with its characteristic tufo clefts and fissures where the cliffs fall to wooded streambeds from the levels of the plain. Approached from Barbarano across the great arch of its modern bridge, this village is seen to be built like the other on one side of a great ravine upon the rust reds of the tufo. But the ravine is wider and deeper here, and from the middle of the bridge one looks down to where seemingly far below the whitish-grey waters of the Bieda run, shut in by steep fluted cliffs and by the slopes of Blera itself, which are punctuated by dark cave-holes utilized crudely for storage and shelter, even as at Barbarano.

Then suddenly one is in the shadow of the village itself and moving along a narrow street between lichened houses and the occasional shop. The place does not have the air of apathy and collapse that shrouds Barbarano. It seems more secure, more confident of survival. Of course there is poverty here too, for it cannot be easy to make even a tolerable living off this land. And the village has the rough plain look of most agricultural communities in the district. These people have never been able to afford refinements. They have lived here for centuries, and perhaps still do, as the vassals of absentee-landlords with absolute power "over the lives and properties of their tenants". Even the electric lighting is of the simplest kind, consisting of a lamp strung across the street. But compared to Barbarano the village seems almost prosperous. The shops display a variety of goods, there is a club room, a Communist Party office, a tiny piazza with a fountain and an ancient leaning stone-porched palazzo. There are even one or two bars, and an osteria (run incidentally by a former professional racing cyclist who had been a prisoner of war in England) where you can get good local wine and a meal of sorts. And the Church beyond its modest Piazza, graced by a carved Roman sarcophagus found in the neighbourhood, contains of all refinements an altar-piece by Annibale Caracci of the Scourging of Christ.

There are two or three signposts to the necropolis carefully placed along the main street to guide visitors. They point down past the church to a steep cobbled lane at the other end that leads back to the cavern-tombs on the cliffside. And from here an earth track branches off in the opposite direction, along the line of the terraced slopes of the ravine. It moves in a gradual descent past occasional tombs, the rock above now and then exposed to reveal at the summit a remnant of ancient wall. Till suddenly, about a mile from the village, the roadway levels out and hardens, cut from the rock, with a channelled water-passage on one side, and begins to pass between solid walls of rock—into which are set a row of tombs, their arched doorways obscured by bramble but not impassable, with the characteristic couches and slanted ceilings of fifth- and fourth-century tomb-chambers inside. And almost at once one is at the ancient bridge itself that crosses the Bieda. And it is from here that one at last gets something of the impact of the context of this necropolis. Already, it is true, the landscape has prepared one for it with its dramatic cliffdrops. But as one comes up to the bridge, there ahead the necropolis emerges suddenly into view—massed rock and shrub, a genuine hill-city, the tombs standing out upon it in tiers and terraces, sepulchre after sepulchre, many of them connected by flights of steps.

The effect is very striking. But almost at the same moment one notices a number of other things about this spot. First, that here the Bieda splits into two, one fork going on through the glen below the necropolis hill ahead, the other turning right under the bridge and itself splitting into two on the other side. Secondly, that the bridge on which one is standing—narrow and humped, its lichened blocks of tufo worn and smoothed—is of course the Etruscan bridge mentioned by Dennis "at the point of junction of the two ravines", its wide arch "based on the rocky banks of the stream, and approached by a gradually ascending causeway of masonry, which as well as the bridge is of tufo cut from the cliffs around".[14] The third point to notice is that the cliff along the side of which one has been walking ends abruptly just before the bridge in a sharp wedge-like spur that drops away on the other side too into another glen. And from its structure it is now apparent that this high tongue of land must have marked the terminating *arx* of the Etruscan town—the modern village lying a mile back and occupying a far corner of the long narrow ridge— "a mere spine-bone between the parallel glens"—that the height turns out to be.[15]

A further point is that a separate road leads directly up to the spur of the arx, forking away from the one to the village and forming perhaps the approach to a gateway into the city— though there is now no sign of that and the summit is obscured by a dense tangled mass of vegetation. But from here it is clear that the tombs exist on all sides, for one can see some half-way up the cliffs to the east of the bridge, and in the cliffs opposite the hill where they seem to be mainly concentrated. In fact, as further exploration reveals, the tombs of Blera are not only more numerous than in any of the other three local sites described, but they are also more varied in structure and in style.

This variety is nowhere more evident or more concentrated than on the cliffs ahead. Even the road itself, hewn from the rock, is lined on one side with tombs, many of them half-obscured. They are mostly single-chambered, some with moulded doorways of the Doric type, others having no decoration at all. There is one at a bend in the road whose plain entrance is cut into a right-angled wall which runs to another right-angle where the road curves and dips, and here in the stepped wall of rock are five niches for urns or votive objects. A few yards beyond this a flight of steps leads up the cliffside from terrace to terrace, one of four or five interspersed between the tombs. There is another at the very beginning of the necropolis, just beyond the bridge, by means of which one is able to examine any of the tombs at leisure, however high they are upon the cliff. And one has only to climb the steps a little way for it to become quite obvious even to the untrained eye that this is no mere haphazard conglomeration of tombs, but a city architecturally planned and constructed.

Here one comes upon simple square-cut doorways with little windows on either side, leading into single rooms containing bench-like couches, and tombs with doorways and windows which have raised mouldings around them as at Castel D'Asso and Norchia, decorating the façade of rock above the real entrance. There are a number of larger tombs also, built in the severe style of that superb temple-tomb at San Giuliano, topped by cornices of differing types—one of them consisting of three squared layers retreating upward—with traces of window and door moulding on the walls, and one or more entrances into the rectangular chambers. At certain chosen points high upon the cliff, blocks of tufo have been split from the face, placed in position, and hewn out as isolated tombs—shaped (even outside) like houses, with sloping roofs and overhanging eaves, their angle, as Dennis had observed, "that still usual in Italian buildings . . . being just sufficient to carry off the rain".[16] The chambers themselves of these and many other tombs here have ceilings that slant away from a great central beam, either raftered or coffered, above columned benches arranged as for a triclinium or banquet. And where there is an inner chamber it often has two narrow windows on either side of the door to "light" the far darkness and add to the decorative pattern of the outer room. One tomb near the top of the cliff has a bench carved outside against the wall, set in a quiet position along a terrace so that seated on it you overlook the whole necropolis, the sheer cliffs opposite, the valley, the bridge, the arx of the acropolis, and the plain. And the steps take one between tombs to the very top of the cliff, where the plain begins and the earth is under cultivation, having long ago perhaps disturbed the pit and trench tombs that would once have been here, as at Castel D'Asso.

And so one moves up and down the steps and along the rock-levels of terrace, noting the beautiful cornice mouldings of the large tombs, an ancient raised door-surround here, half-hidden among the vegetation, the right-angled wall there of a house-tomb, the plainer doorways narrowing upward, the little empty rooms and their empty couches (often adorned with pilasters), the votive niches to be found everywhere beside the entrances—and on one occasion even enclosed within the raised door mouldings where there is no tomb at all. And, lying in the earth, innumerable fragments of pottery are to be seen—bits of impasto and bucchero vase, discarded as worthless no doubt by those who had come here to strip the tombs of their treasures, thrown down contemptuously as the pickaxes broke into the tombs and the hands scrabbled excitedly for marketable objects. I myself once discovered a whole pile of sherds lying in a cleft of rock outside a tomb—valueless obviously to the moneygrubbers, but of great interest to me, because I could see at once that they were all of very early date. There were many pieces, for instance, of seventh-century ribbed impasto bowl, from the curving lip and the body, and of bucchero—some with the fern-leaf motive in stippled white dots on the black. The discovery of these little signs and traces, even at this late date, makes one wonder what happened to all the beautiful intact objects with which the tombs must once have been filled. Probably the necropolis was desolated early, for it is in a very exposed position above a road which must once have been in frequent use as a public highway—if, that is, one can assume this road to have been a section of the ancient Via Clodia, as Dennis thought likely.[17] At any rate there is no systematic display of pieces from Blera in any of the Italian museums, though Viterbo has some, so they must have vanished long before anyone had wakened to the significance of Etruria.

On the Eastern side of the ridge on which Blera lies, more tombs are to be found. And here, lying in the glen, are three or four very striking conical structures, hewn from the rock in circular steps or ledges tapering upwards. There are no others like them anywhere else here, and only at Vulci is one likely to see similar. The cone was probably at one time surmounted by "a sphinx or a lion or a cippus", and within it, approached by a passage cut into the cone, is a double-chambered sepulchre. Finally, away to the south of the modern bridge on the western side of Blera, there is a long narrow three-arched bridge. This is of late Etruscan or Roman workmanship, its central arch, as defined by Dennis, "thirty feet in span", the structure "formed of rusticated blocks, with edges so sharp and fresh that it was difficult to believe it the work of . . . two thousand years since". The central arch had been "split throughout its entire length, probably by an earthquake" a long time ago, and the rock is worn by the passage of innumerable feet into a deep hollow pathway.[18]

Such discoveries are the delight of these small unimportant places, tucked away and almost forgotten by the world that rushes by along the Cassia upon important journeys. They cannot affect the greater world, its decisions and its acts. They, the village and its setting—every contour intimately known by those who live there—hardly exist for that world. But they do, all the same, exist. And returning from the necropolis to Blera in the late afternoon, with the sun setting beyond the opposite cliffs, one carries with one a vivid sense of their existence—secretive and physical and placed, quietly containing all those hints and images from a greater vanished past. And on such an afternoon one is even likely to have one's sense of this particularity confirmed by contact with the peasants, returning after their day's work in the fields. If you ask them they will talk unemotionally and simply about their village and its life. And no doubt each one has his own Etruscan story to tell, like that of the old man I fell in with, gloomily recounting to me how in the rock above his pig-sty he and his friends had one day broken into a never-before-opened tomb to find an ornamented body lying on its bench among offerings of implements and vases. This story, true or not, was well told, and savoured for the gritty character of the words it was couched in, and the gruff directness of the leathery-faced old man who told it—born here, pointing out his birthplace on the cliffside, coming back in the sun with the earthiness and rigour of the landscape in him, and the toughness of the very poor, obliged by circumstances to endure a lifetime of hard labour.

Centuries ago another people used this road, carving and hollowing out the rock for their dead, and shaping the landscape to their own needs. And though only scattered signs remain of what that world once was, they have their place (even as they sometimes have their present uses) rooted here in mute persistent witness to a vanished world—Tarquinia, its territory, the widespread, short-lived splendours of Etruscan culture.

VEII: THE CITY

V EII WAS THE first of the great Etruscan cities to give way before the growing power of Rome. Its territory, stretching inland from the sea between the Tiber and the Arrone rivers, with Caere to the north-west and Falerii to the north-east, had Rome facing it along its south-eastern border. It was one of the largest and oldest of the city-states, including within its domain such towns as Formello, Sutri, Nepi, Campagnaro and Ronciglione, and reached as far as the southern shore of Lake Vico. The city itself must have rivalled even Tarquinia and Caere in importance. The Villanovan burial grounds indicate that a large community existed here from at least the ninth century, and the necropolis that extends all around the area of the city has brought to light evidence of a highly developed and significant culture, especially in the discovery of important tombs of the seventh-century orientalizing period. The famous *Campana Tomb*, and another— the *Tomb of the Ducks*—contained, for instance, the most ancient wall frescoes to have been found in Etruria.[1] But perhaps the most important finds were those made in 1916 and later on the site of the Temple of Apollo on Portonaccio, and particularly that of the superb terracotta statue of Apollo himself.[2] These offered splendid proofs of the city's distinction in the sixth century, when cities throughout Etruria were alike bringing their art and culture to mature expression. The terracotta workshops of Veii, indeed, are said to have been renowned for the quality of their products, and the name of one of the artists (Vulca) is even remembered by Pliny as the man responsible for the statues of the Temple of Jove commissioned by Tarquinius Superbus for the Roman Capitol. He may even have made the famous bronze Wolf that is in the Capitoline Museum, which is definitely Etruscan and was later to become the symbol of the Roman State—though without the Romulus and Remus, added during the Renaissance.

After the final sacking of the city in 397 or 396, those inhabitants who escaped massacre were probably either "driven away or sold into slavery", as Mary Cameron wrote, "and the site of one of the most prosperous cities of the Campagna left desolate, its ruins crumbling away and overgrown by brushwood and rank grass".[3] The vengeance of the Romans was no doubt merciless and absolute enough. Livy writes of "Rome and Veii facing each other with such mutual hatred and ferocity that none could doubt but that defeat for either would mean extinction". And when he comes to describe the actual defeat of the Veientines, he writes of that "famous day" of which every hour was spent in the killing of Rome's enemies and the sacking of a wealthy city, "and the riot of plunder that took place, even to the desecration of the famed Temple of Juno and the transportation of the goddess to Rome, where Camillus had her installed in her eternal dwelling-place on the Aventine".[4]

So the city, after its long and deadly struggle with Rome, was finally crushed, stripped of its wealth, deserted, desolated, never to revive. Though there are Roman ruins on the hill behind the Portonaccio sanctuary to prove that the area was again to be inhabited, the splendours of Etruscan Veii had vanished for ever, leaving only echoes and fragments behind. Rome had taken one more step towards domination of Etruria and Italy and her betrayal of the ancient heritage of the Mediterranean world. So completely in fact did the city disappear from the map that it was only identified again during the last century with the discovery of tombs and walls and temple foundations in that area below the small hamlet of Isola Farnese, twelve miles north of Rome.

The journey from the centre of the capital takes no more than half an hour along the Cassia. There is a yellow signpost for the ruins of Veii, and another for the village of Isola Farnese, just beyond La Storta. The road here runs down into a valley, leaving the noise and the self-importance of the Cassia behind, and moving in among the hills and the tufo fissures of the Campagna. It continues along a ridge above the valley, runs past a group of houses, and then dips steeply down to where a lane turns off immediately below the hamlet. Isola Farnese lies high above on a rock-spur, its fortress-palace at the cliff on one side of the Cremera ravine which separates it from the area of the ancient city. If you go up to the village you will find a charming little piazza flanked by old houses, a church and a bar; and a single street of stone cottages leading from there to the arched portico of the Rospigliosi palace; that is all. But from a pathway that runs around outside the village you can look down across the tumbling vegetation of the ravine slopes to the tree-screened platform of the Portonaccio sanctuary and its ruins, in an area outside the vanished walls on the western side of the city.

To get to the sanctuary, you have to take the lane below, plunging down through its tunnel of green between the walls of tufo, and out into a narrowish valley. This lane curves past the village cemetery, moving among the tangled vegetation and half-obscured crops of tufo to end at a shut red building and the rock-passage of the river Cremera. It is an oppressive and melancholy spot. From the left the dammed water comes over in a thin sheet 8 feet high and perhaps 20 feet long, and on the right it falls 50 feet into a deep ravine, in two falls, the cascade broken at a ledge half-way down and continuing from there to the bottom. The great shut ravine into which it falls reminds one at once of the gorge at Vulci. Although it is of tufo and not limestone, and therefore darker, it has the same kind of fantastic sheer-cliffed structure, the same kind of brooding and ominous beauty, only more closed in; and a desolateness full of the hints and echoes of places once thickly populated that have long been deserted.

You cross the stream by planks laid over the tufo. And from here a path leads up through the rock on to the Portonaccio height, where, below the crest of the hill, a Roman archway serves as the entrance to the sanctuary itself. This archway and the road that continues on from it beside the Etruscan remains, was built three or four centuries after the destruction of the city when it became inhabited by a small colony of Romans under the Empire, referred to as *municipium Augustum veiens*.[5] And it was probably the local labourers, during the construction of this road, who placed the terracotta fragments of the Apollo and other gods out of the way, in the cache of rock where, in 1916, they were eventually discovered. Strange that these workmen should not have destroyed their finds; that we should owe the survival of the Apollo to a race over whom Veii and Etruria must long have ceased to exert an influence. But if we assume these workers to have been Etruscans, hired from among surrounding villages in the Campagna, then it would not be unreasonable to suggest that they might have wanted to conserve these fragments—perhaps recalling the legends handed down to them about their world as it had once been, and suddenly awed by the mystic smiles on the faces of the Apollo and the Hermes, echoing the vanished splendours of their world.

The sanctuary enclosure contains the foundations of the temple from which the terracottas must have come, a rectangular sacred pool fed by water channelled through the rock, and the foundation-stones of two or three other buildings. The whole of the central zone came to light much ruined because of the collapse of tunnels excavated centuries ago as a quarry for building material. But in spite of this, the foundations, and considerable sections of the walls of its buildings, remain as an impressive testimony to the importance of the site. Set on their platform above the choked gorge and the cliffsides at the bottom of which runs the river, the greyish-black tufo blocks lie there massive and rooted among the grass opposite the ashen walls of the palace on the other side.

The main temple, with its sacred pool, retains the shape of its three *cellae*, and was once faced, as many fragments found in the vicinity have proved, with two rows of columns and a terracotta pediment. It is not a large building, being no more than $18\frac{1}{2}$ metres or about 55 feet in length.[6] But then one very quickly discovers that the Etruscans had no use for mere size or the rhetoric of mass. They built intimately and densely, to contain and embody their vision of community—for delight, within the human scale. And one imagines their houses and public buildings also to have been small—in relation, that is, to the size and grandiosity, the pomp and flourish of Roman building.

Further down, beyond the temple, in the middle of an area of complicated inter-crossing walls and canals, lies a large enclosed quadrangle which, in the excavations that took place on the site at the beginning of the century, yielded a great quantity of precious votive objects, figures in bronze, finely shaped articles of jewellery, and vases. Among them, for example, was found a bucchero vase inscribed with the name of one Velthur Tulumni, which is of particular interest because that is the name recorded by Livy when he mentions a certain Larte Tolumnis as having been the Lucumon in 437 B.C. There is anyway little doubt that the sanctuary had been in existence for a long time previous to this. Beneath the rubble of the temple certain walls have come to light which date back to the seventh century, and the famous terracottas of Apollo, Herakles, Hermes and the Goddess with Child, together with all the other fragments from the façade are the silent witness to Veii's fame in the sixth century.[7]

The city of Veii was built upon two adjacent heights, the smaller of the two on the south side taking the form of a huge rectangle more or less isolated from the rest of the city, where the acropolis had its place. It is called *Piazza D'Armi*, and still bears traces, on the side closest to the city itself, of its defensive walls and of a very ancient temple, fragments of the terracotta pedimental decoration of which were discovered and carried away during the last century. The larger height, triangular in shape, was also surrounded by a great wall, said to have measured many miles round. Traces of this wall are still visible at odd points on the hillside, especially to the north-west; but they are not easy to find because the whole area is thick with vegetation, and corn has been sown and ploughed for centuries on every available open space. One is even surprised to find that there are bits of wall still resisting the voracious thrusting tangle of brush and undergrowth that surrounds the stones. And this makes them seem the more impressive.

Leaving the enclosed area for the central part of the city, you turn to the right up an ancient road cut out of the tufo which probably once led through a gateway, either here or further down towards the Cremera cascade. It leads on to the open hilltop— bare and open and dipping away and desolate as a deserted battle- field. To the left there is a crest covered in the fallow year at the beginning of June with tall greyish-green thistles, black and dead at their roots, but thrusting up out of the ground like huge symbols of the phallus. Ahead the road dips to a cleft and up round another curve of hill brilliant with the ripening yellow of the corn, leaving a bowl of land behind that falls in green disorder towards the gorge. It was on the left-hand crest, at the very centre of the ancient city, that excavations undertaken rather haphazardly in the last century exposed the remains of *augustum veiens*, the Roman settlement established here four centuries after the fall of Veii. Among the thistles one treads the hard-cracked earth, moving round the excavated areas, noting the small-brick inner structures of walls and the diamond-patterned *reticulatum* of Augustan Rome, as well as another older part cut from the tufo and probably belonging to the ancient city. A few pieces of Roman sculpture were found here which are now in the Vatican, and the twelve beautiful Ionic columns that decorate the façade of the Palazzo Wedekind in the Piazza Colonna were taken from the ruins during the last century.[8] As for the rest, it has either been dispersed or lies under the earth, still broken into by the plough or by the roots or thistles, and given over to the long bared silences of this hill campagna.

There are thousands of tombs among the hills that surround the city heights, but only a few are now either visible or accessible after more than a century of destructive excavation. It has been said that even in the time of Julius Caesar "painted vases, which had become valuable, were sought and taken wherever they were found";[9] though perhaps only sporadically. The majority of the tombs, however, would have remained untouched, being outside the town in the hills, and soon to be hidden beneath protective screens of vegetation. They lay like this no doubt for centuries, until hunted out and broken into and ruthlessly exposed when the nineteenth-century speculators and explorers began to operate. And this nineteenth-century quest was no doubt a far more predatory and destructive process than either the Romans or the vegetation, reducing hundreds of the tombs to ruins. It began long before state laws had been passed to make sporadic and unlicensed excavation an offence and declare the contents of all tombs the property of the nation. As George Dennis wrote, of what went on at Veii in 1847: "The greater part of the land belongs to the Queen of Sardinia, who lets it out in the season to excavators, most of them dealers in antiquities in Rome, but as lucre is their sole object, they are content to rifle the tombs of everything convertible into cash and cover them in immediately with earth."[10] A kind of "gold rush" seems in fact to have taken place, and a great deal of easy money no doubt came the way of those who staked their claims and struck a tomb.

In this way, many of the riches of Veii were scattered, vanishing into private and public collections all over the world. Nevertheless, these early speculators, excavating in haste and without knowledge, left intact a considerable number of the tombs; and in recent years archaeologists using scientific methods have made many new discoveries. On the heights of Grotta Gramiccia north-west of the city, and at Picazzano, for example, lie the most ancient cemeteries, dating to the nineth and eighth centuries, with well-tombs shaped to contain the Villanovan cinerary urns common to so many of the cemeteries of Etruria, and hundreds of barrow tombs belonging to the period immediately following. These two areas, excavated at the beginning of the century, have yielded enough pieces in the last few years to demonstrate the opulence of the Veientine culture during the Villanovan period. There is a collection of Veii urns to be seen today at the archaeological museum in Florence, and among these are some impressive examples—black, biconical, with geometric patterns of every variety incised upon them. There are many fine bronzes too in Florence—brooches, ear-rings, pins, household utensils, bowls with hammered designs. And a few pieces of exquisite gold, which are to be compared in finesse, if not in range, with the gold-work of Caere, Vetulonia and Praeneste. These were found in the cemeteries of the so-called "orientalizing" phase of Etruscan culture, of the seventh and sixth centuries, which lay on heights such as Casale del Fosso to the west of the city and Vaccareccia to the south-west—chamber-tombs carved out of the rock, many of them long ago ransacked and stripped of their gold, but sometimes when rediscovered still containing the odd fragmented

Corinthian vase or votive bronze. In these tombs some of the most exciting of the early painted vases of proto-Corinthian origin (either imported from Greece or locally imitated) were discovered. There are one or two of these in Florence with their bands of processional animals. They stand beside a very exceptional piece —a large crater with horizontal terracotta bands of varying thickness painted on a cream ground with a vivid rhythmic motive of diagonally rising triangles in black painted between two red bands across the waist of the vase, which makes one think at once of the strange primitive beauty of the Tomb of the Ducks, to be described in a moment, and of vases from the remoter past of Rhodes and Crete that one remembers having seen in the Louvre and the British Museum. As for the black bucchero work of Veii, Florence possesses some strikingly beautiful examples—cups and amphorae and bowls decorated with incised geometric patterns—ribbed sections between raised bands, delicate stippled motives of leaf or fern running horizontally round the neck, and zig-zags and triangles—and with heraldic animals. Then there is the famous Chigi oinichoe, which came from a tumulus tomb (at least seven of which are still visible) in the district north of the city on the way to Formello, and is now in the Villa Giulia. This is a unique and richly detailed vase, of great vivacity, late Corinthian in style (of the seventh century) which must have been imported from Greece. It is decorated with three figured zones. On the upper band, two groups of helmeted warriors are moving towards each other in close formation, their shields decorated with black heraldic birds and gorgon heads, and among them a double-flute player, head raised, pipes to the sky. The middle band has three scenes—a symbolic lion-hunt in which the men are moving swiftly to the aid of a comrade into whose shoulder the lion has already sunk his teeth; a partly vanished Judgement of Paris, and a group of horsemen following a quadriga. While on the lower band one can make out a swiftly drawn scene from a hare hunt. This is altogether an extraordinary work by one of the masters of the painted Greek vase, the fortunate survival of so many of which we owe to the Etruscans who imported them.[11]

These things apart, however, Veii would remain justly famous for its sculptures and for the existence of its two painted tombs, the recently discovered Tomb of the Ducks, and the renowned Campana Tomb, both among the earliest examples yet found in Etruria, and a unique witness to the art of wall painting in the ancient world. These I shall now examine more closely, and since I consider them to be of special significance for anyone wishing to come to a closer understanding of the Etruscan spirit, I shall deal with them in a separate chapter.

VEII: THE PAINTED TOMBS AND THE
PORTONACCIO SCULPTURES

THE TOMB OF the Ducks was brought to light only in January 1958, following an entry by clandestine robbers. It is situated a good distance from the city, to the north-east, on a hill that rises beside the Formello road and the miniature falls of the Piordo known as Cascatella della Ninfa. There is an ancient bridge here, the Ponte dell'Isola, which one crosses to get to the hill, and above the falls a curious unfinished circular house, the plaything (as my guide informed me) of a well-known Roman architect. There had been plans, it seemed, to build upon the hill itself, but with the discovery of the tomb, the land was at once appropriated by the state and systematically explored, to reveal three other tombs, carved out of the rock and contemporary with the first but without paintings.

All four tombs were found to have been already violated and stripped of their contents, though out of certain fragments collected from them, two large and very interesting Italo-geometric olle of the first half of the seventh century, with strange schematic bird-creatures and horses painted on them, exactly similar in style to the ducks of the tomb painting itself, have been reconstructed.

The painted tomb, like the others, has only one room. It is rectangular in shape, rather small, with an archway facing south, which was found on discovery to have been sealed with blocks of tufo. The tomb robbers had apparently forced their way in through the roof, leaving the sealed door undisturbed. But the tomb now has an iron door, and is always kept locked, for obvious reasons. So that for a visit to this tomb you have to ask at Portonaccio for a guide—who will be happy to take you there, and will even add to the pleasure of the visit with his anecdotes and asides, his personal commentaries on the history of Veii and the present inhabitants of the surrounding district.

The tomb is intimate and primitive, painted with an unself-conscious directness and artlessness. Alfredo di Agostino, in his little booklet in the series "Quaderni di Villa Giulia" (1964) dates it between the years 675 and 650 B.C., which means that it is more than a century earlier than anything at Tarquinia. In fact Signor di Agostino calls it "the most ancient wall painting yet found in Etruria . . ." and though "inspired by some oriental prototype . . . executed with a certain independence and freedom of its own".[1] And Mario Torelli refers to it as "a document of exceptional importance both historically and artistically", since it demonstrates the existence in Etruria, even at this early date, of monumental forms of art implying an already developed culture echoing those of ancient Rhodes and Crete. Torelli links this art to the art of vase-painting in other parts of central Italy and beyond Italy itself.[2] Vases found for instance at Tarquinia, Bizenzio and Falerii are very close in style to the vases and the wall-paintings of this tomb. And there is a krater in the British Museum from Cyprus and dated to the fourteenth century B.C. which has striking features in common with the vases in this Veii tomb and the ducks themselves.

Only three colours are used in the tomb: red, yellow and black. The walls are painted up to a height of about three feet from the ground in a beautiful vivid red, and this red is separated from the yellow of the upper wall by five horizontal bands respectively black, yellow, black, red and black in colour, forming a frieze. Immediately above which, on the northern wall, the five ducks move, from right to left, silhouetted or outlined in red against the yellow. The two outer ducks are completely red (for masculinity no doubt), with primitive schematic black lines denoting the plumage. The one in the centre is also red, but has a black inner body. And on either side of him are two yellow (and therefore female) ducks—their red outlines, that is, are not painted in with red so that instead they take the colour of the wall itself, though they have the same kind of schematic black plumage markings as the other pair.

These ducks are primitively yet swiftly drawn, and they move with a curious high-necked stiff assurance towards the sarcophagus—or rather towards the empty raised platform (edged with five rectangular blocks of tufo) where the sarcophagus used to be, and the deeply gouged lines that take the shape of its roof-like lid. Though severely schematic, they carry such vivid conviction most of all because of the unhesitant character of the forms, and the clear sense one gets of their intent as the carriers of spirit and of immortality. They are geometric in structure, executed with the same spirited sense of style that distinguishes the abstract geometric patterns on the two large impasto vases found in the tomb. The heads are done simply by outline, without eyes, the breasts and bodies in a single flowing curve, the necks and legs in hatched triangles and lines, quite effortlessly and with astonishing economy.

Above them the ceiling, meeting at its highest point in the centre, is divided geometrically into four parts, two triangular and two trapezoidal, alternately red and yellow in colour. This pattern, partially ruined by the hole that had been made by the thieves, adds a final consistency to the decorative scheme of the whole; and the effect, as the heavy iron door swings back and one steps into the little room, is indeed vivacious and touching.

The paintings of the famous *Campana Tomb*, first discovered in 1843, are in contrast a highly elaborate and complex symbolism, with a queer, intent immediacy and a richness of pattern that points on to the great tombs at Tarquinia, indicating a date some-where close to the end of the seventh century or the beginning of the sixth. They have now deteriorated to such a point as to be only faintly and partially visible, but the detailed etching that is available at the custodian's office on Portonaccio, and the graphic descriptions offered by George Dennis, Mary Cameron and Torelli among others,[3] are sufficient to enable one to reconstruct from what remains a vivid enough image of the forms and patterns of the original. And the tomb itself would anyway be well worth a visit for its architectural distinction alone.

It can be reached by crossing the fields by a path that leaves the Formello road a little further on from the Ponte dell'Isola and the Tomb of the Ducks, or from within the city itself by moving across the hilltop and out through the north-eastern gateway on the other side of the Formello valley. As you approach it, the first thing about the tomb that strikes you is the entrance doorway. Instead of being carved from the tufo, as most of the tombs in the district, it is built out of carefully fitted blocks of stone laid horizontally one against the other, and is closed at the top by a great flat stone. The *dromos* or passageway that leads to it is built likewise, and has a little open room on the left, no doubt a servant's tomb. On each side of the doorway at the end lies a mutilated almost faceless lion, symbolically guarding the sepulchre, thrusting its blind head forward in symbolic protection of the sepulchre—one is reminded of the Lion Gate at Mycenae, and of many other monuments from the Eastern Mediterranean; and of Solomon setting lions as guardians round his throne.

Within there are two chambers, one beyond the other. The first and larger of the two has a stone couch on each side, and the paintings are to be found on the dividing wall between the outer and the inner chamber. The latter is frescoed with a series of six shields decorated with radial geometric patterns in minutely worked segments, such as are to be seen on the bronze shields and urns of the orientalizing period from Tarquinia and Vulci. Here, a number of cinerary urns were found (three of them in the form of caskets with heads moulded on the lids) which incidentally offer one more proof of the peaceable fusion in Etruria of two races with distinct funeral customs, since they lay immediately beside the sarcophagi themselves.

The tomb was found to be rich in Corinthian and Italo-corinthian vases, figured bucchero, bronze and gold; and there were a number of superb amphorae, both large and small. Many of these, though, vanished untraceably when thieves broke into the tomb at the beginning of this century—for the authorities had decided to leave the contents of the tomb intact after providing a heavy iron door for their protection. It was a loss of incalculable value, but at least the paintings were left—even though they too are being gradually stolen away by time and the weather. And it is they that are the main attraction of the tomb. As you come in through the doorway, you can just make them out where they cover the far wall of the first room, faintly and mysteriously forming before your eyes in the gloom.

There are four scenes—two on each side of the door, the upper and the lower each divided by a horizontal band of the lotus pattern. In the top right-hand scene a small figure on a high-crouped, long-legged horse is being led by a man with a symbolic axe held to his shoulder and a naked groom who walks on the far side of the horse. A little tailless cat sits behind the tiny rider with one paw resting familiarly against his shoulder, and a strange-headed dog lifts its head beneath the horse. The procession moves towards the door, as does the other scene on the opposite side, except that there the figure on horseback moves in the opposite direction. Below, on the right, a species of sphinx, with a small deer-like animal beside it, is being pushed from behind by a leopard sitting on its haunches. And in the lower scene to the left of the door a lioness or similar beast, of great size, walks forward, hanging out a long tongue, accompanied by a couple of smaller animals, one seated with paw raised, the other half in movement, its head turned to look up at the lioness.

"These queer beasts," Mary Cameron wrote of them early i the century, "are as odd in colour as in form, being parti-coloured black, yellow and red, and spotted all over without the least regard to nature. The flesh of the human beings is (apparently according to the convention) painted deep red. And all around and about, the background is filled in with the double-volute symbol of fertility . . ."4 One can, it is true, name the animals leopards, lions, horses, dogs. But the strange consistency and rigour of the scheme of colour (the only colours used being black, red and yellow) and the transformation of the animal forms, give the paintings a compelling intensity which is almost purely symbolic. All the animals, for instance, have spotted necks, bodies and legs, either in white or in yellow, though the near foreleg of the horse on the left-hand wall and the seated dog below it are curiously stylized, almost in imitation of the forma-lized plant patterns curling around them.

The horse on the right has legs of extraordinary length and "tenuity", and a barrel "pinched in like a lady's waist", as Dennis puts it. "His neck and chest," he further observes, "are red, with

Above: 7a AERIAL VIEW OF THE BANDITACCIA NECROPOLIS AT CERVETERI. Left—the enclosed area with seventh- and sixth-century tumuli. Extreme right—the seventh-century Tumulus of the Shields and Chairs with the Manganello valley behind and Vignali (site of the city) beyond it (*p. 145*).

Below: 7b THE TUMULUS OF THE SHIP, CERVETERI. Seventh to sixth centuries. Corridor with chambers on either side leading to main tomb (*pp. 148–9*).

Above: 8a THE TOMB OF THE LIONESSES. Second half of the sixth century. Tarquinia. Far wall, above niche for urn. Heraldic lionesses, musicians and dancers with frieze of dolphin and birds below pomegranate-lotus motif. Two of the four reclining men can be seen on the side walls (*pp. 50–51*). *Below:* 8b THE TOMB OF THE BULLS. Mid-sixth century. Tarquinia. The central panel on the far wall: Achilles (armoured behind fountain) awaiting Troilus (on horseback) (*pp. 48–49*).

yellow spots—his head black—hair and tail yellow—hind quarters and near leg black—near foreleg corresponding with his body, but off-legs yellow, spotted with red." The other animals are similarly coloured, all of them, and particularly the sphinx, with its "red face and bosom, spotted with white", its straight black hair, its short wings, with curling tips striped black, red and yellow, and its yellow body and tail.[5]

These creatures, including the two tiny boy-like riders and the walking men, inhabit their universe with complete conviction. They are like images met in dreams, compelling acceptance, moving silently, with slow hieratic dignity, across one's path, their spotted bodies glowing in the dusk. One peers fascinated, absorbed, at the shapes and the colours that are still there, with an obscure sense of their significance; for they leave their spell upon one. And they are like nothing else one has ever seen outside Etruria. Though the sphinx and the elaborate lotus patterns worked into the background are symbols one associates with Egypt, they have been utilized for a very different kind of vision. The sphinx, besides, has wings, like those sphinxes found in Ionian tombs at Smyrna and other places and on many Caeretan vases, and is standing; and its head, in common with the other heads, reminds one of the features of figures on early Doric vases.

One finds links too with those early proto-Corinthian hydras and amphorae found here in the tomb and in other places throughout Etruria. But the closest affinities are with other early Etruscan wall paintings—with those of Cerveteri (the Boccanera slabs in the British Museum and the five ceremonial scenes in the Louvre, both a little later in date); or with the beautiful reddish-brown chest-like sarcophagus of the Lions in the Villa Giulia, with its couchant lions, one with head turned outward, the other in profile with hanging tongue; or again with the sphinx-like figures of Chiusi. And as one looks at the pomegranate-shaped udder of the lioness at Veii, one is particularly reminded of the Tomb of the Lionesses at Tarquinia, with its frieze of sliced, open pomegranates, and the udders of the two spotted "lionesses" of the pediment.

But even so, the paintings of the Campana Tomb, in so far as

E

they remain, remain a unique and quite distinctive record, earlier than anything else yet discovered, with the exception of the Duck Tomb, in the Etruscan world. These mysterious creatures, solemnly moving through the dusk, are most probably symbolic of the Journey of the Dead to their final resting-place—the small figures on horseback being (as Dennis and others have suggested) the souls of the dead being led through the dark. And the animals have their place upon this journey as protective and positive symbols—symbols of fertility and of immortality, of the vital forces of nature and the cosmos, the guardians of life and death.

The terracottas from Portonaccio, which are now in the Villa Giulia, do not, of course, belong to the "oltretomba" world of the Campana murals. They were intended to stand at the apex of a temple roof in full sunlight. Which gives them a special significance, for the reason that very little evidence of this kind has survived the centuries. So that when the Apollo, the Herakles and the head of Hermes were brought to light in 1916 in a hole in the rock, the archaeologists were justifiably excited and encouraged to a more complete excavation of the area of the temple. And Pallottino's later find close by of the Goddess with Child, belonging to the same group, was one of the many discoveries made in the years since 1916.

These pieces have been a subject for dispute among scholars and critics. By some they are considered peculiarly Etruscan in character. For others they are hardly more than imitations of prevailing Ionian forms such as that of the archaic Kore of the same date from the acropolis in Athens, and may even have been done by Greeks. But those who argue in terms of a common heritage with its own distinctive characteristics would seem to be closest to the truth. From all the evidence we have, it is clear that there were many contacts between the Etruscans and the Greeks, not to speak of other nations. Art was a currency, and artists were welcome in Etruria who could work to the rhythms of its way of life. The workshops of Veii were famous enough, anyway, to attract comment; and they probably attracted artists from "abroad" too. But the point is that they were Etruscan and not Greek, and their sculpture belongs to a style and a taste that can only be defined as "anti-classical". In other words, there is little doubt as to the significance of the Apollo as a representative instance of the mature artistic vision of the sixth-century Etruscans.

There were at first thought to be only four figures, representing Apollo, Hermes, Herakles standing above the trapped body of a hind, and Artemis. But when Pallottino discovered the Goddess, and when at various periods since the Second World War other fragments were found, indicating the presence of other figures, the classical interpretation of Giulio Giglioli (who had made the 1916 discovery) had to be reconsidered. This interpretation, limited to four figures, was based upon the incident in which Apollo and Herakles engaged in combat for possession of the hind Cerinite, aided by Artemis and Hermes (more or less as it is depicted on a sixth-century helmet found at Vulci). It had to be revised and enlarged to include the Goddess, whom Pallottino identified as Leto carrying the infant Apollo in her arms in the act of fleeing from Python, who had been pursuing her round the world. Be that as it may, these figures—obviously conceived as a large group placed high up on the ridgepole of the temple a good distance away from the spectator—probably refer ambiguously to both the Greek myths and the modified adaptations of the Etruscans; and the fragments gathered in recent years indicate the presence at this culminating point of a number of figures considerably in excess of the five that have been identified.[6]

The most impressive of the three standing figures that are exhibited at the Villa Giulia (where all the sculptures are to be found) is the Apollo, not only because he is the most complete, but because of the vivacity of his striding limbs and the superbly active poise of the head, with its intent smiling face. It offers a triumphant resolution to one of the recurrent themes of both Etruscan art and the art of the archaic world in general—that of the human figure in motion. The stride of these massive legs gives this Apollo a dynamic thrusting energy which emphasizes his movement forward while fixing him firmly and bodily in space. And the sense of propulsion is intensified by the plastic treatment of the knee-length tunic, the formalized pattern of its folds pressed against the limbs, and the stylized muscularity of the calf and shin and foot of the left leg. As to the Herakles, it is difficult to form a true idea of the quality of the piece as sculpture, because it has been made up from many fragments, which are only partially connected. But the hind that lies trapped under him on its back with its legs tied together, again has something of the leashed power and energy that is so characteristic of the Apollo; so much so indeed that certain critics have linked the two pieces together as the work of a single artist. And it is more than likely that the beautiful head of Hermes was by the same sculptor too. The features are very close in style to those of the Apollo, though they are softer, more rounded. A soft Ionian smile plays about the lips, and the clear open expression seems a glowing challenge to pleasure and a defeat of the dark, an affirmation, serene and confident.

The Goddess, on the other hand—her body found in about 250 fragments in 1938, her head only six years afterwards in 1944[6]— appears to be the work of a later follower of the maker of the Apollo. For the figure lacks the Apollo's dynamic balance: her legs are a little too heavily articulated and splayed, particularly in relation to the upper part of the body; and the head itself seems only approximately placed upon a pedantically reconstructed neck. But she too is nevertheless an impressive addition to the company—big-limbed, hieratic, stylized, and certainly no part of a merely decorative convention. Looking at her, one sees how much she differs in actual expressiveness and style from the archaic Kore of the Acropolis in Athens—she moves, she is active, she has intent, she is almost aggressively protective.

There are other fragments beyond these: one side, for instance, of another smiling Hermes-face, in profile, dark-skinned and sharply articulated; the figure of a striding female dancer, coloured red, cream and black, and very much like the figure of the dancer from the Tomb of the Lionesses, gliding along sideways in her elaborately flowing robes with long pointed shoes, her arm crooked inward, the body flowing rhythmically beneath the clothes in a fluent slow gliding movement; and a grimacing Maenad or Gorgon-head antefix.

The problem of the influences that have gone to the creation of these superbly affirmative examples of Etruscan art is related to the whole problem of intercommunication and exchange among all the peoples of the ancient Mediterranean world and the extent to which these peoples shared a common spiritual heritage. Undeniably, there are stylistic links between this Apollo and the figures of late archaic Greek art—between the Hermes and the softly smiling faces of sculptures from Asia Minor; between the goddess and the Acropolis Kore—all executed at more or less the same time. It is absurd to speak of "originality" (as if that anyway were an adequate criterion) in a period of such intense and incessant interchange between peoples. But all the same, the sense of a profoundly Ionian expressiveness that gives the Apollo and the Hermes such eloquence is further intensified and particularized by a peculiarly intimate and intent character which one recognizes at once as specifically Etruscan.

The classical ideal is an ideal of stillness, poise, repose, a logic of poise or of stilled act, a rational and almost philosophical equilibrium, an organic anatomical control. And archaic art is often concerned with movement, as you see it on the Attic black-figure vases, or with a kind of hieratic, symbolic, anti-classical stillness. It presents the ceremonial and ritualistic vision of the East, where almost every figure has its symbolic place in the iconography of religious feeling. The roots and sources of Etruscan art, indeed, diverse and varied as they are, brought into being a specially distinctive iconography of forms. Those rigid, mask-like Canopic heads, the winged sphinxes and wide-faced hieratic stone heads of Chiusi, which one links with the Vulci centaur and the lions of Veii, have their part to play in the evolution of Etruscan art. Influences in fact were continually at work shaping and modifying and transforming the styles, internally as well as from the outside world. It is impossible to believe that the idiosyncratic art of Chiusi would not have influenced that of Tarquinia, or Tarquinia that of Veii; or the achievements of Tarquinia those of Chiusi. And certainly the terracotta workshops of Veii, producing their sculptures at the end of the sixth century, would have had their effect upon artists from other parts of

Etruria; upon the painters, for instance, of Tarquinia and the sculptors of those beautiful Chiusian urns in soft sandstone which are such a feature of the museum at Chiusi.

The Apollo has his apparent affinities with the Greek art of the period—with, for instance, the half life-size marble figure of a lady, of about 520 B.C., that is in the Acropolis Museum in Athens. And one sees reflections of him, in the formulation of the hair and the way in which it falls in ringlets to the shoulders, in other figures of the same period from mainland and eastern Greece; even as one sees echoes of him (of the earlier archaic style, that is) in the famous Phidian Apollo of the Tiber,[7] done by a fine anonymous Greek craftsman a century later. But whereas the Tiber Apollo is part of the later triumph of the Greek world and its classical ideals, at a period (the middle of the fifth century) when Etruria was still rooted in the world it was displacing, the Veii Apollo is an authentic symbol of the ancient world, belonging to it, part of its vision, referring to the east, his roots in the old pre-classical continuities.

Here there is no smile of dreamy contemplative interest, no aiming at an abstract logic of proportion, a geometry of the human figure. The smile is stylized, symbolic. It refers to a vision of the universe that Greece was moving away from to produce "those models", as Kenneth Clark underlines, "which were to satisfy our Western notion of beauty till the present day".[8] It is alert and vital and lucid. This could well be the face of the God of Light, who comes striding swiftly forward into contact. It has little of the calm of the Greek ideal, but is quick and spontaneous as the *action* of light, almost as Dionysiac as Apollonian. In its clearly chiselled lines, the face seems to hint at many things beyond the conventions of the classical gods. There is a certain rigidity, a certain tension about it; an intent immediacy. But there is also a remoteness—a remoteness, one may say, not of the abstract concept, but of the elusiveness of feeling. For with his parted lips and his clear-cut nose, the very direction, slightly downward looking, in which the whole face turns, this Apollo has an intent expressiveness which is of the rapt world inhabited by the dancers of the tombs—sexually and sensuously intent, with something of the elusive quick intentness of living beings.

I have more than once been surprised to hear the smile of this Apollo referred to as the smile of a corrupt ungodly creature. But by what criterion, what morality, one would ask, can it be judged in this way, if not that of the classical ideal or of Christian godliness? But these are not criteria we can judge the Etruscans on. The Phidian god speaks a different language, more perhaps or less significant, and no doubt more universal than the Veientine god. It is beside the point. *This* god seems to me to take no part in the debate the moralists are always indulging between good and evil or the aestheticians between degrees of beauty based upon doubtful absolutes; but rather to exist beyond such quibblings, as an image of the uncontaminated quick of life; no dialectic god but a god of the energies of being who exists in terms of his intent swift smile and the dynamic immediacy of his body's movement, contained and undoubting. Set beside the grimacing gorgon or the Maenad head antefixes that decorated the pediment of the temple, there is no essential contradiction, no dichotomy. For the Etruscans of the sixth century, Hell did not exist—or at least if it did, it did not split their world into irreconcilable camps. And death itself, according to their symbolic vision of the universe, was a part of life, a continuation of it—the dead feted by the living in their "oltretomba" world. For them, as for so many of the peoples of the ancient world, there were the unhesitant continuities that define the rhythms of the universe. Christ and the Logos had not yet arrived to detach man from his closeness of community with nature. There was no equivalent of Giotto's Christian Hell with its overt condemnation of the flesh, its division of the spirit *from* the flesh; of Christianity's "casting of filth on the beginning, the very condition", as Nietzsche put it, "of our life".[9] These gorgon heads were the caricaturist expression of those same forces (or energies) of nature and of being which lie coiled in each of us. And it is surely not against such strange and unpredictable energies that we should take our stand, if we have to take a stand; but only against those divisive mechanistic concepts that would deny the strange and unpredictable energies of life. Even in this spirit did the Etruscans perhaps take their stand against the ideas and aims of Rome. They had to, politically and economically, and in defence of their own vision. Faced by the alien power of Rome as well as by the Gauls, with their backs to the wall, they had no choice. But it was a struggle that they could not hope to win. The Romans had the advantage, both politically and psychologically, as in the ferocity of their desire to crush Etruria. And it was to be their destiny to become the instrument which finally brought about the collapse of the ancient world and its structure of values; even as it was their destiny to be the vehicle through which a new scale of values would be brought into being. Dividing materialism had triumphed over the ancient Mediterranean vision of community, just as the Christian spirit was itself later to triumph over Rome's materialism, and later still to establish its own materialistic empire in the wake of the other, "crowned on the grave thereof".[10] And so were the Etruscans defeated, an "inferior", "primitive" people with a vision of life and of death, and a social and political order, too delicately balanced to withstand the harsh, hard-headed practicality of the Romans, with their talent for exploiting situations, their opportunist scheming for place and power. How could a people content to let their destinies be controlled by the mystical authority of a small élite of princes and priests be a match for Roman politics, for a mentality that could interchange expediency and principle almost at will to suit its ends? No. Difficult though it may have been in terms of actual struggle for the Romans to achieve supremacy, the outcome was inevitable. They had the greater organizing power. They were not obscured or burdened by beliefs or scruples that could not be reconciled to their opportunist and acquisitive aims. The Roman state became an efficient and deadly machine for conquest. And so Camillus devastated Veii, killing or enslaving its people and carrying Juno off to Rome in triumph, leaving other gods and goddesses lying broken among the rubble, to be cached away and brought to light again only after 2,300 years of silence.

CERVETERI: CITY OF THE DEAD
(The Southern Maremma)

THE VILLAGE OF Cerveteri, forty kilometres from Rome in the
Southern Maremma, is situated four or five kilometres inland
from the sea. It occupies the north-west corner of a vast tufaceous
plateau called Vignali, the central of three heights above the
plain, whose reddish cliffs drop to the Mola valley on the south
and the Manganello to the north.

It is a poor village. Its three or four restaurants and the shop
that sells cheap imitation Etruscan vases are of course a gesture
to the tourists; and there are now other modest signs—a few new
buildings, bars, a few attempts at renovation here and there—that
the modern world is beginning to notice it. Perhaps also the
reclamation of the Maremma from its malarial desolation has
brought about some kind of material improvement. But looking
at the village alone, it is hard to imagine—in spite of the massive
fourth-century Etruscan walls and the castellated remains of the
mediaeval fortress that rises above them—that this is the site of
one of the richest cities of the Etruscan world—the largest and
the richest city, by all accounts, of maritime Etruria, and at its
height an international centre of art and commerce, with its own
port just up the coast at Pyrgi, to which people from all over the
Mediterranean no doubt came to trade goods and to enjoy the
pleasures of a civilized world. The Greeks called the city Agylla,
but it is known today to archaeologists and laymen alike by its
Roman name, Caere—the name Cerveteri (meaning Old Caere)
distinguishing it from the village of Ceri, a few kilometres south,
for which it was abandoned in the Middle Ages.

In the seventh and sixth centuries B.C., Caere must have presented a splendid sight to its visitors, spread out across the Vignali
plateau with its pattern of intercrossing streets,[1] its temples in
wood and terracotta, its wooden houses, its high red tufo walls,

its great gateways, and on the adjacent hills, its ceremonial cities of the dead, with their own planned streets and tomb-houses. And though it is only from the necropoli that we are now able to form any clear image of what the city was like, the architectural distinction there is such as to suggest a place of extraordinary importance.

For what one thinks of first when one thinks of Caere is the architecture of the tombs—its variety, its richness, the inventiveness and flexibility of its forms, and the power with which these forms convey their image of a people's way of life. It is not that there are not things equally as significant as these to give us a picture of the range and splendour of the Etruscan city, but simply that we think first of the architecture because it is the most immediately striking of all the evidence we have, just as the tomb-paintings are of Tarquinia.

On Vignali itself the remains of seven or eight temples have been discovered, as well as "water tunnels, tanks, drains, the foundations of diverse buildings, underground storerooms and so on", mostly from the period when Rome had taken over.[2] And there are fragments of the ring of walls, of doors and roads cut into the tufo and of gateways, visible all along the perimeter of the city.

But it is in the necropoli, extending in a vast ring around the city, that the richest discoveries have been made—on Banditaccia and Monte Abetone, marking the period of the city's greatest prosperity; at the localities of Pozzolana and Sorbo, where the most ancient remains (of the ninth and eighth centuries) were brought to light, and the seventh-century Regolini-Galassi tomb of the Sorbo necropolis yielded an astonishing treasure now in the Gregorian Museum in Rome. Many thousands of tombs, indeed, have been opened and explored—most of them to vanish again after being rifled, but hundreds remaining to satisfy the curious and to delight the fanatical. And others are being discovered almost daily, either by the archaeologists (when they can spare the time, the energy and the money) or (for purely mercenary reasons) by the *clandestini* and the local peasants.

The territory of the ancient city is said to have stretched for

forty-five miles along the coast between the Arrone River
(dividing it from that of Veii) and the Mignone, which marked
the boundary between Caere and Tarquinia. It extended inland
to include the dark ridges of the Tolfa hills and its many scattered
mining centres, and to embrace the whole of the vast lake of
Bracciano. The city itself, on its elevated position slightly inland,
exercised its commercial and military activity through at least
three ports—Alsium (Palo) to the south, Pyrgi (Santa Severa)
closest to the city a few kilometres to the north, and Punicum
(Santa Marinella) further still to the north, of which much
waterfront equipment from the Roman period remains. Of
these ports, Pyrgi was perhaps the most important, and recent
excavations on the site—revealing the foundations of two fifth-
century temples together with many precious fragments, including a vigorous group of terracotta figures from the pediment and
the now famous gold tablets inscribed in Punic and Etruscan—
appear at the least to indicate the presence here of a significant
monumental area, lavishly appointed, beside the port.

It is difficult of course to reconstruct the history in any detail,
but from the archaeological evidence (and from scattered
references made to the city), it can be established with at least
reasonable accuracy that a settlement of some sort was already in
existence on the site in the ninth or very early eighth century.
Ancient pit and trench tombs, some hewn from the rock, others
sunk in the earth and lined with stones, have been found in
abundance at Pozzolana and Sorbo, the latter containing decorated
cinerary urns in bronze and clay. The number of these tombs
alone would convincingly demonstrate a rich Villanovan culture
and a large community. But they also define two distinct
forms of burial rite, a far more important point that indicates the
peaceable fusion of two races or tribes. Inhumation and cremation
are a common feature of all so-called pre-Etruscan settlements—
of those foundations, that is, out of which the Etruscan civilization was built—and are therefore not unique to Caere. But the
interesting thing is that the two kinds of funeral custom should
have continued to be used even when, later on, the burial embra-
sure "widens out in the seventh century", as Pallottino puts it, "to

form a chamber with a covering of stone blocks beneath an earth mound";[3] for it hints at tolerance and flexibility in religious matters such as to give us a sense of Etruscan confidence in absorbing and reconciling apparently conflicting influences.

By the seventh century, at a time when Rome was probably still a minor centre ruled or dominated by Etruscans, Caere had become a rich and important city, trading with all the great nations of the Mediterranean. This is apparent not only from the architecture of the tombs themselves, but also from the things found in them—the scarabei, the bronzes and the gold ornaments, the vases, the chairs and couches found in the Regolini-Galassi tomb, the great number of early Attic amphorae and Hydriae found in other tombs, and (all together in one Banditaccia tomb) examples of Attic, Corinthian, Laconian, South Italian, Lydian, Ionian and Etruscan vases, that witness the confluence of various civilizations in sixth-century Caere. No doubt there were times when, to protect its commerce and maintain its position, the city would have come into conflict with other traders. So much can be gathered from reported instances of battles in the vicinity. And it would be strange if this had not been so. But Caere seems on the whole to have encouraged interchange with other peoples, and to have welcomed foreigners into the city without restriction. Or at least one has the feeling that far from presenting any warlike or threatening aspect, it would have been a place where gaiety and friendliness and the arts of peace were to be sought and cultivated; where even a foreigner could freely settle; a city of art and of trade where people could speak to each other in the language of common interest.

The fifth century, however, saw the end of expansion and of political stability in Central Italy, with increasing restrictions and threats beginning to put Etruria on to the defensive. And Caere must have suffered as much almost as any at the hands of the Gauls and the Romans among other nations intent on aggression and conquest. In 384 B.C., the fleet of Dionysus of Syracuse is said to have suddenly appeared off the coast and devastated Pyrgi, leaving its beautiful temples in ruins.[4] But by this time anyway the whole of Etruria had begun to falter before the power of Roman and

Gaulish invasions, and Caere was soon to attempt to hold off collapse by maintaining with Rome a kind of "benevolent neutrality", in spite of the fact that other cities in Etruria were being ruthlessly subjected to the "alien yoke". Its ambiguous attitude during this period could not have served to do any more than hold off the ultimate surrender for a while, and to make that surrender the more humiliating when it came; for about 350 Caere was forcibly annexed to Rome and a special prefectorial government established in the city. After which there was rapid and progressive decline, with its people no doubt sold into slavery or lured by the splendours of the New Rome into Roman ways, till reduced to a mere appendage or extension of the Roman state. And though, as a place where people lived, it lingered on through the Empire and into the Middle Ages, apathetic and malarial, its agriculture lapsing into stagnancy and swamp, it must very soon have presented a sorry contrast to the splendours of sixth-, fifth-, and even fourth-century Caere. By the third century B.C., with the area colonized by Roman gentry, that process of land-neglect which lasted till the beginning of our own century, had probably already begun. And in the Middle Ages the town was more or less abandoned for the neighbouring village of Ceri because of malaria, and left to moulder. So that the village as we see it today —built around and out of the ruins of mediaeval buildings and the Etruscan walls of the castle at the centre—is poor and small, and only in these last few decades (as a result of land reclamation by the Ente Maremma) beginning to stir out of its collapse and poverty, the mere echo of an echo of an echo of the Etruscan city.

Its setting, however, is among the most extraordinary of all the settings of Etruscan cities, though the full impact of this depends on how it is approached. Coming along the Aurelia it is the great expanse of the Maremma and the dark outlines of the Tolfa hills behind that dominate. From a distance it hardly seems as if Cerveteri is on anything more than a slight rise in the landscape, so dwarfed is it by the vastness of the plain. But there is another way of getting to Cerveteri—by the Cassia or the Via di Boccea, inland. From Bracciano the road approaches the site along a high plain, coming dramatically into the heart of the setting when it turns and begins to dip under a tangled spur of rock. For at this moment, without warning, the plain falls away to the right into a deep valley, and exactly here the wild shrub-dark cliffs of Monte Abetone begin, under the shadow of which one finds oneself looking across the valley of the Fosso della Mola separating Abetone from Vignali. Down below, along the floor of the valley, the Mola winds between fields, and the Vignali cliffs rise out of the gentle slopes in a thrust of livid red tufo topped and partly obscured by thick bushes.

Those who are moved by such things are likely to find this particularly memorable, not only because of the exultant beauty of the landscape, but because it is evident from the peculiar flatness of the hill itself that this is where the ancient city of Caere once lay. Indeed, so powerful is the impression of a city's foundations made by this first sweeping view that one hardly needs the confirmation that comes from suddenly catching sight among the shrubbery of a few great blocks of tufo wall or of the roadway cut into the rock further down to indicate the site of one of the gateways. It is the impact of the natural walls of those red cliffs and the flat-topped plain above that convinces.

So that going slowly beneath the towering cliffs of Abetone, at first obscured by a rank growth of bush and tree but bared in flaking masses further on, one moves (now with the sea glistening ahead) down towards the plain, as if out of the heart of the land-scape, emerging from it and turning across the little stream to the village. It is an altogether different sense of scale one has here—the Aurelia-view belongs to another, lesser world. From the bridge over the stream, for instance, the flaring beauty of the Abetone and Vignali cliffs declares the presence of the city, setting the scale and the tone of it, so that all larger perspectives come to seem mere pallid abstracts.

Cerveteri is so rich in tombs, and the tombs are so eloquently expressive in their varied forms of a distinctive architectural vision, that even those who have no more than a vague idea of what is meant by the Etruscan world are likely to have heard of them. For many they are of course the beginning and the end of the matter. Tourist buses leave Rome in the summer months to visit the necropolis among these bare Maremma hills, an hour is spent clambering in and out of the tombs, and then Rome calls again, compulsively. Which is as it should be, I suppose. For even in its richest flowering, Etruria cannot compete with the splendours of Renaissance Rome or with any of a dozen other cities in Central Italy. It is hidden, fragmentary, strange, just a little too far off-track perhaps to attract most, except incidentally. Which leaves it to the enthusiast and the lover, to those who have the time and are free enough of the intoxications of the cities to be drawn by the immemorial voices of the ancient world that come to us out of the silences of ruin.

Apart from the earliest ninth- and eighth-century cremation graves (sunken, circular, containing urns) and the oblong inhumation trenches that are contemporary with them, the tombs take the form of rock-hewn or constructed chambers grouped first of all under great circular mounds (the tumuli), then singly or in groups along streets with doorways leading straight in; and later still as *hypogei*, sunk deep underground and approached by flights of steps. These tombs are remarkable above all for the skill and the beauty of their architecture, and for the evident delight with which all kinds of detail are provided.

Among the earliest of the tumuli, the royal Sorbo tomb, discovered by Archpriest Regolini and General Galassi in 1836, and named after them, put Caere "among the great archaeological centres of the classical world", as Massimo Pallottino has pointed out.[5] It was once much larger than it is now—a great tumulus consisting of an outer and an inner ring of tufo, the outer being 48 metres in diameter, and therefore much the largest in the whole area. This outer ring, which now no longer exists, was excavated in the last century, its four tomb-groups found to have been already stripped of valuables. But it must have acted as a protective façade to the more ancient inner ring, lying sealed off at the very centre of the tumulus, for this was found with all its contents intact—a treasure of astonishing richness and variety from the seventh century "orientalizing" period of Etruscan art comparable in magnificence to those found at Veii and Vulci and Vetulonia, and now in the Gregorian Museum in Rome. So one can say that it was the ingenuity (or rather the vision) of the builders of this tomb, in a sense, that saved these marvellous things from the pilferers, and kept them for us to delight in and judge the Etruscans by.

The tomb is part of the great archaic burial-ground in the low-lying country south of the village, and it was one among a number of tumulus tombs, all of which have been exposed and most of which are now gone. But the chamber that contained the treasure is still there. It is sunk a little below ground—a long narrow passage with two small semi-circular side-chambers that widens out at the far end. And it is built of great stone blocks laid in such a way as gradually to converge as they rise, forming a kind of ogival vault. The converging walls do not actually meet at the top. They terminate at a certain point and the space is then roofed in with horizontal blocks, either fitted into the walls or laid across, presumably for greater support for the weight of the huge mound above. The whole structure has something of the massiveness and impact one associates with Mycenean tombs and others of the ancient Greek world, and indeed this kind of vaulting has an almost exact counterpart in the Creto-Mycenean civilization of 600 or 700 years earlier.

The other great tumuli, which are only a little later than this in date and form perhaps the most impressive monumental funerary architecture in Etruria, are to be found on Banditaccia. These have circular rock-hewn or constructed basements with ribbed cornices, and "contain one or more groups of burial chambers contructed in a complex and varied manner to imitate actual rooms".[6] Five or six of them are of great size, the largest (such as the Tomb of the Ship) having a diameter of over 30 metres, but even the smaller ones carry the same monumental impact. They lie among other later tombs dug into the rock or beneath the level of the ground, or along the sepulchral ways—tombs built square or rectangular out of squared blocks, sometimes with steps leading up beside them to a platform above. These are isolated or in rows, in squares or streets such as the Street of the Greek Vases, belonging to the fifth century. And finally, there are the underground tombs, dating from the fourth century onward, which consist of single rooms reproducing (like so many of the others) the interior decoration and even the furniture of an Etruscan house.

This house-like character, and the lay-out of the tombs along sepulchral ways, makes the necropolis a true "city of the dead". Its long main street runs over the crest of the Banditaccia hill for nearly two kilometres. It starts at the western edge of the hill, cuts straight through the enclosed area between a network of inter-crossing streets and lanes and squares, and continues on beyond it till reaching the eastern end it dips downhill through a narrow wooded cleft cut into the rock, with tombs at different levels on each side, rock-cut and moulded. This descends to the valley below the Cava della Pozzolana, and turns south to cross the Manganello stream, where it moves up through remnants of wall and gateway into the area of the city proper, inland and east of Cerveteri.

The main approach is from the west. A lane runs down from the village to the Manganello, much perhaps as it did in Etruscan times, and curves up to the spine of Banditaccia where (on both sides) the tombs at once begin. From here a modern road, lined with cypress, moves straight up to the enclosure. But the ancient road still remains—running parallel with and a little to the left of it, narrow and grass-grown, past the unkempt mounds of small to medium-sized tumuli. And almost at the start of this road there is an ancient street (now nothing but a track) that branches off to the left and goes out in the direction of the open hillside. There, a hundred yards off on its own, carved out of the rock, lies the *Tomb of the Five Chairs*, a chamber-tomb of the fifth-century whose charm is its intimate reflection, perhaps schematized, of the interior of an Etruscan house. It contains three rooms (a large one at the end and one at each side) that are entered through narrow arched doorways. The ceilings are beamed and slanted, giving delicate proportion to the rectangular spaces, and the five small carved chairs are in the left-hand room, which also possesses what looks like a grooved table or drum, while a replica of a table furnishes the room opposite. This tomb has the kind of little surprises to offer in which the necropolis abounds. One emerges from it into the sunlight with a sense of the Etruscan immediacy, the shock of pleasure that comes from contact with things lovingly shaped: the finality and gloom of death have no place here, one feels. It is an auspicious prelude.

Along another track a little further on there is a group of four interesting later tombs. These (of the fourth to the second centuries) have constructed façades and are dug deep into the rock, steps leading down to the chambers. The first of them, the *Tomb of the Triclinium*, still bears traces of painting on its walls which (though faded almost to vanishing point) enable one to recognize the familiar banquet theme, so characteristic of the Tarquinia tombs, and probably once of other tombs here at Caere. Now one has to be content with these faint vestiges, though some idea can be gained of the vividness of early Caeretan painting from the seventh- or early sixth-century Boccanera slabs in the British Museum and the extraordinary series of five sixth-century frescoes in red, cream and black at the Louvre. This tomb, in common with the one next to it, the *Tomb of the Sarcophagus*, has carved benches with head-rests to them, and the latter gets its name from the three alabaster sarcophagi that remain, two of them representing reclining male figures on the lids, that differ from those of Tuscania and Tarquinia in that they do not prop themselves up on their elbows, but lie full length, as that beautiful fourth-century example in the Gregorian Museum —bearded, with a head-band, necklace and armlet, his left hand grasping the circlet of office, the right holding a patera to his belly.

The next tomb along this track takes its name from the funerary inscriptions to a family called *Tarquinii*, which probably has no connection at all with the family that ruled Rome in the sixth century. It has one or two cippi still lying outside the entrance, and goes down past two half-open side rooms to a large chamber with a sloping roof supported by square pillars, and has niches for urns sunk into the walls. Beyond it, a good way out on the hill, is the last of the four tombs along this branch-road, and the most important architecturally. Called the *Tomb of the Alcove—*

a large and beautifully proportioned room—it is divided into four parts. First there is a central area whose ribbed ceiling slants downward from a great foot-wide central beam to two outer beams supported upon two thick fluted pillars with moulded bases and capitals. Then, on either side of this central area, beyond the pillars, lies a room-like space with recessed benches in the walls where the sarcophagi were placed. And at the far end in the centre is the alcove, entered up three steps, a little room within the room, with two plain pillars under the outer beams and the entrance itself framed by two more fluted pillars with layered bases and capitals, within which lies a high, pillowed funeral couch. The effect is so much that of an architecturally calculated space that one finds it difficult to believe the whole room has been carved out of the solid rock. For a moment one is fully convinced that those columns are actually supporting a roof and that the central beam has its own architectonic function to play. But instead everything is simulated. Space and proportion, the sense of balanced weight and stress, have been created out of a solid mass of rock. This, it seems to me, however malleable the rock, is one of the minor miracles of the Etruscan vision.

There is another striking tomb of the early fifth century near to the main road, which has a very large rectangular room, in the far wall of which are carved three doorways with moulded Doric surrounds that lead to three small inner chambers with little windows to them, two on each side of the central doorway. The large "hall" has a bed or bench at each end and its ceiling is carved to represent a series of fifteen beams running across from near to far wall.

And then, close to each other on either side of the main road, come the various tumuli belonging to the seventh and sixth centuries—circular in shape, their domed mounds resting upon tufo bases, either carved direct from the rock or constructed. One of them, among the smaller, is built out of massive blocks closely interlocked and rising to a height of 5 feet or so, the uppermost blocks forming a covering slab for the entrance lintel and jutting out to make a sort of ridged cornice. Another, carved, has double cordoned mouldings running round it, low down, with the rock cut smoothly away above to begin the curve of the semicircular dome. And above each of them is the unkempt grassy mound that conceals the stone superstructure of the chambers themselves. They are elaborately and powerfully built. Even now, though they do not get the attention of those tombs inside the enclosure, they seem rooted, immovably secure among the rank grass and the bramble—built out of conviction, in a spirit of praise, each one shaped with innate care for balance and structural clarity, the logic of stress and mass. In one of them, there is an antechamber with a ceiling formed of blocks laid geometrically in diminishing rectangles and an arched doorway that leads to an inner room, its smooth walls upheld by a carved column, containing a single stone bed. Another has a beautiful little chamber whose ceiling of steeply slanting blocks narrows to a long rectangle. And yet another, this time carved from the rock, like the great tumuli in the enclosure, has a rounded portico with a grooved cornice above which leads into a circular central chamber, elaborately cross-beamed, off which three small chambers lead. Among these, the *Tomb of the Olives* is unique in that it is a seventh-century tumulus on a squared tufo basement, whose simple burial chamber contained many valuable impasto and bucchero vessels and small vases and included a bronze plate with an offering of olives on it, the stones of which still remain.

And so one comes to the open parking area before the custodian's building and the enclosure. And away across the fields in the direction of Vignali one can see the domes of the three great isolated tumuli, almost the largest in the whole necropolis, for a visit to which it is necessary to ask the custodian for keys. The *Tumulus of the Ship* is close to the edge of the cliffs which drop into the Manganello valley, and from behind it one can look across at the livid red of the exposed rock slopes of Vignali on the other side, flaring in the sun. This tumulus, compared with those already seen, seems even bigger than it is. Within its great circular basement, carved out of the tufo and raised to a great height for the support of the dome by square-cut blocks, lie five groups of burial chambers, each with its own long entrance corridor. The severity, the impressive scale of the architecture, brings us very close to the roots of this ancient world, belonging as it does to the period immediately following that of the Sorbo tumulus. As one enters the corridor of the group of tombs after which the tumulus is named, solid walls of tufo rise on either side, to the right and left arched doorways lead into chambers, and above the third doorway at the end the squared blocks continue the structure to a height of 30 feet or more from where the rock itself ends. Particularly striking here is the doorway on the left, formed like the one at the end into a beautifully curving arch, but (unlike the other) elaborated as a frame to the vanished door with four raised cordons. The opposite one on the right is little more than rudimentary, but it leads into the tomb where the few faint traces of the painting of a ship remain on the wall, just clearly enough defined to make one wonder how much else was once there—whether in fact the walls of these tombs were not throughout painted in glowing reds and blacks and creams around their symbolic figures. Through the end doorway lie two rooms, an elliptical antechamber with ribbed ceiling, and the tomb-chamber itself, its slanting roof supported by four columns. And among other tombs in the tumulus there is a very beautiful little room, vivid with the delight of the Etruscans of this period when all over Etruria art was giving expression to their sense of the intimacy of man's place in his world, their unostentatious belief in the forces of the natural world around them and its life-giving forms. At the base of each side-wall are two steps, perhaps for votive objects or urns; and against the end wall is a high couch with capitalled columns at each end and a pillow at the head. The walls end in protruding beams, and the slanted ceiling is ribbed on either side of a narrow central beam which culminates above the bed in a circle from which the ribs seem to issue like spokes or rays. The effect here, quite clearly, is not of the beamed ceiling of a house, as it is in many of the other tombs, but of radiating beams of light, and of the sun (or the patera) as a symbol of the source of light. It is an effect achieved simply, freely, naturally, but with great tenderness, as an act of homage and of praise. And one is moved because one accepts it immediately in this way, emptied though the room is of all the proffered objects that would once have been laid on the ledges of rock—such as the ostrich egg with traces of polychrome decoration, the two golden buckles, the Corinthian krater and the figured bucchero found in the Tomb of the Ship and now in the Villa Giulia.

The nearby *Tumulus of the Painted Animals*, with its four groups of chambers, is equally as impressive. Its most important tomb-group and the only one normally open to visitors, has an elliptical antechamber with a ceiling of ribbed spokes radiating out from a sun-symbol and traces of animals painted on the walls, and two rooms leading on one from the other, the first containing a high boat-shaped couch with an almost unrecognizable animal painted at its head and beautifully arched doorways. It too is vast, massive, built to last; not clumsily or rhetorically but intently and with superb assurance, the great swelling dome containing within its girdling stone outer ring its own intimate symbols of community and continuity.

The third of the great tumuli is called the *Tumulus of the Shields and Chairs*, after the antechamber in one of the groups of tombs, a large rectangular room richly yet austerely decorated with objects symbolic of the household, and one of the earliest examples incorporating domestic furniture in the general scheme. Here, there are six framed and pillared funeral couches set back against the three nearer walls, three on each side of the entrance, and two high thrones or chairs with rounded backs and little foot-stools on either side of the central of the three doors. The doors have raised lintel mouldings of the Doric pattern, and there are windows set into the walls to light the three inner chambers, where the dead once lay on their couches. A protruding dado runs round the walls, which are hung with a series of fourteen shields, perhaps once carved and painted upon though now worn smooth; and the room is enclosed by a flat beamed ceiling.

The same tumulus contains a tomb-group of a quite different kind, and probably fifty or more years earlier in date, the *Tomb of the Painted Lions*. It is severe and plain by comparison, except for the ceilings—which slant steeply from a central beam and (in the four tomb-chambers) are patterned with lines of narrow rectangular cavities. The antechamber from which the rooms lead off again has a great sun-circle carved above the central doorway, but the doorway itself here is wide and uncompromisingly rectangular, and leads to a chamber with funeral beds and another narrowing doorway to a further room. In the side-chamber to the right of the antechamber the faint shapes of beasts in red on the walls, and particularly of a couchant lion, almost gone, may be seen above the sherds of ancient pots and beside two thick fluted pedestals placed at each angle of the far wall, carved perhaps to take some special offering.

Coming out into the sunlight again, into a world of riotous greens, the encroaching earth revelling in its power to command and subdue, one is more than ever conscious of the strange attraction of this tomb-culture and its celebratory delight in the seminal energies of the living world. It may not ever find a place in the public mind among the hierarchy of cultures—as the Romans have done, and the Greeks—but it has its own vision of things, its own idiosyncratic and intimate way of reconciling contradictions. Standing among these fields, in the midst of an area crowded with tombs, it is not I think possible to shrug off these people, as the history books have done, and as many people still do, caught under the shadow of Rome. They have had apologists and enthusiasts, of course. Fashions and crazes have come and gone, and some have written seriously about the Etruscans. But still they remain in the shadows for most of us, somewhere on the edge of things. Looking across to the enclosure, with its clusters of domes, an undulation of curves among the verticals of cypresses and pines, one wonders why. But then Cerveteri is not a shadowy place, and one is in contact with tangible evidence—what has been saved from the acquisitive energies of the conquerors by the earth itself and the rock to speak up for a people and their culture.

Inside the enclosure—with its 200 or more tombs covering no more than a small part of the whole necropolis—the main sepulchral way runs down past the rounded shapes of the tumuli and the lichened grey stone of the tomb façades and roadside copings that line it on either side, punctuated here and there by the dark uprights of cypresses. It is silent and contained here, in summer and in winter. And though winter takes away the heat it leaves intact the peculiar clarity, the inheld quiet of the place. Even when there are other visitors around, the streets and lanes, the green mounds and their shadowing trees absorb and disperse them. One has the place to oneself, walking down past the doorways of the older tombs, level with the roadway, and the façades of the later ones, sunk in the earth, piercing down into the heart of the tufo. And at once one notices the little symbolic stones (or cippi) that here and there still lie outside the doorways. These stones—columnar or chest-like in shape, some found with names engraved upon them—are there as the insignia of the dead within. The columnar shape symbolizes the erect masculine presence— "big and little", as Lawrence observed, "standing by the doors, or inserted, quite small, into the rock: the phallic stone!"[7] And the chest-like form is "the Ark, the arx, the womb . . . that brought forth all the creatures. The womb, the arx, where life retreats in the last refuge";[8] the source that defines the seed and gives it life, and which elsewhere we find symbolized in the circlets of stone, the circlets of leaves, the mundum, the patera, and even in the cippi that once crowned the tumuli, breast-like or nippled in shape—of which there are so many to be seen, deprived of their context, in the museums, and in rare instances (as at Orvieto) in their original places. (Could it be, one asks oneself, that it was what was implicit in these symbols—the phallic delight, the belief in the principle of contact and community, that left the Etruscans so fatally exposed? It is at least possible. You cannot defend yourself against conquest and acquisition and suppression—any more than you can conquer—unless or until you have hardened yourself against the blandishments of peace and fraternization and sexual recognition.)

Among the first of the tombs in the enclosure, beyond three or four medium-sized tumuli, is the famous *Tomb of the Capitals*, which—very close in style to that of the Shields and Chairs as an example of the skills of its sixth-century craftsmen—is if anything even more strikingly formulated, perhaps most of all because of its two Aeolian-capitalled pillars. The room is large, long and rectangular. The pillars stand one on each side of the entrance doorway, seeming to support two great beams, out of which six smaller beams (between alternate plain and diagonally-grooved squares) run the length of the room. The capitals are carved into curling fern-like plant forms, tightly scrolled, and the pillars stand on circular bases. There are four round-headed couches on each side of the entrance doorway; and three moulded doorways in the far wall with windows lead to three smaller chambers, the central of them larger than the other two. Curiously, one notes that the beds in these rooms, a pair to each, are squared *and* rounded, apparently to distinguish the sex of the dead person. One is left with a haunting impression of the proportions of a household, as if these rooms were echoing the structural proportions of the houses of the city itself, those vanished buildings that once stood on the bared heights of Vignali away on the other side of the Manganello. They are there as symbols, registering the closeness of the links between the living and the dead. In the Tomb of the Capitals the dead upon their benches may have been reduced to dust, but they inhabited their house (as the living theirs), sleeping through the long night of death among their familiar possessions. Nor does it strike one as inapt that the surroundings of the dead should have survived so long beyond those of the living. On the contrary, this is as it should be. Death implies permanence beyond change; stillness, arrest. While life is involved in a process of continual change, a movement towards the unknown, a sequence of momentary acts and states of being. All of which the Etruscans seem to have understood. Their dancers celebrating the moment of intent delight in the tombs were one way of symbolizing both the act of life and the permanence they were intended for; of bringing life and death—that which changes and that which is beyond change—into intimate contact, the one reflecting the other, where the skills of stillness have been learned; where stilled act celebrates the roots of song. And so it is with these tombs—dwelling-places characteristic of the living for the dead to sleep on in, made not from perishables in keeping with the fragilities of life but from rock, to last.

On from this lies the first of two very large tumulus tombs, called simply *Tumulus II*. It is among the oldest in the necropolis, perhaps even contemporary with the Sorbo tomb, and the curving breast of the mound is set upon a great tufo drum carved from solid rock and decorated (one might say bound around) with a five-banded cornice of raised cordons. Its several groups of tombs are approached along corridors and hollowed out of the interior. The oldest is the *Tomb of the Hut with the Thatched Roof*, which is low and small and has a steeply slanting ogival roof that rises from a low wall and a stone ledge, the two halves meeting in a narrow beam—below which in the far wall a low rounded doorway leads into a tiny funeral chamber. Another tomb, the *Tomb of the Doloi*, has a number of large ribbed red-clay doloi, or storage jars, as well as Corinthian and bucchero vases preserved upon the benches of its severely geometric cells. Yet another, the *Tomb of the Funeral Beds*, is distinguished by its arched doorways with long narrow windows on either side, its ceilings gently slanted from a wide beam, and the high once-lidded funeral beds that dominate the main chamber. And lastly, there is the *Tomb of the Greek Vases*, again severe in form and built on the three-cell plan, named after the magnificent collection of Attic black- and red-figure vases found in it, which point to its continuous use over at least a hundred years from the second half of the sixth-century, and include a strikingly beautiful amphora signed by the Greek potter Nicosthenes.[9]

Between this and the other tumulus there is a street of chamber tombs of much later date, and the superstructure to other subterranean tombs lying beside the sepulchral way, many with the little phallic or chest-like stones outside the doorways, and some with their tomb-furniture still intact inside. And then comes *Tumulus I*. It is a little smaller than the other, its circular base banded with two grooved cordons separated by the width of a foot, the upper one dividing the tufo from the mound. There are two groups of tombs in the tumulus, very severe, with Doric mouldings to the doorways and gently slanting roofs, delineating the earliest period of Etruscan mastery, the style reminding one of the façades of tombs at Castel D'Asso and Norchia.

The contrast is therefore all the more marked between these tombs and the large, elaborately decorated and sensational *Tomb*

of the Painted Reliefs (or Tomba Bella) which lies close by. This
has a constructed entrance and is approached down a long flight
of steps, at the top of which a great lion's head, half obliterated,
rounded and snarling, stands as guardian. It is indeed unique
among the tombs here for its wealth of detail, and for the sensuous
Hellenistic shapes that are everywhere depicted in it. Though late
in date (of the fourth or early third century) it is not so late as to
reflect the general decline that is so apparent in the later tombs at
Tarquinia. The form is that of a spacious square supported on
either side of a sunken central area by two massive squared
columns with lovely curling Aeolian-style capitals to them.
Spaced at intervals around the walls are other columns, again
with beautifully scrolled capitals, that divide off a series of at least
eleven deep rectangular recesses, simulating beds complete with
coloured pillows, 2 feet or so above the ground. But the most
astonishing feature of this tomb is the richness and beauty of its
decorations. Everywhere, from walls and columns, hang objects
such as would have been found and used in every household, the
weapons and implements and aids of the living, still glowing with
traces of the colours they once had. Above the entrance are the
heads of a bull and a cow and on either side of the doorway a
circular shield. Immediately under the roof are hung swords and
caps, and beneath them, shields, swords, helmets and shin guards.
On the columns hang a rich array of objects—gourds, a fan, a
staff, a satchel, an axe, a truncheon, an unsheathed slaughtering
knife, coils of rope, a large mirror, a pair of pincers, a pot, a jug, a
pan. At the base of the left-hand column a long thin dog with
curling tail, down on his front paws in play, and at the base of
the right-hand one a kitten teasing a little mouselike animal, add a
final domestic touch to the images. While below the central bed
(between two elaborate columns depicting the carved wooden
legs of the bed itself) another creature—three-headed within a
curling necklace, dog or fawn or horse—steps daintily on before
the only human figure in the tomb—a man with curling snake-
tails for legs, who seems to be holding the animal in rein with one
hand, while the other holds a wide-bladed implement (perhaps an
oar) across his shoulder as he glides along; a symbolic sea-figure,

his head perhaps a portrait of the dead man himself who once lay sleeping in his pillowed recess.

The colours glow—the traces of red, blue and cream bands below the recesses, the red of the pillows and many other objects, the blue of knife-blades, the red and cream of shields and sheaths. This deep underground chamber is rich with incident and detail, and the massive structural proportions of the room contain it all easily. And though it may not reflect the Etruscan culture at its most significant, it is nevertheless of great interest and importance in giving us an intimately observed glimpse of the everyday life of the Etruscans of Caere as they lived it in the period when the Hellenistic influence was at its height. Though Roman supremacy was not far off (and the weapons seem to hint at the state of preparedness that must by then have become necessary) it had not yet stifled the Etruscan gaiety and sense of delight and the solemnity that is here, gesturing to a spirit as unRoman and as intimately expressive as that of mediaeval Tuscany.

Beyond this tomb there is a junction where three streets come into the sepulchral way. Here are many small archaic tumuli, some with stairways leading up beside them to a higher level, most of them cut directly from the rock with rooms of varying shapes and sizes on the three-cell pattern, decorated with various motives. One of these is particularly notable. It has four little interconnecting rooms with arched doors and long narrow arched windows. The first two rooms (on either side of the entrance passage) have beds in them with moulded columns, and the central room is peculiarly striking in that on each side there are two beds, one large and rectangular, the other small with carved pillars supporting a lovely ornate carved head-rest, perhaps for a child. Close to this tomb is a group of squarely constructed chamber tombs, two of which have rooms with columns in them. And then a little way down one of the two streets leading off to the right is the *Tomb of the Cornice*, another superb fifth-century structure formed on the pattern of the Tomb of the Capitals and the Shields and Chairs. It has two preliminary chambers approached along a high walled passage with rectangular coffered ceiling, past which one enters into a large rectangular room with benches and a curious square-carved altar-like piece of furniture with two circles mounted on pillars as backing on either side of the doorway. The main feature of the room, however, is the cornice that runs around three walls, curving outward so that the top edge forms a kind of shelf a foot below the ceiling. In the far wall, as usual, three moulded inner doorways with windows lead into small chambers, and the ceiling itself is heavily beamed.

From here the main road goes on beyond the public enclosure to where the authorities are still excavating and restoring. Here there are a number of small to medium-sized tumuli with circular drum basements, some of them containing chambers of a very archaic type. These stand between and behind chamber-tombs of the same period (the seventh and sixth centuries) and later, one-roomed or two-roomed, with single central pillars. And among them stands another very large tumulus, the *Tumulus of the Colonel*, the mound built as usual on a great tufo base banded by a cornice of grooved lines and containing four corridor entrances. Not far beyond which the road dips downward through the rock into a thickly wooded area riddled with chamber tombs, including one on the right (earlier than most) whose ceiling is supported by two octagonal pillars narrowing towards the top and surmounted by heavy whorled capitals.

In the excavation area, there is a whole street of constructed fifth-century tombs already half restored, the moulded Doric lintels coloured black and with black dados around the walls as well as internal door surrounds. I myself spent a whole morning there once, watching the men as they worked to bring new inches of wall and many fragments of pottery to light, in the slow pains-taking process of systematic exploration, during which everything has to be recorded. The experience made me realize just how much work—remedial and exploratory—has still to be done, even within the restricted limits of the enclosure. And of course there is always the necessity of keeping the place in good condition against the periodic onslaughts of the weather.

As for Banditaccia as a whole, the problems of coping with it, given the small working staff available for excavation, must be well-nigh insoluble. I have been told that there are still, for instance, many undiscovered or unexplored tombs in the district, with their treasures still intact. The villagers know this, and so no doubt do the *clandestini*. In fact I myself was once an inadvertent witness to the illicit activities of the locals. I happened one day to be sitting with my wife and daughter picnicking on the crown of a hill outside the enclosure when suddenly from the dense bushes below, close to where the sepulchral way dips down through the rock, two men emerged carrying vases under their arms. They stopped dead when they saw us, and promptly vanished into the bushes again. And I'm certain they could not have been more surprised than we were to have our privacy so violently obtruded upon. But at least their presence seemed to demonstrate clearly enough that the underground wealth of Caere had not been totally exhausted, in spite of the avarice of generations of thieves and tomb-seekers. Maybe somewhere in the area there is another Royal tomb waiting to have its fabulous treasures brought to light. If so, we must hope that the right people find it, for there can be no illusion that if these treasures were to get into the hands of the buyers and sellers there would be a moment's thought about the irreplaceable patrimony involved. Fortunately many tombs excavated in recent years with their offerings intact have been discovered by the state authorities. And although one now has to go to the Museums in Rome and other cities to seek them out, one can there at least attempt to complete the links between these beautiful works of art and the architecture that once enshrined them.

Caere holds its magic, however many visits one makes. It has the spell of poetry about it. And there is always something new to discover, for it stretches over a vast area. The necropolis of Monte Abetone, for instance, is said to have been as varied and as highly organized as that of Banditaccia. And though now, after extensive excavation, it has sunk back into desuetude, it is still an area of great interest for those who wish to know Etruria.

I remember on one occasion coming to Cerveteri along the high Maremma plain. That time (after lunch at a trattoria with tables in the high-walled courtyard of the castle) I paid a visit to Monte Abetone, taking a guide with me. From the heights the sea glinted in the distance beneath a sky of pewter clouds. The Mola valley lay exposed under the cliffs of Vignali, seeming to flow out into the flats of the sea-plain like a river or a great green lake. My guide suffered from a serious impediment of speech which often prevented him from getting a sentence finished and made him stab at the air with his hands in a frustrated attempt to complete his meaning. Yet he managed to tell me many things as we stood high on the open ground above the cliffs. He told me that he had worked on many tombs up here, both officially and unofficially; that he himself had been to prison three times for clandestine diggings; that he and his friends had found gold rings, necklaces and amulets, and many painted vases, some of which they still possessed. He even asked me if I wanted any vases, and said he could let me have one for a "small consideration". And he declared it was inexplicable to him why finding such things on their own land should be rewarded with prison. Gesturing across the hilltop he asked me what it was that gave others the right to profit from what came out of land that belonged to him and his friends. I tried to explain, in my Anglo-Saxon manner, how important it was that the authorities should have access to everything that was found. But he either couldn't see the point at all, or didn't wish to.

He took me across the open fields, stopping to show me where there had once been excavations, now grown over, and where—according to calculations—other unexcavated tombs were situated. He pointed out tombs and tomb-groups among the dense undergrowth, and a sepulchral way with open chamber-tombs along it leading down through a cleft in the rocks to the valley. Then we moved across to the famous sixth-century *Campana Tomb*, which lies on the lip of the cliff overlooking the valley, and has remained open since it was discovered in 1845.

This consists of a great central room and two flanking rooms approached along a corridor cut from the tufo to a depth of 20 feet or more. The wall of the room on the left has been broken open or has fallen in to reveal the moulded interior of another tomb on a slightly higher level, which has its own entrance from outside. The striking features of this room are the three fluted pedestals that stand in a row at the end beneath a beamed and slanted ceiling. They rise to a height of about 3 feet, forming the base of an altar or funerary shelf that probably once held symbolic offerings to the family buried there—urns, vases, jewellery, votive figures such as the little seated man in terracotta in the Capitoline Museum, wide-faced, serenely waiting with hand held out, or the thin flat elongated bronze Augurs of the Villa Giulia Antiquarium. Opposite this is a single room with three carved beds in it under a slanted ceiling.

But the central room is very elaborate. A round-arched doorway leads into a kind of antechamber which is divided from the inner space by a thick beam projecting at least 2 feet from the slanted ceiling, with a flat grooved pillar at each end to simulate support. The elliptical ceiling of the antechamber is here closely ribbed to symbolize the intent rays of the sun; for the ribs fan out from a carved disc that lies not at the centre but close to the beam, therefore creating the effect of the setting (or the rising) sun. And beneath it, on either side of the door, is a piece of furniture, the one on the right carved into the form of a high altar-like table with rectangular cavities in it, surmounted at the back by a three-strutted top out of the sides of which project two strange curved shapes like bull's horns. Finally, beyond the beam, a coffered ceiling lies above a clear central space which gives on to the funeral beds themselves against the far wall.

The tomb with the broken wall, higher up, also has its walled approach with two flanking rooms. And inside, the doorways have beautiful Doric outlines in ribbed relief upon the wall. But the undergrowth invades, the earth silts up the entrances, the walls and roofs crack and fall. At the top of the cliff, from where (despite the rabid growth of bramble and bush) a sepulchral way clearly begins, one tomb lies roofless and almost unrecognizable except in plan—and a few traces of moulding remain exposed amid broken chunks of roof and vegetation. So gradually the sepulchres are vanishing, being wiped out, reduced to rubble. Though the Campana tomb is still miraculously intact, there will come a time when it too has crumbled and collapsed beyond repair, unless the archaeologists decide to save it as they have so

Above: 9a THE TOMB OF THE AUGURS. Second half of the sixth century.
Tarquinia. Salutation to the dead. On the side walls: ceremonial contest
with wrestlers and 'phersu' (far left and near right) (*pp. 49–50*).
Below: 9b THE TOMB OF THE CAPITALS. Sixth century. Cerveteri. Interior of
main chamber with two of the three moulded doors leading to inner
chambers, and one of the two columns with Aeolian capitals (*pp. 152–3*).

10b CAERETAN HYDRIA. End of sixth century. From Cerveteri. Representing the myth of Hercules and Eurystheus.

10a FAÇADE OF A TOMB. Sixth century. The necropolis at Norchia. Architectural detail with moulded cornice and false window (pp. 98–99).

many of the tombs on Banditaccia. Its iron gateway, which once
kept the vandals out, now lies discarded on the ground, suggesting
that even guardianship has been dispensed with and the tomb
abandoned. Standing here, or listening to one's guide recounting
his exploits, one wonders how it is that so many of the tombs and
their contents managed to survive. The truth of course is that
many of them didn't. They and their treasures were, as Pierre
Grimal has it, "lost or irretrievably damaged as archaeologists,
scholars, collectors and dealers in antiquities failed to take the
necessary precautions. Frequently, no inventory was made, and
interesting objects were removed and dispersed at random."[10]
And one is no more clearly aware of this than when moving
among the remains of these Abetone tombs. On Banditaccia,
with its carefully maintained enclosure, one can forget it, but
not here. Here the violations and thieveries have left their mark,
and neglect is desolating the remains.

On Vignali too, standing near the cliffs above the Sorbo area,
one finds only hints that this was once a corner of the great city of
Caere, perhaps close to the arx. Here a semicircle carved from the
tufo lies exposed, and a track, deeply rutted, leads down through
the rock to an old ruined chapel built in an open space between
the remains of further tombs right under the Mola cliff. Here, or
somewhere near here, was the temple of Hera, where a number
of sixth-century Maenad-head antefixes were found. It is mostly
farmland, with olives and vines that stretch away across the
flattened top of the hill. But objects and fragments of objects
have been found everywhere—heads, pottery, jewels, figurines,
vases, terracotta slabs from temple or house façades—and are
scattered in museums throughout the world. At the nothernmost
point the great stones of an ancient gate and its jambs remain.
Here and there above the cliffs one finds blocks of stone that once
formed part of the walls. There is a large section of wall with a
ditch in front near where the road from the necropolis turns up
to the city, and the site of a temple, the Manganello temple, on a
tufaceous platform just outside the village and above the river. But
that, apart from a few remains of the urban centre, mostly
Roman, is about all. The rest is gone, obliterated, sunk into the

F

earth and into silence, where the olive groves in their hieratic twisted stillness and the shaggy tree-growth on the cliffs takes over.

Yet much in the silence remains, a sense of inheld presences, of something having once been here—a people, a history, a past, a spirit, a great city and its buildings; now reduced to echoes, intimations, the echoes of the echoes of a world; reduced to myth, dissolved into the air. From here, a December sunset celebrates and intensifies for me the sombre beauties of the landscape—the flat plain below, the dulled horizontals of the sea, the dark blue-grey of the clouds. And as I stand within the semicircle of tufo on this open height I watch the sun flashing its intent particles of light through the air, alive and vibrant on the fields—part of the daily ritual of life and light, a quotidian splendour. And as it is now, so this undiminished ceremonial was for these people, worshipped by them as the source of life, a declaration from the potency and mystery of the universe. One finds the symbol of it in the tombs, the votive figures and the paintings, the ornaments and implements, the little phallic stones—that sense of a people celebrating the solemnity and delight of life, endowed with a feeling for its rhythms and its continuities; rooted in the particularities of their world.

THE ARTS OF THE CITY OF CAERE

IF THE TOMBS of the Banditaccia necropolis offer us a more immediately striking and coherent image of the civilization of the ancient city of Caere than can be got from superficial contact with the wealth of material collected in the museums, this is not to say that they are more important. Certainly, we can have no adequate picture of the significance of Caere without also taking into account the objects recovered from the site throughout the last 150 years. For these works not only confirm and complement the architecture. They are the unmistakable evidence of a vigorous artistic culture sustained in quality for more than three centuries, from the seventh to the fifth and beyond, from the so-called Orientalizing period to the century preceding the ultimate surrender to Rome.

The story of Caeretan art really begins (for us at least) in the ninth century, with the Villanovan cinerary urns of Cava Della Pozzolana and Sorbo. We may think of the ninth and eighth centuries in fact as a kind of seminal prelude to the development of a specifically Etruscan culture. What is interesting about this period is that the material surviving from it does not significantly differ from that found at the sites of other great cities. In other words, Caere shared roots common to the whole of Etruria, as part of a widespread native culture, upon which the sudden explosive injection of powerful influences from abroad was to act to produce a complete transformation of the pattern of life—that phenomenon of the civilizing spirit which, with its affirmation of ancient religious customs and an awakened artistic curiosity, was to bring about the achievement of the Etruscan world.

In the eighth century the people of Central Italy were still quietly unexpansive. But they were neither inactive nor incurious. The collection of armlets, fibulae, bronze necklaces and pendants, coloured glass-paste beads and implements in the Villa Giulia displays a quick delight in the shaping of things which is at the root of the Italic vision. And this is nowhere more evident than in the Italo-geometric impasto vases and the biconical cinerary urns collected from early tombs, which are sometimes astonishingly beautiful. They have about them a vigorous undeliberated rough beauty—the clay black or red or grey in colour, decorated with varied geometric patterns of zig-zags, parallel lines, dots, meanders and swastikas incised or embossed upon lid and bowl. These are the primitive root forms "of an evolution peculiar to Italy, possibly affected by currents from the North, which integrated extremely diverse ethnic substrata",[1] and was to develop in diverse ways according to the influences exerted upon it, whether from the local elements that prevailed in Latium or from the Tyrrhenians in Etruria. The idea that "a pre-formed culture" was suddenly "imported in one piece into Italy" is seriously open to question. Much more likely is it that the Etruscan culture was "the outcome of a regional quickening, a sudden acceleration similar to that which, at about the same time, the Greek world . . . was experiencing", on the basis of direct contact at some given moment "between the Etruscan peoples and the people of the Eastern Mediterranean".[1]

As Etruria began to prosper (establishing contacts with Egypt, Carthage, Corinth and Attica) so she began to awaken to her own potentialities; to accept and absorb the major influences that came her way and to shape them to the needs of her people. In this manner were the skills of her craftsmen brought into play and organized towards the achievements of the seventh century, which at Caere are richly represented by the early tombs and their contents, and particularly by the dramatic discoveries of the Royal Sorbo tomb itself.

When the tomb was excavated in 1836 its treasures established the Caere necropolis as a place of singular importance in the ancient world, testifying to an artistic culture at once richly expressive, complex and integrated, springing from the powerful influence of the Eastern Mediterranean. Each piece was recorded as it was found, and its position defined by contemporary drawings.[2] Along the entrance passage, for instance, were placed a tall bronze tripod, two laminated bronze vases decorated with bands of processional animals and plant motifs in relief, a great bronze-plated four-wheeled carriage with orientalizing motives worked upon it, and a series of hammered bronze shields. This passage ends in two small side-chambers. On the left were found many fragments of broken Egyptian vases, and on the right two rows of little clay idols, squat and primitive, their hands raised either to cheek or neck or sometimes both. Between the two chambers a full-length bronze bed was placed, upon which the body of the person for whom the tomb was built was no doubt carried before being placed at the far end of the tomb. Alongside it, to the left, another row of little idols stood. And then, in the funeral chamber itself, was found a rich array of objects—decorated silver and bronze plates hanging on the wall; three small silver vases all inscribed with the name Larthia; a beautiful Egyptianized silver cup; twelve ribbed patere; a bronze vase with six long-necked griffin heads projecting from the lip, the body depicting winged bulls and lions with long flickering tongues; and above all, many pieces of jewellery in gold, including clasps and brooches, decorated with geometric patterns and figures in filigree and granulation, more than twenty in all. The gold lay at the far end, around the body. And where the body itself lay, among the dust and the bones, was found the famous gold fibula, with its embossed and granulated figures, and a great gold figured breast-piece of breath-taking quality.

The gold ornaments are the most extraordinary of all the pieces in the tomb, comparable in virtuosity and refinement with other collections from Praeneste, Populonia and Vetulonia. Sheets of embossed gold shaped in a variety of ways are further enhanced by geometric motifs in filigree and granulation to produce effects of great elegance. As Raymond Bloch observes: "Gold wire of incredible thinness was braided, crossed and interweaved into finely-wrought patterns." Or "tiny gold granules were applied",[3] looking like strings of little gold beads, to give the forms an added lustre, the techniques demanding a skill of the greatest delicacy, because the globules or the wire had to be soldered to the sheet without in any way modifying the figures embossed on it. Such techniques are astonishing, and still defy imitation. They may be observed at their most accomplished in the Sorbo pieces, and particularly in the elaborate fibula. This has a laminated upper sheet portraying five lions—embossed and outlined in filigree—enclosed within two rows of interlocked palm-leaves, and a leaf-like sheet suspended below the patterned clasp with serried ranks of standing griffin above outlined lions.

The work is intricate and assured. Oriental motifs and Greek techniques are blended into a distinctive style which enables one with certainty (as Mario Torelli affirms)[4] to attribute these masterpieces to local artists. Such consummate skills are handed on into the sixth century to achieve ornaments of great beauty, as examples from all the sites prove. But with the fifth century there is a sudden decline in quality, as if all the great craftsmen had died off, taking their secrets with them—for by then the techniques of filigree and granulation had ceased to be practised. And though one still finds many fine pieces, they are of a different order altogether, to be classed among the lesser arts.

Apart from the gold discovered in other seventh-century tombs, material of every kind was brought to light to indicate the scope and variety of the culture of that period. From a tumulus on Monte Tosto, outside Cerveteri, came necklaces of amber, an incised bucchero vase, and a number of objects in bone and ivory including a magnificent carved group representing a lion attacking its prey and part of a comb decorated in relief. In the so-called Bell Tomb were found a series of impasto vases with incised geometric patterns. Tomb 53 in the enclosure yielded a superb Corinthian oinochoe decorated with bands of processional animals, a small Egyptianized vase, and two little proto-Corinthian perfume jars. From another tomb nearby came a series of bucchero and impasto vases of great beauty, among which a small bucchero oinochoe is outstanding—its high tapering neck decorated with stippled triangles and lines, and the swelling body depicting two delicately-stepping spotted winged horses and a hind, very close in style to the animals of the Campana Tomb at Veii and to early Faliscan vases. The great tumuli outside the enclosure (and the tumulus of the Colonel inside) also contained many pieces—Corinthian vases, a variety of bucchero goblets, cups and jugs, large proto-Corinthian hydriae in red, black and cream decorated with impressed circles and bands of striding animals; objects of all shapes and sizes. And even as early as this (though perhaps towards the end of the century) began to appear those miraculous black-figure pieces from Attic Greece which were only a little later to be imported in their hundreds into Etruria, and to take pride of place in the tombs, both here and elsewhere.[5]

Before and during this invasion, the Etruscans were producing much impasto and bucchero work of high quality. And the bucchero, developing out of earlier impasto forms as an exclusively Etruscan invention, is particularly striking—destined, as Torelli has it, "to become a typical form throughout the Etruscan world".[6] It is even possible that the Caeretans invented the form, since by the middle of the seventh century they had clearly established special workshops for the production of it. Whether or not this is so, there is no doubting the fact that they produced pieces unequalled elsewhere in quality and inventiveness. The lustrous jet-black colour of the clay (black throughout) was achieved either by a special method of firing the vase or by blending a manganese substance with the clay during its preparation. And the earliest forms (called *bucchero sottile*) are very thin and delicate. They are decorated with abstract geometric motifs, patterns of stippled leaves and plants, with animals and even human figures, engraved upon the surface to produce a white linear impression. Later on the form changes. It becomes thicker and heavier in structure (hence the name, *bucchero pesante*), and the figures are now moulded in relief upon the bowl, with details of hair and feature continuing to be engraved upon them. Both kinds are vigorous and inventive in shape, and are indulged at times for the pure delight of play and fantasy. There is one seventh-century Caeretan piece in the Gregorian Museum in Rome, for example, that exploits the medium to such limits that it becomes almost sculptural. The vase has a double neck in the shape of two long-necked stag-like creatures, heads raised, their antlers turned into crowns. A man stands behind, reining them in upon the body of the vase, which represents at once the animals' body and the form of a chariot. The engraved geometric patterns on the vase include on each side a pattern of circles enclosing a flower, symbol of fertility and also signifying no doubt the wheel of the chariot. The man is faintly Egyptian in cast. His only clothing is a short skirt, cross-hatched; and the handle of the vase issues out of his back to fall straight to the swelling of the body. The whole thing stands on a beautiful inverted bell of a base, ribbed, and rises vertical, narrow and phallic to a height of nearly 1 foot. It has the exuberance, the gaiety, the idiosyncratic energy one comes to associate with the Etruscans. And it carries on an ancient tradition of animal-shaped pottery, found in abundance on Greek sites, in Rhodes, in Cyprus, in Lydia, and Italy too in the ninth and eighth centuries.

Between such forms and the sculptures that Caere began to produce from at least the end of the seventh century is little more than a step. Those that have survived may be few and scattered, but two or three of them are among the masterpieces of the Etruscan world, and offer a further proof of the importance of Caere in the seventh and sixth centuries. The earliest, coming at the end of the seventh century, are the three seated votive figures —two female (in the British Museum) and one male (in Rome's Capitoline Museum)—found among an offering of gold ornaments in a small tumulus tomb on Banditaccia. Made of terracotta, seated upright, all dressed in long, diamond-patterned robes, each holds out the right hand (palm upward) in ritual offering. The faces are open, wide-eyed, the mouths moulded to convey the faintest suggestion of a smile, the hair brushed back behind the ears, the two women wearing thick circular earrings. They have an expressiveness at once grave and serene, with something of the rapt spell of internal composure about them, that speaks through the outstretched hands, the eyes set large and wide apart in the oval of the head, and the sensuous generosity of the mouth. Their weight and volume, embodied in terms of their substance and the space that surrounds them, is genuinely sculptural, and their repose and stability seems the reflection of a world now sure of itself and confident of the future. From this point onward, judging from the wealth of evidence available, Caere was to develop into full maturity, assurance and power.

The tombs are one impressive proof of this. The continuing production of bucchero in new and varied forms, is another. And during this period a new class of pottery emerges—massive red-clay doloi (or oil-vats), braziers and wash-bowls decorated along the rim with stamped motives of isolated figures and processional animals, very small but minutely observed, together with more complex tableaux illustrating obscure mythologies and scenes from daily life. But from the middle of the sixth century, sculpture again dominates with the beautiful series of temple antefixes —some with, some without, the nimbus or halo around them. These smiling Maenad heads, some still retaining their polychrome colouring, all have long plaited hair falling in curves along the shoulder lines. Some have earrings and necklaces. Two, in the Capitoline Museum, incorporate a patera on each side of the head, lying in the curl of the plaits, the second of these offering a head of bewitching loveliness and a remote Eastern smile, the patera on the shoulders supported by two pert crouching monkeys. Another, in the Gregorian Museum in Rome, wears a high diadem and has extraordinarily long curving eyebrows and large slanted eyes. There are other examples in museums throughout the world, including seven or eight, all offering variations of the theme, in Rome's Villa Giulia.

These pieces, with many fragments of terracotta gable-slab, frieze and facing, survive to hint at the opulence of the numerous temples that arose in the city and its immediate vicinity in the sixth century. As to the temples themselves, only the foundations remain, so that one can have little idea of the actual architecture. The only plausible reconstructions, based upon Vitruvius, have been of the later Etrusco-Italic type.[7] But there is no doubt that the sixth-century temples were richly adorned—this can be verified from the Villa Giulia fragments alone, not to mention those that lie hidden away in the basements of other museums.

No monumental sculptures remain from any of these temples, though the pediments must once have carried groups of figures similar to those from the Portonaccio temple at Veii and to the magnificent early fifth-century figures which were discovered on the site of the later of the two Pyrgi temples a few kilometres from

Cerveteri. But the tombs have yielded at least three pieces of funerary sculpture from the second half of the sixth century which confirm the presence at Caere of an important school of practising sculptors. Two of these, the famous *Sarcophagi degli Sposi* (one at the Villa Giulia, the other at the Louvre) are masterly achievements in their own right. The third, though much more modest in scale and conception, has the same kind of direct and compelling lucidity. The influence is Ionian, as with so much of the art of this century, an influence triumphantly absorbed and redirected to celebrate the Etruscan vision of things. The figures of the Villa Giulia piece, embodied within the flowing contours of the terracotta (which is a honeyed brown in colour), seem caught and held in a mood of rapt intimacy, alert and vivid, delighting in the immediacy of contact. They recline at ease on a sumptuous couch, almost life-size, their bodies closely interlinked, each complementing the other, the woman slightly leaning into the man, their hands uniting the interflow of contour and volume that defines the intimacy, the sexual community, of their contact. The man rests his right hand lightly on her right shoulder, and his left —outstretched, palm upward as in offering or as if he were presenting her to the assembled company at a banquet—lies gently upon her left forearm. So that she seems tenderly contained, drawn in to the area of his body, the rectangle of his frame. Her hands are more active, the left held out cupped, the right with the two forefingers pointing up diagonally across her body as if to acknowledge her husband's presence, though it might once have held the handle of a bowl. The four arms and hands set up a complex counterpoint of rhythms and angles within the rectangle bounded by the man's left shoulder and arm and the woman's right. Moreover, the balance of the forms is intensified and fixed by the contraries of horizontal and vertical: for while the couch and the lower bodies (terminated by the woman's curved and pointed boots) move horizontally, the line of the torso and the heads is vertical. And since she reclines in front of and lower than he, her form seems to reflect the gentle downward lines of the couch from its raised pillow to the foot.

The faces are only half-particularized. The man's pointed beard, his hair parted in the middle and falling in braids down his back, the expectancy of the parted lips, the slanted set of the eyes, the long eyebrows, the prominent nose and high forehead, are Ionian in cast, but informed with a quick intentness similar to that of the Veii Apollo. The face of the woman is more rounded, her expression buoyant and amused. She has large ears, exposed below a conical hat, and her plaited hair falls each side of the full cheeks. Her gown seems to be pleated under the bodice, covering her small breasts, but the shawl has slipped down to leave her left shoulder bare, a detail of delicate suggestiveness.

Altogether, then, this sarcophagus is a beautiful and complex grouping, symbolic of sexual and social community between man and woman, with the woman taking her place beside her husband instead of being relegated to an inferior position in the world. As for the Louvre couple, I shall content myself with simply referring to it as an achievement of a similar kind, formed to the same general design but differing in the disposition of volume, angle and mass.

The Villa Giulia also contains the other smaller piece, which came from a tomb on Monte Abetone. It is a terracotta ash-chest in the shape of a *kline* like the others, very close to them in style but only $2\frac{1}{2}$ feet long. On it, reclining in a half-upright position supported by her left elbow, is a young woman. Dressed in a long gown and shod in curved pointed boots, she is richly adorned, with a bracelet on each wrist, a necklace of huge ribbed stones falling round her small breasts, and circular pierced earrings. Her hair is concealed beneath a close-fitting cap, and she has a bordered cape around her shoulders. There are traces of red colouring that define the girdle at the waist, but otherwise the colours that must once have glowed upon the figure have disappeared. But what is most striking about her is the intent almost trance-like expression of the face, which gives intimate significance to the act she is engaged in of pouring the contents of a little perfume jar into her outstretched left hand. It is as if each drop of oil or perfume were being inwardly counted and registered; as if it were some precious life-giving substance to which she must give her undivided attention. For the eyes are shut, and the lips seem to be shaped to form

some kind of murmured incantation. This, in other words, is no
mere toilet preparation she is carrying out, as women do (even
perhaps from their couches), but a symbolic religious rite involv-
ing her whole being, which the artist has tenderly conveyed
through the moulding of the face, the lifted right arm and the flat
stretched palm of the offered left hand.

To turn from sculpture to painting is to turn to another important aspect of the culture of Caere. Though not much remains, and
though it may be true to say that painting in Caere cannot have
had the dominating place it assumed at Tarquinia, there is enough
to prove that it was being widely practised from at least the end of
the seventh century. Certain of the most ancient tumulus tombs
retain vestiges, even now, which make it seem highly probable
that they were decorated throughout. The painting was then
applied direct to the tufo, as in the Tomb of the Painted Lions, and
would have been constantly attacked by damp and the sweating of
the rock. Perhaps it was an awareness of such deterioration that led
the sixth-century artists to abandon this method, and to paint their
scenes instead upon specially baked terracotta slabs. Anyway, the
change has resulted in the preservation of two important series of
slabs—the Five Boccanera slabs in the British Museum, and the
Campana slabs in the Louvre, each set from tombs on Banditaccia.

The Lastre Boccanera are probably the earliest in date, painted
somewhere between 575 and 550 B.C.,[8] in the wake of the influence of Corinthian painting, which had already made itself felt by
the end of the seventh century. Many Corinthian vases had been
imported into the city by then, and from the first decade or so of
the sixth century there exist a number of large column kraters
with bands of figures in black, red and white on a cream ground,
including prominent harpy figures, which bear some affinity to
the sphinxes on the Boccanera paintings. But the slabs are peculiarly distinctive for the way in which they make use of these
Corinthian elements in the presentation of an essentially Etruscan
ceremony.

All of the figures were apparently painted in after the preliminary designs had been scratched upon the clay with a pointed
instrument. The outlines are black, enclosing plain areas of red

and black over a cream ground, and cream serves also to define the flesh of the women, the men according to convention being red in colour. Apart from this, white is used, for the eyeballs and for details such as the dotted borders of certain of the garments. But there is no monotony, for these colours are cunningly varied from figure to figure.

Two of the slabs depict winged sphinxes—one facing right, the other facing left. And on each of the three others, there are three figures, all taking part in some kind of solemn ritual procession. The sphinxes are queer, lithe-bodied, hieratic creatures, with big wide-eyed faces; drawn seated in a pattern of interlocking flowing curves, the wings curling back, fern-like, with alternate white, black and red feathers, their line continuing the curving line of the leg, breast and shoulder. They have long hair and curling black tails. And each raises a foreleg in a grave symbolic gesture of salutation.

It is likely, as Modona has pointed out, that they were placed on either side of the doorway within the tomb, with the other three slabs occupying the far wall facing the entrance. Whatever the arrangement, the latter clearly form part of a continuous procession. On the left, a priest (facing right and holding a seven-leafed branch in his hand) greets an important male functionary carrying a sceptre, who leads a group of three female votaries with offerings —a circlet and two fruiting pomegranate sprigs. The last two votaries, wearing their black hair long, are on the second slab; and the third, who holds a lidded pot in her hands, together with two more in cowled cloaks on the final slab, are painted moving in the opposite direction, led by a long-haired woman in a red chiton.

The figures are clearly differentiated according to the symbolic function they have to fulfil in this vivid ritual ceremony. They are boldly executed, the complex patterns of colour and form conveyed with directness and economy rather as the figures on mediaeval frescoes. And because the frieze-like scheme was apparently designed for the walls of a very small tomb, the human figures (in their band between treble *guilloche* borders above and vertical red and cream stripes below) are no more than a foot in height. They seem diminutive beside the sphinxes. For the sphinxes fill the whole space of the band, even seated—being the dominating forms, both in size and by nature of their strange exotic condition as the mysterious extra-human guardians of the sepulchre.

The Lastre Campana (to be seen at the Louvre) have been dated to the beginning of the second half of the sixth century, though R. P. Hinks maintains that "their somewhat more advanced style ... is to be attributed to a difference of skill rather than of date".[9] They too display the influence of Corinthian vase-painting in a distinctive monumental frieze of five scenes. The central slab shows the figure of a nude male in the act of sacrificing at a high altar (curiously constructed in symmetrical layers of rectangles) where a small fire is burning in front of a red bowl set upon a tall column. To the left of this three young bearded warriors and two women with offerings are painted on two slabs moving processionally towards the altar, each raising a hand in salutation. While approaching from the other side, in perhaps the most vivid scene of all, are three figures—a young bearded man in a short tunic moving upward and forward, his right knee lifted, carrying a bow and arrows and raising a hand in salute, followed by a god with striped wings and winged boots who carries in his arms a small black-haired woman wrapped in her gown. These figures move lightly, quickly, on their journey, as the appointed guardians of the dead, the death-guides, clear and sure in face of the unknown. And behind them, on the final slab, two elders are shown seated, facing each other—one white-bearded with a staff in his left hand talking, the other black-bearded, his chin supported on his right hand, listening intently. Above them, her arms outstretched in their direction, a small winged female flies through the sky, perhaps emblematic of the spirit of the dead woman in the next scene.

The impact of these scenes comes first of all from the clarity with which the figures are drawn, the linear consistency of the style. But the clarity is not merely illustrative. The figures have colour, body, weight, and a kind of sensuous vigour (even though badly restored in parts); but they are not individualized. They are governed by a ceremonial, symbolic vision of life and death, a sense of the mystery of the journey beyond the tomb, of myth and ritual. Their movements and gestures, the alert faces, the bodies held within their flowing outlines, enact this vision, conveying homage and respect with a simplicity untouched by morbidity or gloom, even in the presence of the tragic unknowns of night and the dark and death.

Does the question of the originality of these pieces really arise? Is it not, as I have already suggested, misleading to engage in disputes about the influences absorbed and utilized by the Etruscans for the expression of their view of the world? Was this not a heritage shared with other peoples of the pre-classical Mediterranean world? To denigrate the Etruscans (as some have done) by saying that there is "virtually nothing in this art which is truly original"[10] —by talking of Greek domination or of Greek tutelage, as if Caere and Etruria were no more than a Greek dependency populated by an acquiescent and gullible people—is to suggest that nothing that came out of Etruria could not have been formally expressed elsewhere. Such denigration can only be made, I think, by those who have not seen or experienced with their own eyes the manifest distinctions of Etruscan art and architecture and its mature achievements.

The tombs have of course brought to light many superb examples of the ceramic arts of Greece. But what does this prove, other than that the Etruscans openly delighted in the possession of such things? One can imagine the enthusiasm and excitement with which they would have accepted the series of vases found in the Tomb of the Greek Vases, the Tomb of the Doloi and others, for these contained some of the undisputed masterpieces of Attic black-figure ware, including a number of magnificent amphorae by a master potter named Nicosthenes, and a seventh-century krater signed by Aristothonos.[11] And with their own series of hydriae, known as Caeretan hydriae, made in all probability by an Ionian artist established in Caere and his assistants, we have what is perhaps the most beautiful pottery produced on Etruscan soil in the sixth century. But there is no confusion. There is positive acceptance, and there are clearly definable influences, which the Etruscans felt no particular need to disguise. The figures on these Caeretan hydriae, for instance, are vigorous but weighted, they glow reddish black against the rose background, caught in eloquent and even humoristic situations, as in the myth of Hercules and the people of the Egyptian King Busiris, where a gigantic Hercules, scattering opponents right and left, makes his way to a figure crouching in open-mouthed terror at an altar. The colours glow, the patterns are bold, the figures are quick with life. Which is not to argue that Etruscan pottery in general, either during or after the sixth century, was the equal of its Greek counterparts. It is simply to point out that its vigour and charm and its expressionistic sense of delight in the shaping of forms ought to be sufficient argument against the dismissive attitude and the deprecatory comment.

From the fifth century onward, Caere began rapidly to decline, both politically and economically. The Temples of Pyrgi have produced their superb pedimental group of terracottas, clearly made in workshops adopting the same high standards as those of the sixth century, and possibly these were also the models for the remarkably similar pieces salvaged from the ruins of Satricum, south of Rome. Also, sculpture of vigour and distinction continued to be produced even up to the second century, as a number of pieces prove, such as the portrait head of a man from the Manganello temple site. But by the fourth century the artistic and cultural momentum had begun to slacken—even though the pottery workshops were still in action, and new variations of the old architectural forms were still appearing. The zenith had passed. Caere, rising swiftly into prominence, almost as swiftly declined, till at last it had degenerated into little more than a provincial Roman town. Such is the fate of all cultures. Sooner or later they weaken, and are taken over. It is a sad but inevitable fact. In the end there was nothing left for the people of Caere to do but to acquiesce,

> "To grovel in the shadows of white togas,
> And to die to Latin epitaphs,
> To be forgotten, to forget, to let
> Themselves be travestied by Roman laws
> And Roman lies till there was nothing,
> Nothing of them left, except the dead."[12]

But we at least are fortunate in being able to go back beyond
the period of decay and death, even by means of the dead; to re-
live their moments of consummate unity and acknowledge with
the hind-sight of time on our side the pride and triumph of their
maturity.

VULCI: THE CITY AND ITS CEMETERIES

NORTH OF TARQUINIA the Maremma runs on between the hills and the sea, narrowing in to the heights of Ansedonia before continuing as part of the Grosseto plain. Here, stretching from the left bank of the Arrone River to Lake Bolsena, and including the mountainous country inland to the foothills of Monte Amiata and the coast beyond Talamone, lay the territory of the great Etruscan city of Vulci. It is a strange, impressive and varied landscape of dark hills and riven valleys, of earth and limestone and tufo, formed like that of Tarquinia from the eruptions of now extinct volcanoes. The ruins of the city itself and its necropolis are on the plain, about ten kilometres inland from Montalto di Castro. They were not even brought to light until after the fortuitous discovery in 1828 of the first of the tombs. For centuries every trace of Vulci had vanished and even the site was unknown. All that remained were a few references by Latin geographers and a record of its defeat by the Romans preserved in the Capitol.[1] But from that moment in 1828 when a peasant's plough broke through the roof of the first chamber tomb and the excavations began, it was only a matter of time before the vestiges of the city would be unearthed. The incredible richness of the tombs, yielding material from the earliest Villanovan period to the time of the late Etruscans and the Romans, and including over 5,000 Attic black- and red-figure vases, left no room for doubt. Vulci, prominent among the cities of the Etruscan League from the first, conquered by the Romans in 290 and finally destroyed by the Saracens in the early Middle Ages, had been found again. Its position, close to the gorge-like cliff-banks of the River Fiora, is defined by the great bridge and its castle that are the most conspicuous features of the district. Indeed, the bridge is such a startlingly beautiful piece of work to stumble across in a desolate countryside that one wonders why it was not linked earlier with the idea of the city. It crosses the boundary formed by the river between Lazio and Tuscany, as a frontier-post for the Papal States, and was clearly part of the ancient Etruscan road connecting Tuscania with Vulci and going on beyond Vulci to the Vulcian port of Cosa. Though strengthened and restored by the Romans, and again in the Middle Ages, it is essentially Etruscan in spirit and style, soaring high across the gorge to the area north of the north gate of the city.

When Vulci was the capital of its territory, the Maremma plain must have been even more fertile than it is now, now that it has been reclaimed or partially reclaimed from the malarial marsh and heathland that was its condition for hundreds of years. Parts of it were probably covered with pine, as the slopes of the mountains are still, the rest being drained by an elaborate system of canals for the cultivation of fruit and wheat. Even after the Romans had come the fertility and richness of the land would have been maintained by the people, till the adverse effects of the Second Punic War and after that of immense surpluses from abroad had begun that slackening of effort, that neglect and apathy in the midst of surfeit which lowered standards of local agriculture all the way up the coast from Rome and started the gradual decline of the land. The Romans could get corn from Sicily and elsewhere. They didn't need to work for it themselves. They had their slaves build villas. Their direct control of the land lapsed. Who cared? The known world (almost all of it belonging to the Romans) was prodigal with riches. Even the Etruscan Vulcians could afford to sit back or go to Rome. So gradually, as Lawrence put it, "the streams threw their mud along the coast and choked themselves, then soaked the land and made marshes and vast stagnant shallow pools where the mosquitoes bred like fiends . . . and with the mosquitoes came the malaria. . . . The marshes became deadly, and human life departed or was destroyed",[2] to linger on only in isolated pockets, diseased and poverty-stricken among the ruins.

Vulci had flowered, lapsed as a city, and lingered on miserably into the Middle Ages until finally wiped out and abandoned to the swamp and heath. But now at least its foundations have been recovered, and its lands are again being cultivated. All the farms and villages on the plain are associated with the Ente Maremma, under which development of the land is being systematically and communally controlled. But still it has an air of desolate loneliness about it, even at its most fertile, even with the corn growing rich and strong. It is this which gives it its peculiar stamp, its tone. It is this and what it contains and refers to of history and of fact that dominates. You cannot wipe out centuries of neglect in a few years. The grasses are rank in gulley, cleft and stream-bed, the farmsteads dotted about seem isolated, small, inadequate. Great parts of the plain remain empty, villageless. There is no malaria now, but what villages there are, such as Capalbio, Canino and Pescia Fiorentina are poor, their older men sunken-cheeked and yellow-skinned and bowed. If prosperity is returning, it has taken a long time and a great toll in life and in suffering.

On a late May afternoon, the road from Canino to Vulci seems endless, a dusty white reflection of the sun amid the heat and the silence. Tracks pierce the fields on either side to an occasional low hut or house. Old riddled stones, a fossilized statuary, lie beside the road. Though the signs of hard work are everywhere present, now it's deserted. Now the corn lies trapped in the sun, and the thickness of May closes round. Then suddenly the plain gives way a little, and the blackish-grey tower of the castle rises into sight, startling the prevailing horizontals, barring the way, stamping itself like a seal upon the background. As you come down to it, tower and walls seem to sink a little into the fields, and you notice the new bridge cutting straight across the river and the ravine, off to the right. But the ancient bridge springs out and away from the limestone cliff and the wall—very thin, humped at the centre, rising in a high wide arc from its massive supports, with great beard-like stalactites of lime hanging from the edge where an aqueduct had once crossed.

At the centre it is as if the bridge were suspended in mid-air, 150 feet above where the river trickles through between great boulders and sheer yellowish cliffs. From here one gets a curiously particularized sense of the landscape. Not only is this a gateway into the province of Tuscany, it is also an introduction to the panorama of Vulci itself, and a rare survival—there before the Romans, and no doubt crossed by them when they conquered Vulci. Nor would

the Romans have been blind to its strategic position in the plain.
Though probably it was less important after the building of the
Aurelia, it obviously continued to have its place as an alternative
route for those wishing to travel north, and must owe its survival
to later isolation and the accidents of history. The new bridge,
going straight across, seems in contrast the dullest commonplace,
a mere connecting link, an unremarkable utility.

The path from the bridge to the city moves to the crown of a
hill and then dips steeply downward to an offshoot of the Fiora,
below the walls. Here one comes across a few abandoned chamber
tombs, and along a path by the stream, the site of a Villanovan
cemetery, beyond which lie the remains of the once extensive
Osteria necropolis. In Dennis's time the cliffs all round the city
must have been thick with tombs, for according to his reckoning
in 1840 at least 15,000 had already been excavated.[3] They were
broken into, rifled, and left in ruins. Because in those days excavation was mostly unscientific and indiscriminate, and the diggers
out for nothing but that which could be turned into cash. They
were after the Greek figured vases, the gold and the bronzes.
When the Prince of Canino ordered his trial diggings and began
to find things, his men set to work with such zeal that in a very
short time more than 2,000 painted vases among numberless other
objects were dragged from the tombs.[4] This was a treasure of
inestimable value; but a great number of the tombs were left
irreparably ruined, for *they* could not be bought or sold. They
were merely there to get into, safes to be blown. No one had eyes
for the architecture. It was what was inside that mattered. Soon
enough, with the Prince of Canino displaying his riches—at a
lavish party he once even presented his wife adorned exclusively in
Etruscan jewellery—Europe had become aware of Vulci, and for
a while the Etruscans were in fashion.[5] And it was from about this
time (perhaps encouraged by the fashion) that archaeologists and
scholars too began seriously to turn their attention to a study of
this problematic people, largely as a result of the dazzling discoveries at Vulci. Their work went on slowly, painstakingly,
laying foundations, even in spite of the feverish activities of
dealers and robbers. All through the century discoveries were

being made, haphazardly and indiscriminately on the whole, and it was not until the twentieth century that the area was scientifically explored; and by then much of it had been ravaged. Even today, with an Antiquarium on the site and the area policed, the thieving continues, and illegal diggings have developed almost into an industry, urged on by the pressure of the middlemen and the dealers. So that archaeologists are being forced bitterly to accept the disappearance day by day of evidence invaluable to them in their efforts to reconstruct the Vulcian world.

The tombs that remain accessible from this devastating invasion are to be found up the cleft beyond the acropolis at Cavalupo and in the François necropolis. Others on the Lazio plain have either been ruined or are still awaiting discovery. They are of every kind. Apart from the many pit and trench tombs, there are the vestiges of the great *Cucumelle* or tumulus tombs of the seventh and sixth centuries, of chamber tombs cut into the cliffs with Doric lintelled doorways and interconnecting paths, and the later hypogei, sunk deep in the ground. And it is still an impressive enough image you get as you clamber down the paths among the François tombs towards the Ponte Rotto. Many of them are ruined, but there are fragmentary details of carving everywhere around doorways, and the rooms contain benches, sloping ceilings and internal mouldings characteristic of those at almost every major site, and one or two early tombs have antechambers with ceilings symbolizing the spoked rays of the sun, as in the Campana Tomb at Cerveteri. In the nine rooms of the famous François Tomb, of the fourth century—its frescoes detached and now in the Villa Albani in Rome—there are even fragments of the painting left, and the central chamber has a beautiful coffered ceiling. Then there is the recently discovered fourth-century Tomb of the Inscriptions, which has a central hall and six rooms, with inscriptions above or to the side of the doorways, ten in Etruscan and three in Latin. A carved sarcophagus was found here with various other fragments and a great doorslab, with a female divinity carved upon it, that sealed the dromos.

And what of the tumuli? There is one in particular on the plain, half-ruined, that stands out—"a strange, strange nut indeed, with a kernel of perpetual mystery", as Lawrence has it.[6] Two stone sphinxes were found guarding the entrance when it was opened up in 1829, and there were two small chambers at the centre of the mound, with two shafts of masonry passing up to its apex—probably once for the support of the phallic cippi that crowned it.[7] Other tumuli dotted about the plain have long been rifled and deserted and left to collapse, like those at Tarquinia. But perhaps there will be some attempt in the future to restore or reconstruct them within their circular stone girdles. On the great bared plain, only now beginning to respond to the efforts of the Ente Maremma, they are landmarks symbolizing what Signor Bartoccini calls "the most mysterious and fascinating city in Etruria".[8]

It was only in this century, with the laying of a hydroelectric canal across its western side, that the city really began to come to light. After various sporadic digs a systematic excavation of the area was started in the 1950s, and has been going on slowly ever since under Renato Bartoccini, revealing more and more of the foundations. There are the basalt slabs of a Roman road, the ruins of shops and public buildings, part of a vast Piazza with the bases of columns upon a travertine pavement, and a cluster of buildings with remains of a triumphal arch at its edge, where two roads cross. Here one finds the rectangular form of a great temple, built of huge squared blocks of reddish tufo, and standing 8 or 9 feet high. This is late Etruscan, but the layout of the city forum around it is part of the centre of the third and second century Roman *municipium Vulcentium*, reshaped upon the foundations of the Etruscan city, so that there is hardly a sign of Etruscan workmanship. True, down towards the East gate and the river, one comes upon the great tufo blocks again, around a Roman shrine to Hercules. And at the site of the gateway itself a section of the Etruscan wall, built of massive blocks, very thick and solid, has been exposed. This comes right to the edge of the road and retains stones for the base of the gateway. It is an impressive position, for the road dips down through a cutting to the flat land below, to the river and the Roman Ponte Rotto, the great gorge-like cliffs and the vast desolate sweep of the plain beyond. From here one gets something of the full impact of the strange beauty of the

place and its secreted past. Behind and to the right and left lies the
city. Ahead lies the François necropolis. Away to the left out of
sight beyond the spur of the acropolis lies the Cavalupo necropolis. And looking across the city height towards the acropolis, or
walking to it through the long grass, one wonders how much still
lies undiscovered under the earth. Much, one feels, reaching the exposed tract of road at the North Gate, dug out of the 3 to 4 foot
crust that covers the rest. A great deal, one thinks, remembering
the rich deposit of votive objects found near here, and now in the
Villa Giulia in Rome.[9] The tombs have been voraciously explored,
but the foundations of the city, and possibly much that belongs to
the Etruscan Vulci, have yet to be recovered from the earth.

But it is of course the tombs themselves that have revealed most
to us of the Etruscan world. For though so many of them were
stripped and their contents dissipated beyond record across
Europe, we can accept this philosophically because such a rich and
impressive variety of objects still remains. To visit the Vatican or
the Villa Giulia Museum or any of half a dozen others is to have
the proof of this. The evidence available in those clinical surroundings may not be complete; but it is extensive enough to bring us
close to the nature and spirit of the civilization of Vulci. For those
with sufficient curiosity and patience, and even a little of the
scholar's passionate attentiveness to detail, rich discoveries are to
be made, discoveries that bring a dead world to life and turn
silence into speech.

First of all, the cemeteries of Osteria and Cavalupo have yielded
a collection of impasto and bronze cinerary urns together with
many more intimate pieces which put Vulci among the most
important of the archaic Villanovan settlements that flourished
throughout Etruria between the ninth and eighth centuries. The
biconical urns with covers in the form of bowls or helmets, and
the elliptical or circular hut urns, rank with those of Tarquinia and
Caere in vigour and expressiveness. Their geometric decorations,
combined in varied and interesting ways on black or grey, are
either incised or impressed upon the clay, or applied to it with tin
leaf. And the hut-urns are of especial interest because of the con-
structional details they display. At the apex of the roof, for

instance, interlocking beams protrude after crossing, and there is usually a protected hole representing the flue for smoke from fires. Also the lip of the roof overhangs the walls as it would have done in the actual huts, against rain, and the rectangular doorway is wide, as if to let in air and light.[10]

On the biconical urns the helmet-cover is sometimes in bronze, as at Tarquinia—full-sized, crested, with a rectangle of studs and beaded lines above the forehead, the studded crest rising to a point. And there are a few magnificent examples in which the urn itself is of hammered bronze, with intricate embossed patterns on it, initiating the bronzework for which Vulci is particularly distinguished and which must quickly have given the city a reputation, not only among neighbouring cities but also with traders from abroad. Even before the orientalizing seventh century and the rich productivity of the established sixth-century workshops, Vulci seems memorably to have exploited this material. One group of pieces found at Cavalupo a few years ago consists of a sword, a drinking flask and a large biconical urn. The bronze scabbard of the sword is strikingly decorated with parallel incised lines. Its upper handle end has a primitive figurine on each side, male and female, leaning against a double circle—nude, smiling, overtly sexual; and the tip culminates in two discs. The flask is circular, decorated with concentric rings and embossed studs. But the most prominent of the three pieces is the urn. It has a saucer-shaped lip and a shield cover, and the thick high neck widens to the ridge of the shoulder and a central belt-like band embossed with three lines of studs before the ribbed body narrows sharply in to the base. It is to be seen among many lovely pieces at the Villa Giulia.[11] A group of objects found, for instance, with a rounded biconical ossuary in a circular limestone container in the Osteria necropolis, included fragments of a bronze belt, a series of discs and of boat-shaped fibulae; little rings, studs and spirals; and a marvellous small bronze votive warrior in the Nuragic style, probably imported from Sardinia, who wears a conical hat and a long cloak, holds on the left arm a large shield and stretches out the right arm, hand raised, as if to warn the onlooker not to come any closer. Dominating all these, however, are the bronze

carriage and situla, not actually from Vulci but from the Bizen-
zian necropolis of *Olmo Bello* on the edge of Lake Bolsena and just
within Tarquinian territory, which I refer to here because they
reflect the common traditions of Vulcian and Tarquinian bronzework in the eighth century. The situla is an especially memorable
piece. Its body is studded and decorated with bands of scored
lines; and around the disc-like lid and shoulders are two rings of
little male figurines, dancing a propitiatory phallic dance (their
flesh erect, some armed or carrying cymbals or shields), around a
bear chained at the centre of the lid by a long chain fixed to one
of the handles. There is one little man too, on the shoulder, who
(unlike the others) is portrayed driving a yoked bullock to work;
and he echoes the activities portrayed by the women, peasants and
bullocks on the struts of the incense-carriage.[12]

There are many more striking bronzes from this early period.
They point to the existence in Vulci and the whole area, of highly
skilled craftsmen working to high standards for a people demanding quality in every kind of article. Such skills are absorbed and
utilized in that sudden richening acceleration (brought about by
contact with the peoples of the Eastern Mediterranean, with
Egypt, Corinth and Attica) which occurred in the seventh century. There are collections of bronze, gold and impasto from this
period scattered about everywhere—for instance, a gold necklace
of dazzling quality, with meanders and triangles in granulated
filigree, consisting of a central disc and eight "w" shaped pendants,
exists at Munich. But unfortunately many of the pieces are either
difficult to trace or have gone abroad into the Museums, inade-
quately recorded, as the loot from those indiscriminate nineteenth-
century diggings.

But there is one tomb, discovered intact in 1839, the material
from which is comparable to that of the Cerveteri Sorbo Tomb in
interest if not in richness. This is the Grotta d'Iside, an underground tomb with antechamber and three inner rooms at Polledrara, where many objects were found—including six ostrich
eggs (one painted with winged sphinxes similar to those on the
wall of the Campana Tomb at Veii, the others carved in low
relief), two small seated figures of Isis in the form of ointment jars,

a number of Egyptian and early Vulcian vases, two bronze four-wheeled carriages, and an assortment of other pieces, all showing a very strong oriental influence—which date the tomb to the end of the seventh or the beginning of the sixth century. Most important of all from this tomb are the two female effigies, one in gypsum standing full-length and almost three feet high, the other a bust in hammered bronze, now in the British Museum. For they provide important evidence of the art of Vulci at the turn of the century, when the archaic or Daedalic styles characteristic of the orientalizing tombs were giving way to more sinuous linear forms. In the stone goddess or votary, known as the Polledrara Kore, with her mysterious hieratic severity, her static pose and weight, the archaic quality still remains—rooted in the long tradition of the Greek Korai. The eyes are large and wide open, both arms are held out rigidly, the right hand making a gesture of offering. But these stern ritualistic features are softened by the moulding of the face and the richly braided hair, falling in two coils in front and gathered behind by eleven bangles. Moreover, the rhythmic continuity of outline and surface looks forward to the bronze and stone figures of the middle of the sixth century.

The bronze bust, on the other hand, has affinities with the Canopic urns of Chiusi. She stares out, stiff, intent and unyielding in the archaic primitive style of those early Chiusian heads. There is no softening here; the face is discouragingly unattractive. She holds a horned bird on the closed fist of her right hand, and the left is crossed on the chest, leaving the breasts exposed—for she is nude except for a necklace fastened tight and high round the neck. In addition she is adorned with thin strips of metal representing hair, which hang from two nails behind her ears in tight coils, and the base on which she stands depicts a band of fabulous animals embossed on the sheet.[13]

Of the stone guardians that once stood at the entrances to sixth-century tombs—among them sphinxes and winged lions—few have survived. But these include the nenfro Centaur and the Youth Riding a Hippocampus, both to be seen at the Villa Giulia in Rome.[14] They and the Polledrara Kore give Vulci a place comparable in importance to Vetulonia and Chiusi as a centre for the production of monumental stone sculpture. These pieces, it is obvious, are the survivors of a tradition. They could not have come into being out of nothing. They imply an intensive activity in the city of sculptors working in stone.

The Centaur is probably almost contemporary with the Polledrara Kore—perhaps a decade or so later. He has certain features in common with the monumental sculptures of Chiusi, but the conception of the form can be traced to the iconography of mainland Greece, to the archaic Apollo forms of the seventh century, and perhaps even to Cretan forms. Vulci by this time had established trading links with the Peloponnese, and between the end of the seventh century and the first two or three decades of the sixth, Corinthian pottery was in great demand. We know this not only from pieces found at Vulci itself and the imitations made in the city's workshops, but also from deposits all over Lazio. And we have to take into account also the phenomenal number of Attic black-figure vases that began to come to Vulci from the second or third decade onwards of the sixth century, even at the same time as themes and motives arriving by way of Asia Minor and the Ionian Greeks of Southern Italy were beginning to have their effect upon Etruscan art.[15]

The Centaur is a kind of herald. He is rooted in the archaic past, but he also points forward, standing in the midst of cross-currents of influence. The stylized ritualistic stance, upright and attentive, is modified by the softening and expressive impact of the huge wide-open eyes, the broad expanse of the face and its frame of braided hair. He is conceived as a young virile athlete, the arms held close to the thighs in the manner of the archaic Apollos but with the fingers outstretched, and the rounded equine body issuing behind in rather primitive juxtaposition. The legs are a little apart, and there is hardly any attempt at modelling the subtler surface planes of the body. All attention is concentrated upon the large quasi-triangular form of the face, emphasized by the thick coils of hair falling to the shoulders on each side, and the genitals —their modelling accentuated by the plain rounded surfaces of legs and trunk. It is as if the intention had been to delineate the two poles of being, spirit and flesh—the eye as the mirror of the soul, the penis as the root of the body. Unmistakably there is this interrelation between overt sexuality (symbolizing the life-giving energy and sap at the root of the physical world) and the mystery of the inner world—the world beyond this world that the great eyes gaze out of and the tenderness of the face reflects. This is not an intellectualized image. The crudities have not been smoothed away by consciousness. They are part of the impact of the form, conveying energy and vision without deliberation, as a child would but with an adult's feeling for and knowledge of the essences of things. Those who look for the triumph of "light", for sophistication, subtlety of balance and proportion, judging from the standard of the classical Greek nude, are of course bound to find this disappointing. For it conforms to a very different standard, based upon the values of the ancient world, by which man was still content to pay his homage to the universe containing him, and had not yet been set up as the measure of it or the challenger, "the culminating point of the process of nature". It is instinctive rather than intellectual, and it functions as a propitiatory image, an offering that acknowledges the supremacy of "a mysterious and implacable world",[16] and gives man his vivid place in it.

The second of these pieces, also in nenfro, depicting a young nude male riding a sea monster (probably a hippocampus), clearly betrays the influence of Ionian art, and is therefore later in date than the Centaur. It remains (like the other) a schematic, primitive image of virility, but its expressiveness is achieved with quite different means. There is no exaggeration or enlargement of the face or the eyes, for instance, no stressing of the sex. He sits astride the (headless) sea-horse, leaning against the animal's raised back, his head thrust forward from the long cap of hair, his arms bent— a smallish figure in relation to the high arched curve of the fish-tail and the thick of the sea-horse's body. For it is this form, the animal he rides, in its exaggerated curves, with the lost head rising between his legs, that provides the sexual phallic image. The attention is concentrated upon the interrelation of the fish-like curving form of the sea-horse with the more angular and oppositional rhythms of the rider—its effect being almost one of outline and of relief. Outline, in other words, predominates, in the

Ionian manner (if in a very early and schematic form of it) and especially in the ridge created by the distinction between the animal's outer casing and its inner body.

The Ionian influence became intensified from the second half of the sixth century in the bronzes of the local workshops—the tripods, candelabra and incense-bowls with their elaborate tiered forms, usually incorporating a human figure, either between the base and the upper levels or (on the candelabra) at the very tip. The figures are young, active and alert—votaries, athletes and dancers, male and female. And the flowing curves, the taut, swift modelling of limb and body enhance the vivacity of ritualistic gesture, the health and grace of the body, whether in motion or repose. Their sensuousness is further enhanced when they are depicted clothed—where the breasts, buttocks and thighs of female dancers (whether as votives on their own or as part of a candlestick) are moulded in firm rounded curves beneath the clinging garments. Contemporary with these beautiful if minor sculptures, made to add decorative elegance to the articles of the household, are the bronze bowls, helmets, vases and mirrors decorated with figures incised or in relief. The mirrors are particularly interesting. There is one mid-sixth-century example in the British Museum, for instance, which may have come from Vulci, of Orion crossing the sea. It has a superb economy and lucidity of line, an edge and flow which gives the nude figure a marvellous spontaneous vigour as he runs above the waves and the small fish swimming the sea within a border of leaves and fruit.[17] Such articles, among the many elegant accessories made for women, are one indication of the position enjoyed by them in Etruscan society as the equals of their menfolk, even as the many images of men and women shown together in social intercourse are another. To the Greeks and the Romans such equality would have seemed perhaps immoral and a little shocking, for they were accustomed to having their women play a much more passive and purely private role in society. But it is one of the distinguishing features of Etruscan civilization, which we today are likely to accept with alacrity and delight, especially since there is such evident joyousness in the sexual community thus defined.

If the bronzes of Vulci were a distinctive aspect of the city's culture throughout the sixth century, as they had been before and were to remain, the local pottery workshops were at the same time providing vivid idiosyncratic variants of the prevailing styles of painted vase. In the early decades of the century came a series of vases based upon the Corinthian pottery that had by then begun to reach Etruria in great quantity. The painters of these vases mingled native and Ionian elements with Corinthian motives and themes to create a style of their own not to be confused with the originals they imitated. And later, when the Attic traders brought with them those masterpieces of the potter's art for which Vulci is renowned in the world at large, local artists—again responding to the impact of the cross-currents—began producing a kind of vase which is distinguished for its eccentric but vivacious reconciliation of Attic and Ionian elements. These—the so-called *Pontic* vases of the mid-century—are the equivalent of the series of beautiful hydriae being produced at about the same time in Caere upon similar models, and are quite as distinct from their Greek sources as they are from those peculiarly Caeretan pieces.

Their own work clearly enough demonstrates the positive response of the Vulcians to the dazzling beauty of the many masterpieces of Attic art that came their way. But who would be likely, one might ask, to have remained indifferent to a work of such supreme artistry as the celebrated François vase, signed by the potter Ergotimos and the painter Klitias, that was discovered in a tomb at Vulci and is now to be seen at the Archaeological Museum in Florence? Not at least a people so given to enthusiasm and delight as the Etruscans. For on this huge krater the painter has lavished all his skill, presenting a series of ceremonial scenes from Greek mythology arranged in six bands teeming with animal and human forms around the body and on the handles. It has been dated somewhere between 580 and 550 B.C., so it probably arrived in Vulci around the middle of the century, among countless other pieces, now scattered throughout the world, to provide new incentive for the vasemakers of the city.

Through the fifth, fourth and third centuries, Vulci continued to produce works of distinction in pottery and bronze and terracotta, carrying on the traditions established, and utilizing the prevailing Hellenistic styles. Although the forms became gradually impoverished, cruder and more derivative as time went on, there was no cessation of activity. In many ways the fifth century marks a definite decline in quality—so much so that it is even possible to speak of the Hellenistic fourth century, with its beautiful incised mirrors and caskets, as a period of revival or renaissance. And there is in fact particular support for the theory of renaissance in the existence of the paintings from the François Tomb, dated to the end of the century. Almost all other evidence of painting in Vulci has vanished, but these paintings survive practically intact, and are of exceptional quality, taking into account the general drift towards decadence. They present scenes from Greek mythology and others from a peculiarly local saga. Figuratively, the portrait of one of the owners of the tomb, Vel Saties, is the most striking. He wears a rich *toga picta* and a laurel, and he looks upward, perhaps intent upon interpreting the flight of the birds that the little figure at his feet is setting free. The portrait, though idealized, is clearly defined, in profile, and his face stands out the more because the body is shrouded from the shoulders in its long toga. Of course, neither this nor any of the figures has the vivid active spontaneity of those of sixth- or fifth-century Etruria. It is too late. Even in battle (however well composed) there is a kind of passivity about them; and the demons Vanth and Charun are also there standing ominously beside Achilles in a bloody episode concerning the Trojan prisoners, intruding upon an alien theme.

The very end of the Etruscan culture at Vulci is almost uncannily symbolized in a fascinating collection of heads, of seated or standing infants or infants lying cocooned in their swaddling clothes like mummies, all in terracotta.[18] They are skilfully, even observantly done, but they seem the images of a people sunk into a state of passivity in which all movement has been reduced to a minimum or has been stilled to an approximation of the stillness of death itself. Two hundred years before, such images would have been inconceivable. But then much had happened in that time, and Vulci was soon to be lost even to the memory of its former splendour.

11 HEAD OF APOLLO. Sixth century. Detail of the famous Veii Apollo, a full-length striding figure found on Portonaccio in 1916 (*pp. 131–5*).

12 SEPULCHRAL CIPPUS. 510 B.C. From Chiusi (*pp. 214–16*).

It may be that this place will always remain something of a question-mark, for there are facts that we shall never know, a history lost to the scholar and perhaps not ever written down. A great city, with its customs, its culture, its trade, its daily comings and goings, had existed on this desolated Maremma, surrounded by rich lands, only to vanish almost without trace. But if we are not likely ever to have anything so particularizing as an eye-witness account to break the silence, we do have the silent record of the funerary art of Vulci to define for us something of the pattern of the city's life—the drama of its development, its rise to maturity, and the pathos of its decay. And art does after all have its own authentic voices, even if these do not speak in words, to document a people's mood and spirit.

G

THE VULCIAN TERRITORY

WHAT WAS ONCE the territory of Vulci, stretching north-west along the Maremma and the coastline and north and east into the Tuscan hills, retains the sites of a number of its dependent cities and towns. The massive polygonal walls of Saturnia and Cosa and the ruins of their Roman settlements are matched by the cemeteries carved into the tufo cliffs at Castro and Sovana and those, both carved and constructed, above the Albegna valley at Marsiliana and Magliano. And there are many other signs of ancient habitation scattered about around the villages and hills of this lyrical and sparsely populated countryside.

Cosa, in its commanding position on the top of a macchia-covered hill at Ansedonia, looks across at Monte Argentario and down upon the Bay, and was probably once the main port serving Vulci before it became a Roman colony in 273 B.C. Apart from the extensive remains of the Roman town inside its polygonal walls, there is a necropolis with tombs dating from the seventh to the third centuries below the hill near Orbetello, the remains of ancient harbour walls in Orbetello itself, and to the south a striking canal, the *Tagliata Etrusca*, cut sheer from the tufo to channel off the sea. The great dark mountain, over 2,000 feet in height, must have offered perfect shelter for ships on the landward side. There is the curve of the Bay below Cosa, and there are the unruffled lagoons of Orbetello, quite apart from the natural harbour of Santo Stefano on the semi-island of the mountain itself.

Cosa was abandoned in the Middle Ages by the descendants of the men who built it. The exodus, they say, was one of panic, caused by a ferocious outbreak of malaria. Since when, the whole of the broad flat crest of the hill it covered has remained deserted, given up to grass and shrub and the great gnarled olives that must have seeded centuries ago among the ruins. The massive grey stones of its wall dominate the hill, rising out of the tangled greenery to give on to open ground within and a full view of the surrounding landscape and the sea. At the highest point here the grey-brown lava-stone walls of a Roman temple rise upon huge travertine blocks—the ruins of a Temple of Jupiter on the *arx* of the third-century town. And from it the stone paving of a large piazza leads to the remains of an archway, and beyond that into the grass and the thick silvery green of the olives, the quiet ominous beauty of stilled places.

Almost nothing remains here of the Etruscan settlement. Only the walls in fact betray the presence of a native population. And recent excavation has established that these, though archaic in style, were not likely to have been raised before the Romans arrived. They extend in an almost unbroken ring around the hill, and remain by far the most impressive feature of the site. The great polygonal blocks of the Eastern Gateway are especially striking, rising on either side to a height of 20 feet and forming a walled passage that once obviously supported an arch. The architectural skill is at once apparent in the rock-like stability of the structure, with each stone locked mortarless to the next. And there is little doubt that the Romans would have used the natives, making use of skills the Etruscans had long mastered in the building of earlier cities in the area. Their organizational hardheadedness would have made sure no resources were wasted. They had come to man a fortress against the impending threat of the Gauls, and to make it impregnable. By 225, when the Gauls actually began to move south again, the town had become a flourishing outpost, and must certainly have sent detachments to help defeat the invaders in the Battle of Telamon, at Talamone (another Etruscan centre) twelve miles to the north. It must also have played a part in trying to defend the Roman state against Hannibal during his disastrous occupation of Italy.

Its remains indicate the existence of a small town at a time when Rome was expanding in all directions and dragooning the people of Italy into military service for the imposition of its political aims. Cosa was but one tiny link in a vast chain that was gradually to cover the whole of the then known world, and one wonders how many "volunteers" from among the people its masters would have managed to catch in their militaristic net. There is no knowing. But beyond the excavated area a huge dark pit puts ominous thoughts into one's mind about Roman methods of persuasion. One side of it slopes steeply down to the bottom of a sheer cliff of rock which encloses it. Could this have served as some sort of sacred grove? One is reminded more of a dark open dungeon, a place of punishment for the recalcitrant minority perhaps. The quiet at the top reassures. Here one can more easily think of sacred groves and the inhuman innocence of the natural world than of prison pits. Among the olives evil seems a long way off, a tiny echo in a world with a record of atrocity as long as history itself. But then, to the civilized, evil seems always a long way off—till it suddenly emerges, unmasking itself, stripping away the veneer, erupting in the midst of enlightenment.

Anyway, at Cosa everything is quiet now; and to the north, almost half-way between it and the northernmost Vulcian port of Talamone (or Thlamu) the River Albegna runs inland, fed from Monte Labbro and passing very close to the ruins of Saturnia. Along the river valley many tombs have been found, isolated or in small groups, often constructed rather than carved from the rock. These indicate the existence of small agricultural settlements in an area as much influenced by the culture of Northern Etruria as by Vulci and the South. Here there are no great tufaceous plateaux such as those on which Vulci, Tarquinia and Caere are situated. The landscape is closer to that of Vetulonia. And at *Marsiliana d'Albegna*, which lies on a low hill about twelve kilometres from the sea, in a position similar to other smaller settlements, a very rich necropolis was brought to light, dating from the seventh century to the first decades of the sixth. Here, in an area rich in iron, a small city must have flourished, briefly but intensely —perhaps the focal point of the *Ager Caletranus* mentioned by Pliny and at a period almost exactly contemporary with the rise of Vetulonia. It was soon superseded, as the remains have proved, by Saturnia and by Heba, a few kilometres to the north, but the treasures from its tombs, now in the Archaeological Museum in Florence, indicate the existence at Marsiliana of a kind of lesser Vetulonia. Not only are there tombs of every description, but they were found to be rich in gold, bronze and ivory. The gold ornaments in particular betray influences from both the North and the South—the more plastic figurations of Southern styles (as exemplified in the ducks and lions of the Corsini fibula) mingling with the inimitable and dazzling surfaces characteristic of Vetulonian craftsmen.

Magliano lies a mere eight or nine kilometres north of Marsiliana. It is close to the site of the Roman colony of Heba, and the necropoli that lie around it in four different localities—with tombs carved out of the rock, now mostly ruined—witness the existence of an important Etruscan centre, perhaps displacing Caletrani, from the early decades of the sixth century right through into the Roman period. From here, in fact, came the famous sixth-century Magliano plate of thin convex laminated lead with a long ritual inscription in archaic Etruscan script engraved upon it, which is among the most important of the many inscriptions available to scholars.

About thirty kilometres east of Magliano, inland from Vulci above a tributary of the River Fiora, is the necropolis of *Castro*, isolated upon the sheer sides of a wild gorge. It is hidden away beyond a farm in an almost totally uninhabited area. One comes first upon a cluster of tombs carved out of the tufo into quadrangular chambers on two levels at the side of the path, and then across a stream and a field to the tip of a great wooded gorge where the cliffs are riddled with tombs—some of them mere caverns, others taking the form of *columbaria*, with their rows of pigeon-hole niches, and yet others carved into house-like shapes with moulded doorways and little windows. And above these in the thickly wooded hill that crowns the cliff are the hidden ruins of the mediaeval city of Castro, once the capital of a Duchy, which in 1647 was razed to the ground by Pope Innocent X because its bishop had been murdered. It is a place of chaos now, of broken column and cornice, choked and broken into by the riot of the natural world, left to the appetite of the forest.[1] The tombs of course have all been explored and emptied, but there is a notable small collection of seventh- and sixth-century impastos and bronzes in the Villa Giulia.

In these Tuscan landscapes, the Etruscans have been superseded by so much else. Other people have come, other places have been built over the roots, towns like Pitigliano rise gaunt and towering upon the flattened hill-sites of Etruscan towns, as if in extension of their life, but belonging to another world. Yet underlying it all a strange stilled expectancy remains. As one moves up from Lake Bolsena through Valentano, Ischia di Castro, Farnese and Pitigliano towards Sovana, the wooded slopes and fields, the sudden gorges and clefts, the tense clusterings of houses on their walls of cliff, seem to echo back the secretive diversities of a lost world, to hold its actualities suspended for a moment as if they *were* that world or still belonged to it, or as if the Etruscans had never wholly let it go. This is more than mere illusion induced by the intensity of the imaginative response one makes to such tragically beautiful and stricken places. After all, it comes from what is there to be responded to, an atmosphere invested with meaning and rich with evidence.

And there is nowhere in the whole area that quite so tangibly confirms this, or that puts one quite so closely into contact with the ancient roots, as *Sovana*, set on its ridge among the green six kilometres beyond Pitigliano. For its vast necropolis rivals even those of Norchia and Blera in scope and architectural variety. And even the village, itself a broken vestige reflecting the minor splendours of its mediaeval prime, is interesting. It consists almost entirely of mediaeval buildings—broken-walled, crumbling, lyrically desolate, retaining the poetry of abandoned fallen places, but still lived in. And with the hovering yellowish ruin of its castellated gateway at one end and the eighth- to twelfth-century Duomo rising intact on the edge of the hill at the other, it is now scarcely half a mile in length, and little more than one long silent street—widening at the centre to form what was once a civic square marked by a blinded Palazzo Communale with an open belfry above it.[2] Hard to believe that this was once a city with its own laws, "the residence of bishops and a powerful race of counts . . . which in 1240 was even able to oppose Frederick II and to sustain a siege". Yet it can claim the distinction of being the birthplace of Hildebrand, Pope Gregory VII, the great ecclesiastical reformer of the eleventh century. And centuries before this, as the Roman colony of Suana, it is even mentioned in the catalogues of Pliny and Ptolemy.[3]

But not until 1843, and the discovery of the tombs below the (by then squalid) village, was Sovana in any way linked with the Etruscans. To the local peasants, indulging the whims of a pedantic Englishman (Ainsley, the first discoverer), the massed sepulchres had been mere "scherzi", and no one else apparently had ever troubled about them before.[4] They had lain there for centuries, useless, neglected, perhaps already rifled of their possessions and left. Yet these tombs offer conclusive proof of the Etruscan origin of Sovana. On the city site below the western side of the Duomo there are even portions of the ancient wall, and traces of roadways cut deep into the tufo. The town was probably not of any great size or importance, in spite of the tombs, and no doubt functioned as a local centre dependent upon Vulci.

Descending through the broken gateway to the west, one soon comes upon the first of the tombs, on both sides of the road, in the cliffs below and opposite the town—"a long range of architectural façades, in general form, size and character like those of Norchia and Castel D'Asso", though differing from these in many of their details. They have the familiar narrowing Egyptian formulation of outline, and the characteristic raised Doric mouldings, often with inscriptions above the door. But "here we find cornices not receding but projecting, and actually taking the concave form, with the prominent *torus* beneath, so common," as Dennis puts it, "on the banks of the Nile; and this repeated again and again".[5]

The tombs are separated, as at Norchia and Castel D'Asso, by flights of steps hewn from the rock and rising to the plain above; and on the façade there is often a hollowed recess incorporating a bench. Then in front of each monument a long passage leads down to the tomb entrance itself, which has a moulded door similar to the one on the façade and gives into a spacious undecorated chamber with benches along the walls.

These sepulchres (in the cliffs called Poggio Prisca on the one hand and Sopraripa under the town on the other) are a deep red in colour, and rich with inscriptions, none of them complete, though some contain deep scored letters nine or ten inches high. They make an impressive sight, even when seen only through the screen of summer vegetation. And there is one on the Poggio Prisca that stands out uniquely among its neighbours because of the pediment with sculptural reliefs that crowns its façade, the Doric-style frieze below this and a round-arched recess that displaces the door. This pediment (late Etruscan of the third or second century) has as its central figure, now much defaced, a mermaid or marine deity, similar to those displayed upon certain Volterran and Chiusian ash-chests. She probably functions as the symbol of some half-forgotten creed, like the little man in the Tomb of the Painted Reliefs at Cerveteri, honouring the godhead of the sea. From her naked body, sexually exposed, the coils of her fish-tails roll thickly away; and on each side a winged male figure, one bearing a shield on his arm, is seen flying away from her. The carving remains vigorous in its riotous setting, though a great tree rooted above it has split the façade down the whole of one side, triumphing over the rock.[5]

From these tombs the road goes down to a valley, the far side of which is closed in by another range of wooded cliffs, the Poggio Stanziale, itself profuse with tombs. Here there are many like those to be found immediately below the village, archaic sepulchres of the sixth century carved into the rock with narrowing moulded façades and cornices projecting or receding, some of them topped with pedestals intended perhaps for a figure or a cippus. But there are others too, shaped almost in the round rather than as mere façades. One of these has a rounded roof with projecting beams like the roofs of Villanovan hut-urns. Another has a portico flanked by pilasters and surmounted by a corniced pediment. And on the pediment of yet another, a large half-obliterated head stands out in high relief above a portico with a diamond-coffered ceiling.

But the two most imposing tombs on Poggio Stanziale are the monumental temple-façades, close to each other, of the *Tomba Ildebranda* and the *Grotta Pola*. These are late tombs conceived on a large scale in the shape of the porticoes of Italic temples. The

13 THE TOMB OF THE TRICLINIUM. 470 B.C. Tarquinia.
Flute-player among trees and birds (*pp. 71–72*).

Above: 14a SARCOPHAGUS: "L'Uomo con Cerviatta". Third century. Tarquinia. Hellenistic battle scene in relief (*p. 61*).
Below: 14b THE TOMB OF THE PAINTED RELIEFS (Tomba Bella). Fourth to third centuries. Cerveteri (*pp. 155–6*).

Tomba Ildebranda retains its portico, much ruined, with the remains of a number of huge columns in two rows, two of them intact, the others mere stumps. They support what was once a great double architrave with a coffered ceiling, carrying a lower and an upper frieze, fragments of which remain. The columns are fluted, with capitals that incorporate the acanthus leaf around what looks like a human head, and culminates in a ramshead scroll. They stand upon a high base, and the entrances to the tomb-chambers lie in the cliff, the room on the right having an intricate coffered ceiling.

Close to it and forming part of what must once have been an imposing group of monuments occupying the whole of the cliff-side, is the Grotta Pola, of similar structure and dimensions, though it seems as though the portico consisted in this case of four columns with an internal pilaster at each end. One column only, supporting the end of the pediment and a square pilaster behind it remain, both fluted, with capitals on the pattern of the Ildebranda tomb; and the rectangular recess of the portico, cut deep into the rock, bears traces of stucco on its surface and even of colouring.

This necropolis then is among the most interesting in Etruria. For nowhere, as Dennis pointed out, "are the mouldings so singular and varied", or the façades laid out to quite such con-centrated effect.[6] Though in common with Norchia and Castel D'Asso it seems not to have exploited the tumulus form at all, in every other respect—in the variety and inventiveness of its archi-tectural forms—Sovana represents yet another impressive cele-bration of the Etruscan spirit, symbolizing their reconciliation of the frontiers of life and death, a resolution for the dilemma by which "everything that is generated must be prepared to face its painful dissolution".[7]

FALERII VETERES

THE SITE OF the Etruscan city of Falerii Veteres, today occupied by the small town of Città Castellana, lies at a distance of thirty miles from Rome, off the Via Flaminia. Its territory, bordered to the west and north by Veii, Tarquinii and Volsinii, by the wooded Cimini mountains and the line of the Cassia, once stretched from Capena to just short of Orte, with the Tiber forming a natural boundary to the east. This is an area small but concentrated, rich in contrasts. It takes in desolate brooding stretches of the Campagna, its cleft green concealing small villages like Calcata and Faleria to the west—while on the Tiber side the hills are softer and more sensuous, dominated by the massive ridged form of Monte Soratte, rising from the landscape in an austerely beautiful triumph of stone over the low flowing contours. Soratte indeed is visible for miles—sometimes black against the sun, or blue-hazed, or set harsh against the bone-white tips of the Sabines in the distance—forming an essential backdrop to the setting of Città.

The town itself, clustering above the reddish cliffs of its ravines, is prosperous enough. It boasts a great Sangallo fortress, one or two ancient decaying churches and a beautiful thirteenth-century Cosmatesque portico to its vacuously restored Cathedral. Its most extraordinary features are its dramatic setting and the nineteenth-century Ponte Clementino that spans the 250-foot deep ravine between the old town and its extension, which Dennis judged "worthy of the magnificence of Imperial Rome"—combining "with the ravine, the town on its verge, the distant Campagna, Soratte, and the Apennines to form one of the choicest unions of nature and art to be found in the whole of the Campagna".[1]

More to the point, there are many traces here of the ancient city—sections of tufo wall at the edge of the cliffs, roads cut in the rock with gutters sunk beside them, and the mouths of several sewers such as are to be found upon many other Etruscan sites—

visible in the rock-face, with half-obliterated tombs on either side.

Most interesting of all, however, are the cliffs below the town, where the Ponte Terrano crosses the ravine of the Rio Maggiore. For they are pierced in every direction with sepulchral niches and the doorways to tombs—tombs with little antechambers and spacious sepulchres supported by central pillars or divided into two, with recesses or niches for urns and tiers of benches for the bodies, with cornices carved in relief, with little external vestibules and plain doorways. These are linked by paths and steps from level to level, and the effect is that of a vast planned necropolis.

Nor is this all. The ravines and heights around Città are rich with Etruscan remains. The foundations of five temples have been located, together with a mass of material from their façades, dating from the sixth century onward, and other cemeteries and groups of tombs lie hidden away along the great glens. In addition, the contents of the cemeteries of Monterano and Celle have revealed important evidence of the early artistic culture of the Faliscans—who from the eighth to the sixth centuries produced a variety of impasto pottery of a very high quality and often of startling beauty. The colour of the clay is brown or grey or red, and the shapes are strikingly original, particularly of the early thin-walled kantharoi and the tall incense bowls. But it is the vivacity and subtlety of the decorations incised upon these vases, dishes, bowls and cups that gives them their real distinction. There are many kinds of abstract geometric design, forming patterns of exotic plants; but most memorable of all are the high-stepping, long-legged horses that adorn small and large forms alike. These pieces are uniquely associated with Falerii as the beautiful products of a people poor, even in the orientalizing period, in natural resources, but using those resources vividly and creatively, till able to expand through direct contact with the great coastal cities and therefore obtain other materials.[2]

Finally, three miles north of Città Castellana, close to Corchiano (another important Faliscan town) lie the monumental walls of the Etrusco-Roman city of Falerii Novi, with fifty of its towers and two beautiful arched gateways still standing, built in the third century, sometime after 241 B.C. when the Romans conquered Falerii and drove its people into the plain.[3] And to the south, beyond the mediaeval villages of Faleria and Calcata decaying on their tufo cliffs, is the hill of Narce, site of an unknown Faliscan city, where a vast necropolis brought to light a large and rich collection of seventh- and sixth-century Faliscan objects in bronze, impasto and bucchero, including many richly decorated pieces of high quality.

All this indicates a culture of considerable interest. But not much is known about the origins of the Faliscan people. They probably had close ties at some time or another with the Sabines and the Umbrians. They may even have been a Latin-speaking people, as certain inscriptions with mixed Latin and Etruscan elements in them seem to suggest, though this is not very likely.[4] Their geographical position (with the Tiber as a dividing line) must early have tended to set them apart anyway from their Eastern neighbours and bring about some measure of independence. And with the rise of the great Etruscan cities it was inevitable that they should have turned for cultural sustenance towards coastal Etruria. By the beginning of the sixth century, if not before, Falerii Veteres had established itself as an important Etruscan city, invigorated by Mediterranean influences coming through from the coast, as we can tell from the evidence of the large and small temples found on the Vignale plateau just north of Città, with many fragments belonging to the first, Ionian, phase of the three classifiable phases of Faliscan temple decoration.[5] From this point onward, Falerii was to prosper, opulent and assured, for at least three centuries, right up to the time of its defeat, as excavation has abundantly proved—for apart from the temple sculptures and facing decorations in terracotta that survive from one or other of the five known temples throughout this period, there is much other material, including a whole range of distinctively Faliscan vases produced from local workshops in richly decorative not to say sumptuous variants of Classical and Hellenistic models. The fifth-century temple terracottas (of antefixes, standing figures, battle scenes) are particularly vigorous, many still with their polychrome colouring on them; and the upper section of a life-size nude Apollo from the end of the fourth century is remarkable for the suppleness and control of the modelling and again the vigour with which a predominating Hellenistic style (based on Lysippus and Scopas) is interpreted at a time when elsewhere in Etruria the artistic impulse had already begun to stagnate. This Apollo is one among a number of excellent pieces from the Scasato temple. And even the third-century fragments suggest that, before their brutal suppression by the Romans, the Faliscans were not played out, even in decline.

As for their vases, among the most justly celebrated of these is the large fourth-century red-figure krater in the Villa Giulia representing the abduction of Cephalus by Aurora and of Oreithyia (surprised in her bath) by Boreas. Aurora is seen rising out of the sea with her prize, in a chariot drawn by four horses, with sea animals below and a flight of birds above. There is a frieze of bulls and griffins round the neck, while four delicately observed deers'-heads project from the shoulders. It is a beautifully composed work, the opulence and rhetoric of the prevailing style lightened by the restraint and skill with which the figures are drawn and placed, and by the balance of the vase-form itself. While many of these large Faliscan kraters, stamnoi and oinochoi may, like their Apulian and Campanian counterparts, seem overcrowded and coarsely drawn, there are nevertheless others—finely judged and executed, like the Aurora krater—which achieve a perfect equilibrium.

From the fifth century onward, Falerii fought periodic wars against the Romans, which probably intensified after the defeat of Veii in 396. And with one Etruscan city after another falling to the enemy, the Faliscans must have found themselves in an increasingly dangerous and impossible position. Defeat, in other words, was bound to come; and when in 241 it did, Falerii was to be overwhelmed and razed to the ground, bringing the Faliscan culture with it to a sudden violent end. It had been smashed, uprooted, neutralized, superseded by the Romans.[6] Though the walls of Falerii Novi and the lovely curve of its arched gateway would seem to suggest otherwise, these are in actual fact the walls of a dependent city ruled by alien laws and an alien spirit, symbolizing the triumph of the politics of Rome, not simply as a military power but also in terms of cultural persuasion.

And so Falerii Veteres was to lie for centuries in ruins, an un-inhabited site, its temples abandoned, its walls crumbling, its streets overgrown—till in the eighth century A.D. the people of Falerii Novi, driven back to it again from their vulnerable position on the plain, came to build over it the first dwelling-places of the town we know today as Città Castellana.

THE CHIUSIAN WORLD

IT TAKES TWO or three hours to drive from Rome to Chiusi by the Autostrada del Sole. The transitions are rapid, effortlessly accomplished. Very soon, Rome begins to seem a long way off. Its campagna, uninhabited and unkempt, sapped and stricken by centuries of ruinous squabbling and neglect, is in another world. Coming off the Autostrada close to Chiusi, one approaches the small town past slopes of rich tilled earth, past terraces of olives, past oaks and cypresses, and vines heavy with the dark purple of the Chiana grape. A square grey Lungobardo tower rises out of a mass of trees on the crown of a hill, and then the road moves upward to reveal a wide flat fertile valley spread out below.

At a glance, there is little about the town to give one any sense of its links with the Etruscan past, with Chamars, the city of the legendary Lucumon, Lars Porsenna. Nevertheless, Chiusi is rich with hints and images from that past. It is a beautiful little town, poised above the Chiana valley on the borders of Umbria and Tuscany. Its Cathedral dates back to the sixth century A.D., and takes the Roman basilican form, with pillars and capitals salvaged from the ruins of the old (Romanized) city, and lovely narrow arches that remind one of the arches of Santa Sabina in Rome. The houses, the little piazzas, the gardens, public and private, the narrow streets, the old walls out of which the greens of trees and vines and the façades of houses rise, the Campanile built of great quadrangular blocks above an Etrusco-Roman pool off the Cathedral square, the two mediaeval towers on the summit of the arx, all serve to express the prevailing intimacy and charm of Chiusi. It is an instinct, perhaps. There is the same pride and care about the town that keeps the hillslopes ordered and fertile.

It is of course mainly in the tombs hidden away among the hills, and in the museum that stands to one side of the Duomo, that the Etruscan Chiusi survives. An astonishing collection of funerary ornaments and images has been gathered here to put us into intimate contact with the vivid hieratic forms of Chiusian art, covering seven centuries of continuous activity from the ninth century to the Hellenistic age. But the town itself, in many details as in its very setting, reflects and refers to these ancient roots. Even as one wanders round one finds them, resonances trapped in stone that pervade the atmosphere like a strange remote music, like voices coming from a long way off. Along the pathways of the Public Gardens, laid out on the tip of the hillside overlooking the great flat valley, one comes across a furred cippus here, the half-obliterated form of a sixth-century lion (its faceless head thrust forward) there; a sarcophagus with fish-tailed creatures carved upon it at the end of a long straight path under a cypress; two ancient stone scrolls on either side of a short flight of steps; an alabaster urn with the patera carved upon it between two crescents; a Doric capital in nenfro; everywhere among the shrubs and trees the fragments of symbolic forms and images in which a world comes haltingly and discontinuously to speech. And looking down from the wall one can visualize the ancient setting of the city. For where the flat green floor of the valley stretches away between the low hills on the near side and those which rise in gentle slopes on the other, are the topographical outlines of what was once a great lake—above the shores of which and along the headlands of which Chamars is said to have stretched, its buildings mirrored in the water. This lake dried up in the Middle Ages, leaving swamp and poisonous marshland to decimate the town, until the draining of the valley in the last century. All that is left now is the small lake of Chiusi out of sight beyond the town, fed by the Chiana from its source in the Arno; and the lush green of the fields. But it must have been a magnificent sight for the people of Porsenna's city, looking down from this same spot on the heights 2,500 years ago.

A little below the gardens and a little further round one comes upon a tiny square, the Piazza Cesare Battisti, shaded in October by the yellowing leaves of its planes, where a great bluish-veined porphyry column stands, topped by another of those strangely assertive almost faceless lions. Here one looks out and down towards the long finger of a hill dark with the verticals of cypresses where the modern cemetery lies, and beyond it round a hidden contour the famous fifth-century *Casuccini Tomb of the Charioteers*. In the morning, early, a thick white mist often completely obliterates the Chiana floor, and out of it the hills emerge dark and weightless, spiked with cypress. It stays until the autumn sun has risen high enough to disperse it, leaving Chiusi isolated above an ethereal world, as though floating in a lake of cloud. Up at the highest point of the *arx*, where on a spur the two mediaeval towers rise, the Piazza Vittorio Veneto looks out upon a teeming hill that rises directly from the deep hollow below, a hill crowned by the almost indistinguishable bump of a tumulus, out of which a tall cypress thrusts like a phallic cippus to define the exact position of the so-called *Tomb of the Monkey*. From the parapet of the Piazza early in the morning, you can see the mist flooding the valley, outlining and isolating the hill, lapping against it, silhouetting the two towers and their trees. And here, if anywhere in Chiusi—even as you watch the mist dispersing very slowly under the warmth of the sun, or walk among the fragments of column and capital, the lions and the urns—you have the sense of the mythic past of the Etruscans, remembering Livy perhaps and his account of Porsenna's preparations for the siege of Rome.

There is a famous episode from Livy recorded in a Veronese fresco at the Castello Colleone at Thieni. It depicts an aged, richly dressed Porsenna receiving the young Roman nobleman Caius Mucius, who had attempted to assassinate him. Mucius had come to rid Rome of the enemy at his city's gates, but had stabbed the king's secretary by mistake. Having been dragged before the king, he had fearlessly revealed his intention, and to prove how little a man values his life when the honour of his race is at stake, had thrust his right hand into the fire and let it burn. The king, astonished and impressed, had set Mucius free, "because you have dared to be a worse enemy to yourself than to me". After this, Livy cannot resist recounting another little story concerning the nobility of Porsenna, which has much the same tone—about a young female hostage called Cloelia, who escaped from the Etruscans at great hazard and swam off across the Tiber. Porsenna's anger at having lost her soon gave way to admiration of her courage. Insisting she should be returned, he nevertheless made it clear that if the Romans surrendered her, he would himself voluntarily hand her back safe and sound to her family. When the Romans, trusting his word, duly delivered the girl, Porsenna kept his promise and even publicly praised her for her exploit.[1]

Such stories are no part of history. They record no facts. They are records of old myths handed down perhaps through generations. They tend to flatter the Romans. Yet Livy—the Roman, the Augustan, the partisan—also treats the Etruscans with respect, and remembers Porsenna, King of Chamars, "rex Etruriae", as a man of nobility and dignity. He may have been writing as an artist moved by the legends and traditions of prehistory rather than as a historian. This makes him scientifically unacceptable, since history has to base its findings upon fact. But it does not invalidate his record, which remains a symbolic gesture to the realities of a past not then recorded as historical fact—even as the images remain that lie scattered about Chiusi.

At every turn of a street one comes across the physical signs and proofs of a prehistoric past, a specifically Etruscan presence—even sunk into the wall of a house or to be glimpsed through the wrought-iron gates of a private garden. And all around, you have the atmosphere, the rich quiet of the Tuscan landscape out of which the echoes come—which you may or may not feel, and may or may not accept, but which are all the same obscurely there, as links to the buried realities of Etruria and to the evidence the earth has yielded in confirmation of a people's claim to have existed here among these hills, even if not in the history books.

The museum displays its evidence as a concentrated visual record that brings us as close as we shall ever come to the actualities of Ancient Chiusi. In stone, in terracotta, bronze or clay, these objects offer an eloquence far more representative than many a document of the life of a people. And the first thing that strikes one on entering the museum is the idiosyncratic expressiveness of so many of the early cinerary urns. Their impact is that of a symbolizing vision of great originality, reflecting the unique con-

tribution that Chiusi has to make to the art of the Etruscan world.
To start with, the earliest cinerary urns (from ninth- and eighth-
century burial-pits) are either roughly carved tufo bowls with lids,
sometimes found cached within a huge brown oil-vat, or large
impasto urns with incised geometric patterns on them of the
familiar Villanovan type. But these urns often have attached to
their sides a funeral mask, first in terracotta and later in bronze—
elongated, severe, reminding one of the tight-stretched face of that
famous hammered gold death-mask from Mycenae. There is no
counterpart to these masks anywhere else in Etruria, and they lead
to a startling innovation incorporated into the earliest seventh-
century urns, known as Canope. For with them, the urn becomes
a body, a symbol of the body perhaps of the dead person, male or
female, and the lid itself a head—a head rigidly schematic and
taut, fiercely dignified, fixed as if in death, or shut into its own
trance-like inner world. This is indeed a bold and powerful
innovation, for by it, at one stroke, pottery has become sculpture.
and though these masks are not large in scale they have a monumental dignity and stature of their own, a potent solemnity, grave
and intent, with something of the stern fixed expressiveness of
African death-masks. Moreover, each of them has features that
distinguish and in some sense particularize. Though in the earliest
examples there is a kind of elevated hieratic simplicity about the
faces and forms, even here they are differentiated in expression and
in shape, in the plastic moulding of the features—usually tight-
lipped, with shut eyes, implying a portrait. Particularly impressive among these is a small round hairless female head with
projecting circles for ears, from which hang coiled gold earrings.
The clay urn is plain except for the two tiny protruding swellings of
the breasts and—starting wing-like from the shoulders of the urn
—the raised curves of the arms, ending with schematic hands, the
fingers of the hands extended across the belly. Finally there are
two little angled supports attached to the base representing the
feet. The effect, using only these primitive means, is astonishing
—tautly expressive, alert and concentrated, symbolic of the
person, a container and a guardian of the spirit of the dead.

Another head, this time of a man, stands upon a bronze winged throne studded with mundum-like circles and geometric patterns interspersed with winged lions in the orientalizing style. The urn itself is of bronze, with small serpent-shaped handles, and above it in terracotta the head rises—sharp-nosed, tight-lipped, his eyes shut, his chin thrust out, his hair defined by deep scored lines, flat to the head and coming low down to the neck behind the ears like a headdress. In expression he seems held in, proudly concentrating, rigid, internally alert, as if listening to voices, in fierce meditation, forbidding and austere.

And then come the Canopic urns of the sixth century. They have the same taut simplicity, but now some of them have their eyes open, rigidly staring, and they have little figurines attached to the shoulder of the urn, surrounding the head. On one speci-men, these standing images take the form of priestesses draped in high copes and long gowns, Ionian in style, acting as guardians to the dead man whose head rises above them. And there are two or three memorable examples at Chiusi depicting the female, which extend the canopic idea to include the whole body, standing among its encircling figurines. The figures, almost as large as the urn, have closed eyes, but their faces are softer, and the solemnity of their meditation tenderer than before, invested with a poignant stillness and poise. They are also ceremonially dressed in cloak and gown, with plaited hair. One, in a square-patterned dress reaching to just above the ankles, has one arm bent across her waist, the other lifted towards the face, its little spread hand gently touching the chin. She is surrounded on an upper rim by a circle of ten little human figures, arms crossed at the chest, and below that by screeching long-necked griffin-heads between more figures—protective monsters functioning in the same way as the gorgon heads of temple pediments, to keep away those who might come to despoil. Another has one hand delicately touching her breast, and is guarded by four griffin-heads, overtly phallic, with pendent testicle-jowls. She, like her companion, stands held in a trance fo contemplation, quiet and still amid the livid open-beaked creatures that surround her.

After these pieces—and there are many others in other museums throughout the world—we come to the monumental stone figures that once guarded the entrances to sixth-century tombs in the vicinity. They too stand out as distinctively Chiusian, though they have their affinity with the nenfro sculptures of Vulci, those in sandstone from Vetulonia and the massive heads of Orvieto. They take the form of fabulous animals such as the sphinx and the winged lion; of warriors or of goddesses. A rather plump-faced sphinx at Chiusi, with large pupil-less eyes and headdress falling to the shoulders, sits long-legged, almost 3 feet in height, its fern-like wings curling round behind. It is a powerful creature, with a genial and somewhat vacuous expression. But the Xoanon in sandstone, representing an Etruscan divinity, is among the most beautiful things in the museum. Her face is moulded to an expression of sensuous tenderness by means of the large almond-shaped eyes, the full downward-parted lips, the curve of cheeks and chin around the mouth; and everything about her—the gown she wears, the long plaits that fall from her braided headdress, the hands gently crossed and touching at the chest—is in harmony with this. There is a head in the Cortona Museum which is close in style and spirit to the Chiusian goddess, though here the slightly open mouth does not turn downward and conveys a more active and expectant mood. Another female head at Chiusi, wearing a similar kind of headdress with long braids, is much more severe in expression, less giving, the lips down-turned but pursed within an extraordinarily wide face and skull, the eyes very wide apart, the whole head conveying a sense of mingled gentleness and tenacity, pride and aloofness.

These creatures take their places symbolically between the frontiers of life and death. Behind them lies an unknown universe. They seem to be gazing out upon the world of the living with something of the knowledge of the mystery of that other world in their faces—inhabiting a thin line between reality and reality which may not be crossed, symbolizing the tragic dilemma of man in his endless search for community, the trance of being.

The museum has a large collection of seventh- and sixth-century bucchero, of the thin-walled and the later thicker type decorated with figures in relief that move around the body of the vase, images of the play of life within the ritualized circle of life.

This latter type predominates as a distinctively Chiusian form. To take only one example—an amphora crowned with a bull's head. It has two narrow bands divided by a raised cordon at the neck and shoulder and a frieze-like processional scene on the body of the vase. The neck is decorated with four flower-petal circles, the mundum image, below which run the heads of leonine beasts, their features drawn with incised lines on the black; and the main scene is of four bulls, each held by the left horn and the left hoof by a little striding nude human figure. Above, the bull's head has huge eyes, long curving eyebrows, pointed ears, and a kind of head-band between the horns . . . half-humanized yet accurately observed as an animal form.

Contemporary with the later bucchero and succeeding them into the fifth century, are the Etruscan painted vases based upon Attic black-figure with Ionian elements, richly individualized and painted with a peculiar spontaneity and vigour of line, of which there are two magnificent examples in the museum. Not that in the art of vase-painting the Etruscans could have excelled the Greeks. They probably would not even have wanted to. But their own pieces carry the delight of the maker on them, and as in one or two instances here at Chiusi, to quote Raymond Bloch, "the modifications made by the Etruscan artist in the ornamental motifs adopted from classical painting in Greece amount to a greater expressive intensity . . . closely related to the contemporary frescoes in tombs".[2]

Bronzes of all kinds were made at Chiusi too—among which the elongated votive warriors and priests common to the whole of the Val di Chiana and poised on their long legs like dancers are pre-eminent. And the museum has a large circular washing-bowl, supported by four claw-footed gorgon figures, which is chiefly notable for the vivacity of the rhythmic dance-like postures of the seven male and female figures ranged around the rim.

Nothing in the museum, however, is more expressive or more eloquent of the skill and distinction of Chiusian art than the collection of sixth- and fifth-century base-reliefs carved upon sandstone ash-chests and funeral cippi which is assembled here. These pieces, blending Attic and Ionian elements into a style completely

Etruscan in feeling and in theme, are distinguished for the exquisite clarity of the carving, the sensuous flowing rhythms of the outlines, and the gaiety and delight with which the great variety of figures depicted respond to the ritual music of the dance and the feast. Here the spirits of Apollo and Dionysus combine, for harmony and gaiety are the keynotes of these beautiful reliefs. The faces of dancers and feasters (always in profile) turn smiling intimately to their neighbours. The bodies move lightly and fluently in the rhythms of dance, or lie reclining at ease on their couches. And the arms raised in ritual greeting—hands turned back at the wrist or bent forward from a vertical forearm, the fingertips curved or curling, the whole hand open flat and stretching across to contact, acknowledging the gifts of friendship, indicating welcome and response, grasping the circlet, the egg, the wine-cup—link person to person in a vivid ceremonial enactment of the delight of contact and interchange.

The ash-chests are rather small, often no more than 18 inches long and 12 inches high. Notable among them is a relief of five female dancers dressed in long clinging gowns with cloaks falling behind and pointed boots, hair covered by a close-fitting cap. The rippling flow of movement is indicated by the modelling of the limbs under the gowns as the dancers raise their knees in the swift steps of the dance, turning away or towards each other, heads twisted in the opposite direction to the bodies, one arm raised vertically, the other horizontal, the hands curled sharply back. Each of the little figures is ecstatically intent, caught in the trance of the music.

In contrast, another relief depicts a solemn slow-moving ceremonial procession—three couples of tall, long-gowned female votaries carrying their raised offerings, led and followed by a priest. And then, among the many banqueting scenes, one particularly gay and crowded relief stands out, for its taut placing and control of the forms within a very limited space, and again for that touching sense of recognition which everyone and everything in the scene shares. Two couples are reclining on high couches with carved legs. A naked servant stands waiting to one side. Between the two couches a man in a long gown is playing the double flute. There is a low table laid with plates and cups before each couch, under which a goose and a dog lie, the dog chewing a bone. Behind on the wall hang four circlets. And while each of the women holds a circlet in her left hand, the men (legs crossed) hold fertility offerings. One of the women has turned her head towards the flute-player, even as her companion has towards the servant. But the other couple are turned to one another attentively, the woman raising her hand as if to emphasize something she is saying. The whole scene teems with incident, and is invested with a sense of quick conviviality and sexual pleasure. But all the pieces celebrate such community—the touch, the look, the gesture of sexual recognition. And this has its most positive expression in a beautiful fragment of a man and woman on a couch—she leaning back, eyes closed, he leaning towards her, almost touching. They both seem held under the spell of contact and sexual recognition, their singleness and separateness forgotten in the acclamation of the moment. As a symbol of the lyrical intensity of passion, of the rapt immediacy of the moment of being, "the holy spectral shiver",[3] as Pepys once vividly put it, this little scene is itself a sheer enchantment and an acclamation of the essences of human love.

The bases to columns and to funerary cippi present scenes similar to those on the ash-chests, though they tend to be mostly processional. On one base a pair of winged sphinxes sit facing one another, their paws crossed in greeting. On another, the frieze of figures moves below a cornice decorated at the corners with winged lions, between which four female beasts with parted legs form an overtly sexual symbol. Finally, there is a sixth-century sarcophagus relief, 6 feet in length, the only one among the ash-chests, which has seven reclining male figures on it and a little nude servant refilling wine-cups from a jar. The long narrow frieze is bound together by the rhythmic pattern set up by the figures themselves and the gestures of greeting that link them one to the other in the characteristic mood of intimacy and shared delight.

Later, from the beginning of the fourth century onward, the ash-chests, in alabaster and stone, become rather massive, with

Above: 15a THE BRIDGE OVER THE RIVER FIORA AT VULCI. Fourth century (?). Repaired and reinforced by the Romans, and again in the Middle Ages, when the castle was built on the frontier between Lazio and Tuscany (*p. 180*).

Below: 15b TUSCANIAN SARCOPHAGUS. Second century. Tuscania. In terracotta, representing a woman, the head a portrait (*pp. 90–91*).

16 CINERARY URN. Second century. Volterra. Such foreshortened figures are characteristic of Volterran and Chiusian urns. The scene depicts the Journey of the Dead, as on many other Volterran urns (*p. 247*).

violent battle-scenes from Greek mythology carved in deep relief on the chest and curiously telescoped figures (often richly adorned and gowned, some of them with their polychrome colours still clinging to them) reclining on the lids. These are similar to the ash-chests produced in such numbers at Volterra. Their vigour is conveyed by peculiar (almost Gothic) distortion—whether the figures are engaged in combat or slumped back in their places on the lids. In them, all delicacy, all that delight in the celebration of shared interest, all that seriousness and awe in the act of life, has gone, and pathos triumphs. The superb flowing rhythms of outline have become heavy, turbulent. A kind of Gothic weight of suffering takes over. Life still breathes, the Etruscan vitality is still somewhere there, but war and devastation have become the obsessional themes and ecstasy is a thing of the past.

Of the hundreds of Chiusian tombs that have been opened, few are now fit to visit. But these few include two important painted tombs of the fifth century—the *Tomb of the Monkey* and the *Casuccini Tomb*. The first of these may be compared to tombs contemporary with it at Tarquinia, and especially to the upper fresco of the Tomba delle Bighe, both in theme and in execution, though it is probably a little later in date. In the central room (off which three small chambers lead) a woman under a parasol, representing the dead owner of the tomb, watches a number of athletic contests being enacted in her honour. Before her, a girl dances to a small flute-player wearing a false beard. On the far left, a young man seems in the act of vaulting from one of a pair of horses being driven past. Next to him, a pair of nude wrestlers are being judged by an intent and dignified referee, and one of the two athletes is about to be thrown to the ground. Watching them under the painted door lintel a small monkey sits chained upon a leafy branch. And on the other side of the door, a naked servant boy looks back at the wrestlers. In his interest he ignores the tall javelin thrower who tests the weight of his javelin as he waits and the two nude boxers (their clothes on a stool between them) clearly engrossed in the ancient game of Morra as they too wait.[4]

The figures are swiftly and observantly drawn, especially in the right-hand frieze. The two Morra-players have just opened their fists after calling out the number—one thrust forward, the other drawing back in surprise, oblivious of the wrestling match. But the young javelin thrower has his head turned, like the servant boy, to watch, and his face registers the quick delight of youth as much in his own prowess as in the action of the near-by contest. He and all the actors in the scene exude confidence. Though simply, even in a sense crudely drawn, they convey something of the energy, the glow and the vigour of living creatures caught in the pride of health.

The Casuccini Tomb is more distinguished for its architecture and the decorative scheme in general than for its paintings, which are much inferior to those of the other tomb—though the three charioteers with their pairs of blue and red horses are effective enough. It is set under the brow of a hill rich with dark Chiana vines, and the central chamber is entered up a long *dromos* passage through a door made of two great slabs of travertine that swing outward. This chamber has three rooms leading off it, also painted, with benches for the urns, and its mouldings are painted in stripes of red and blue, the friezes of paintings being high up and narrow. The doorways lean inward as they rise, and have painted Doric surrounds, and the elaborate coffered ceiling slants from a thick central beam.

There are a few other later tombs to be seen at Chiusi, among them one or two (like the *Tomb of the Grand Duke*) constructed with interlocking travertine blocks whose special feature is the barrel vaulting of the central chamber. Besides these, the tumuli to a number of now ruined early tombs are visible in the hills around the town. But as for the most sensational of all Chiusian tombs, the vast tumulus of Porsenna described by Pliny in his report of an account by Varro from the first century B.C., no trace of that remains anywhere.[5]

It is not vastness, anyway, one is likely to associate with Chiusi. Pyramid upon pyramid though the Porsenna tomb may have been, such a monument seems grossly out of scale with both the present Chiusi and its Etruscan remains. For nothing is inflated here. The Etruscans do not boast or swagger. Out of the silence, for three or four centuries, their art celebrates the tragic essences of life and its intangible gifts. For three or four centuries, from those little thin-lipped canopic votives of hope and pride staring out of the dark to the dancers and banqueters enacting on the edge of darkness the delight of recognition, the Etruscans of Chiusi were able to maintain their place in the world, to hold themselves clear of the abyss. And even afterwards, even with the world closing in around them, with the atmosphere darkening and their confidence ebbing away, they managed to carry on, into the Hellenistic era—lessened perhaps, constrained and restive and finally resigned, but still vigorous, as the violently active scenes on ash-chests demonstrate. But then here the figures on the lids seem to grow more and more passive, apathetic, slumped, and all joyousness, all desire to get up on their feet even—let alone dance —seems gone, and there is only the immobile dreamer left, dreaming of life, unable any longer to act or to be, robbed of the present, thinking of the past, or of the amorphous unborn future perhaps.

VETULONIA

VETULONIA IS SITUATED among the hills that rise out of the Grosseto plain, south-east of Populonia. The road winds up to it between slopes of ancient olives and fruit trees, rising gradually to reveal the flat Maremma map-like below. Till suddenly the tower of the village church comes into view, and the grey stone walls appear on a rounded crest. It is a poor village and an ancient village, its mediaeval houses built of lichened grey stone, the stone of the hills. Around it the fields drop away below the parapet of the main square in tilting curves, dipping through a series of hills and spurs to the distant sea plain. There is about the very nature of its position a sense of hiatus—high, suspended, as if at the crest of a stilled wave—the village grey, gnarled and hard as old trees from which the sap has begun to drain away.

Until 1887 this tiny community had been known as Colonna di Buriano. It was given its present name after excavation in the 1880s of an exceptionally important necropolis among the hills below the village, which established the area beyond doubt as the site of Vetl or Vetulonia, one of the earliest and greatest among the cities of Northern Etruria.[1] For centuries before this the remains of the cyclopean walls must have offered their hint of significance to the chance visitor—massive dark-grey blocks exposed below the mediaeval walls to which they served as foundations, rooted on the high eastern spur of the village, and perhaps invested with legendary significance by the local people, as isolated survivals from an immemorial past. But with the discovery of the Pietrera Tomb, foremost among the hundreds that the necropolis yielded, and the extensive remains of Roman buildings and roads immediately below the walls of the village, suddenly the ancient stones, rescued from oblivion, could take their place again, and be renamed, even as the village built above them.

For the archaeologists this discovery was an event of the greatest importance. For the Vetulonian tombs have yielded unique and exciting material, "covering the most extraordinary period of the nation's existence, before the powerful influence of artistic forms imported from Greece had redirected the creative spirit of the people",[2] and centuries before subjection to the military democracy of Rome had reduced them to servitude.

Little is known of the history of Vetulonia. That it was a maritime city with its own port has been proved by numerous Vetulonian coins found on the Roman site embossed with marine symbols (the trident and the dolphin) and by the personification of the *Vetulonienses*, on the throne of a statue to Claudius, as a young man carrying a rudder on his shoulder. Dionysus of Halicarnasus recorded the help given by the people of the city in his struggle against Tarquinius Priscus, and Silius Italicus, a Roman poet of the first century A.D., wrote (in his epic "Punica") how the Romans appropriated as their symbols of power the Vetulonian Lictor's hatchet with fasces, the ivory curule chair, the purple-bordered toga and the battle trumpet. Apart from these and a few others, there are topographical references to Vetulonia's position by Ptolemy and Pliny, and certain mediaeval documents alluding to a "podium de Vitolonia" and a "castellum de Vitulonnio". But the archaeological evidence attests, more firmly, to the existence of a vigorous cultural life on the site from the end of the eighth century to the end of the sixth. And this was succeeded by a period of unaccountable decline, due perhaps to the terrorist harrying of the Gauls and lasting till the third century—when, under Roman domination, Vetulonia again became a centre of some importance because of its convenient position close to the great Aurelia highway. Finally, in the first years of the Christian era, it seems to have been abandoned and left to settle gradually into the earth. From which time, until the last century, all traces of it were lost except for that obscure "castellum", its ruins eventually built over by the stones of the village of Colonna.

Impossible though it is to define precisely the Vetulonian territory, we can say with certainty that it lay between Populonia to the north and Roselle (another important Etruscan city almost visible from the village) to the south. It probably included along its coastline the Gulf of Follonica that looks directly out upon Elba, and what is now the little fishing port of Castiglione della Pescaia; and stretched inland across the plain to the hills around Roccastrada and Massa Maritiima as far as Monte Alto and Monte Quoio. Its prosperity during the seventh and sixth centuries would have come from the mineral deposits of Elba and the inland hills, in a sharing of resources with Populonia and Roselle, both of which rose to prominence and fame at the same time.

Almost all the evidence of Vetulonia's growth and prosperity comes from the tombs themselves, but the great sixth-century polygonal blocks are still there to define the eastern boundary of the ancient city's walls, the platform of which must once have been the site of the *arx* of the acropolis. The necropolis lies below, scattered over a vast area among the wooded hills that overlook the inland plain. On the hillocks closest to the city lie the Villa-novan cemeteries, mostly on this eastern, though also on the western or seaward, side. Here are the stone-lined pit-tombs sealed with stone slabs often in the form of shields, containing biconical cinerary urns and hut urns in impasto with complex geometric patterns incised upon them. Many of these urns, together with the intimate ornaments and implements in bronze and paste-glass deposited with them are to be seen in the Vetulonian rooms of the Archaeological Museum in Florence. Their quantity, richness and diversity, and the high quality of the crafts-manship that went into the making of even the smallest object indicates a culture among the earlier Italic inhabitants already flexible and vigorous enough to convey an articulate formulation of attitude and feeling towards life and death. Wherever we find such evidence (and it is to be found in all the cities of Etruria) we find it linked almost inseparably to the customs and the rites of that other people who came among them from abroad, the people of the patrician Etruscan race, as if those customs and rites were an organic consequence of an invigorating influence. In the trans-formation of the culture that came about early in the seventh century, at least, there is no sign of violent suppression or absorp-tion, but only of continuity and of peaceable fusion, a sudden concentration and expansion of energy, as of a people suddenly awakening to its potentiality.

In clear confirmation of this, the seventh- and sixth-century tombs which have put Vetulonia back on the map are to be found lower down the slopes or protuberances of the same hills that contain the Villanovan tombs, which had been left intact. A people's customs, in other words, do not have to be stamped out to enable their successors, if that is what the Etruscans were, to assume control. They can be respected and absorbed and encouraged to play their own creative part in the pattern of life. By the middle of the seventh century, at any rate, a sudden and astonishing development had occurred, as in other cities. Suddenly, encircling the ancient Villanovan tombs, all around them in the hills, emerged the great circular tumulus tombs of the Vetulonian city-culture. The earliest ones were of modest proportions, their quadrangular or circular rooms constructed (as all of them are on this site) in stone, culminating in a kind of cupola, and containing rich funerary trappings in bronze, gold and silver of the orientalizing style common to the whole of Etruria.

Most of these tombs are shut now, but there are two along the sepulchral way that are not, and these more than bear out the claims made for Vetulonia. The Pietrera Tomb and the Diavolino Tomb (sometimes called Pozzo dell'Abate or the Abbot's Hole) both represent the last and richest phase of the orientalizing period, somewhere around the middle of the seventh century. Both are tumulus tombs, and both are constructed on a monumental scale, as tholoi. Of the two the Pietrera is the more impressive because it is still almost completely intact, whereas the Diavolino lies half sunk in the ground. On its hillock it is itself a great artificial hill, its mound rising above the surrounding vegetation and delineated by a circular drum of stone the diameter of which, being more than 60 metres, exceeds that of even the largest of the great Caeretan tumuli. It is approached by a long walled dromos built of squared blocks, probably once roofed in as the lower of two passages. For the central area itself is divided into two chambers, one above the other, the quadrangular plan of the upper of the two forming a basis of support for the cupola. Since the floor of the upper chamber has vanished, one enters the tomb past two rectangular side chambers into the lower one. This has an entrance porch with a curved roof, and retains one of the two great door slabs. It is a large roughly circular chamber, the original construction of which is now unclear, since it lacks its facing stones. It is dominated by a quadrangular central pillar rising to the floor level of the upper chamber, and the immediate impression one has on looking up is of monumental proportion, an uninterrupted rising thrust of stone—not the effect intended of course, because originally the roof would have shut off the sweeping dome of the upper half, but the more striking for its exposure of the plan and scale of the architecture. It is Aegean, almost Mycenaean, in scope. Indeed, the tholos form is to be traced back to neolithic beehive-shaped houses in Cyprus and Iraq, to Mesopotamian tombs, and later to similar tholos tombs in Crete, with rectangular ante-chambers, which themselves anticipate the form of the great "Treasury of Atreus" at Mycenae, built 600 years before the Pietrera tholos.[3] And now it has its place in Italy, coming by way of Asia Minor rather than Greece, with a cupola formed of narrowing circles of interlocking stone slabs that give a firm support to the weight of the earth mound above it.

The Diavolino tomb, clearly contemporary with the other, is very like it in form. Though it lacks its mound and is not intact, it retain a well-preserved quadrangular chamber and part of its stone-ringed cupola. Many such tholos tombs were discovered during the excavations, and though most of them have been sealed in again, in the area surrounding the Pietrera Tomb one sees on both sides of the track among the trees the swelling forms of intact mounds, their entrances blocked, their stone girdles almost obscured by earth and grass, so that sometimes it is difficult to distinguish between tumulus and natural hillock. But they are still there, and perhaps it is not too much to hope that one day some of them will be reopened and restored to preserve something of the unique nature and quality of these architectural monuments.

Meanwhile the contents of these tombs are of unusual importance, representing what Mary Cameron called "the finished products of the Golden Age of Etruscan art and power".[4] From tomb after tomb emerged the evidence of artistic skills embodying in bronze, gold and stone a passionate celebration of the intangible energies of life, something of the essence of the Vetulonian culture. In other words, a people here declares its underlying conviction and certainty, its "commerce with the cosmos and with death",[5] identifying the cosmic with the commonplace, the prosaic with the passionate. One is reminded somehow of E. M. Forster's injunction: "Only connect! Only connect the prose and the passion, and both will be exalted."[6] For in these Vetulonian things the prose and the passion seem indissolubly fused.

And the quintessential embodiment of such fusion is the miraculously precise and minutely ordered work of the Vetulonian goldsmiths; for their skills are nowhere else excelled in the ancient world, even by the Greeks themselves. Indeed, the abundance and variety of the pieces displayed at the Archaeological Museum in Florence alone is sufficient to demonstrate that the Vetulonian craftsmen were masters of the subtlest techniques and skills. The pendants, bracelets, earrings, rings and necklaces found in so many of the tombs make it seem inadequate to refer to this art as a minor art, for it has produced works of great beauty and interest.

Unlike the goldwork of Southern Etruria, which is treated plastically, the basic shapes of Vetulonian ornaments remain simple, with the hammered sheets formed into discs, globes, crescents or tubes. What gives them their lustre and eloquence is the way in which the gold is used to create minute and complex patterns upon the surface of the hammered sheet. The effect is achieved, almost exclusively, by the technique known to jewellers as granulation. On the earliest pieces, minute gold globules, so fine as to resemble gold dust, are arranged upon the plates or discs or globes of the ornaments in varied geometric patterns of triangles, stars, crescents, meanders and zig-zags, or into the figures of lions, horses, dragons, sphinxes and birds, and even sometimes human beings. The peculiarly soft lustrous texture thus produced transmutes the gold into something richer and stranger than one could have thought possible. By the alchemy of this skill, the result seems as superior to the gold itself as gold is to brass. But

H

then comes the further refinement of this globular technique known as granulated filigree, the triumph of the Etruscan goldsmith's skill, here as elsewhere. When you glance at an object employing this application of the technique it appears to be covered with a tracery of threads of the finest gold wire, "twisted and worked into all sorts of forms, volutes, rosettes, palmettes, circles, flowers, leaves, and numberless other tiny and exquisite forms"[7]—delicate figurations that enchant the eye. But when on closer examination you find that the "wire" is in fact composed of a chain of the tiniest globules welded one to another, not only does it seem a feat of extraordinary skill, it also confirms the peculiar vividness and intensity of the effect. Mere wire can never produce such softness, such a rippling play of light, such depth and lucidity, such gossamer delicacy.

For two centuries, the Etruscan jewellers demonstrated an effortless mastery and produced pieces of great virtuosity—such as the Pietrera pendant, encrusted with minute traceries of globules and an exotic hinge of an animal hung by the middle with head and hind-quarters curved inward to fit into an oval frame. And then, from the beginning of the fifth century onward, granulation ceases, and one of the high achievements of Etruscan craftsmanship has passed. As with everything—even with the flowering of the simplest summer plant—there is a time when the urge or the will has gone. And then, though the flower comes again, it is duller, smaller, more familiar, a homelier, lesser thing, however beautiful.

There have been many attempts to emulate these seventh- and sixth-century pieces. In the nineteenth century Roman jewellers spent years studying them, but had to admit that their own examples could not rival the ancient masterpieces. "The Etruscans were acquainted with some chemical process of treating the globules used in this work," said one famous jeweller, Castellani, "which escapes us."[8] But perhaps it is not so much the process which escapes us (for it is surely possible to emulate this) as the spirit in which those things were made, the feeling that brought them into being.

Apart from the gold ornaments and their lesser equivalents in silver and bronze, there are the bronze weapons and implements used by the people, among which the large hammered bronze vases embossed with geometric motifs in narrow bands across the body and studded at the shoulder are particularly impressive. And from the Tomb of the Lictor came the symbolic hatchet with fasces (together with some of the richest gold pieces) which was to become such a famous and ominous emblem of power—even as late as the present century. But it is the monumental stone sculptures remaining from the period of Vetulonia's early maturity that are most to be noted. I shall confine myself to two. The first is a *stele* from the second half of the seventh century. It depicts the figure of a warrior incised upon fetid limestone. He is drawn striding to the left, in a magnificent plumed helmet, bearing a circular shield decorated with intersecting semi-circles in a floral pattern; and he holds up in his right hand—the forefinger of which points actively forward—a double-bladed axe. He is enclosed within a rectangular frame, bordered on three sides by an inscription in archaic Etruscan characters which commemorates his name, Avle Feluske; and between his legs a strange torch-like plant thrusts upward, emblematic of the phallus, the fertilizing root of energy and being.

The other comes from the Pietrera Tomb, and forms part of the wall decoration of the lower chamber. It is really a group of fragments. There are three or four trunkless heads sculptured in the round and headless bodies in base-relief. In these, oriental and Greek influences are still muted, and are dominated by a distinctive local style—hieratic, severe, symbolic, and at the same time sensuous and rooted in the physical world. In the heads the features are moulded to convey the taut inheld rule of the spirit, the implacable rule of the unknown gods. The eyebrows are sharply drawn in towards the nose above the large eyes, focusing them, giving them an expression of intent concentration akin to the tight-held line of the mouth. And the cap of hair above the narrow forehead, together with the braids that frame the face, emphasize its fierce introspective poise. But the headless female trunk at Florence that is displayed below one of these heads has four heavy coils of hair falling around the swelling globes of its exposed and nippled breasts, between which the hands lie ritually crossed. Again, as in the Vulci Centaur, there is the portrayal of the two poles of being—where in the face the spirit stares out intent upon the world, and in the sensuous swelling of these breasts is symbolized the fertility of the flesh-roots. But not in any mere crude juxtaposition. These sculptures have an eloquent gravity and dignity which unite both head and body as complementary forms reflecting each other. They seem to have emerged out of a remote past that goes down and back, bringing with them something of its mysterious essence and energy, containing it silently and confidently before the enigma of life and death.

And they have their affinity (not in form but in spirit and in feeling) with the little Egyptianized statuette of the goddess Mut, holding a child on her knees, that was found in the seventh-century tomb named after her. For she too refers back to the obscure past, and carries upon her an inscription oddly moving in its directness. She is "the goddess who speaks, the life-giver".

There is also the little bronze ship from another early tomb symbolizing the journey of the dead, as the Egyptian death-ships a thousand years before. This carries a "number of small animals, lizards, moles and mice, in the bulwarks, and two oxen amidships, their yoke stretching from one side of the ship to the other". There is a figurehead in the shape of a stag's head with a nimbus of rays around it; "and forward on the poop is a queer little two-faced figure, the lower part of whose body consists of four pilasters joined into one column". This last image has been linked by Professor Milani with "the oldest idol of Apollo adored at Amyclae in Laconia", and the creatures accompanying him with "creatures sacred to Apollo".[9]

But Vetulonia was not an Apollonian city, any more than that little two-faced image can really be thought Apollonian—not at least if we think of Apollo as the god of rationality and light. Its roots are in the pre-classical, prehistoric world of the ancient religions, before the personal humanizing gods emerged. The sculptures of the Pietrera Tomb are not images of human reason and control, but symbols of the elemental powers, at once sensuous and forbidding, the keepers of the keys. They symbolize an essentially tragic and subjective duality, of life and death—life the giver (to be celebrated as a gift) confronting the unknown, death the taker looking out upon life—and the subjective control of the great natural powers under which the Etruscans lived. They represent the kind of world which can maintain its equilibrium and continue to prosper only so long as it remains intact and confident of itself against external pressure. Once get through its guard, and such a world becomes intensely vulnerable. Being too much like a single interdependent organism, with too little mistrust and too much concentrated in too few hands, it tends not to have the organizational resources or the rationalizing hardheadedness to combat threats to its stability, and therefore leaves itself dangerously exposed. Vetulonia, in other words, was not equipped to cope with the objective materialism and cunning of the Romans when it began to be felt, not any more than anywhere else in Etruria. At any rate, it appears suddenly to have weakened and languished—perhaps even through some kind of internal conflict or sense of doubt, even before the Romans actually moved in. Its collapse was only one more small manifestation of that general collapse of the ancient world which Rome hastened, prospering from it to immense advantage to impose upon the known world its "New Deal"—by which, for the first time, as Nietzsche says, "the political instincts hold absolute sway"—to "secularize" everything in its path. A similar situation exists today, in the aftermath of Christianity. What, one might ask, as Nietzsche did, "does our great historical hunger signify, our clutching about us of countless other cultures, our consuming desire for knowledge, if not the loss of myth, of a mythic home, the mythic womb?"[10]

POPULONIA

Six or seven kilometres from Piombino, a bared green hilltop overlooking the island of Elba on one side and the Bay of Baratti on the other marks the site of the acropolis of the Etruscan city of Populonia. It lies next to the small fortress-village of the same name, on its own green headland above the bay, within sight of the circular stone tombs of the archaic necropolis scattered about the flat ground a little inland from the curve of Baratti beach.

It is a unique setting, for Populonia seems to have been the only great Etruscan city built quite so close to the sea. All the others were placed inland and served by separate ports, whereas Populonia was both city and port combined—or, rather, its port lay immediately below the heights of Massoncello in the shelter of Baratti Point. There is a tradition that the city was established later than the others, probably by people from Volterra, the next great centre to the north. Whether or not this is true, there can be little doubt that, with the discovery of minerals in the area (both here and on Elba), Populonia would have had a significant part to play in the development of the Etruscan civilization. Its iron in particular—so much sought after by merchants from all over the Mediterranean—must have been a principal cause of its transformation in the seventh century. When the archaeologists came upon Populonia in the early years of this century for the first time perhaps since its collapse and disappearance, they brought to light not only many beautiful early tombs and their contents but also fragments from the city itself and much other evidence to confirm the existence of an important city culture fully established by the end of the seventh century and continuing into the age of Roman supremacy, as well as the presence before that of a Villanovan settlement.

Populonia is also at the edge of an area rich in Etruscan remains, stretching northward into Volterran territory as far as Cecina and beyond. And excavation has confirmed the early development of this area with the discovery of seventh- and sixth-century tombs at Casaglia, Bibbona, Castagneto and Casale Marittimo, and its continuing expansion into the period of Etruscan decline—where at Quercianella and Castiglioncello on the Volterran coast, complete necropoli of late Etruscan tombs exist, and where in the Cecina Museum objects from a number of other cemeteries are exhibited. Most impressive among these are the seventh-century constructed tholos tombs of Casale and Casaglia, echoing others further north on the banks of the Arno at Quinto Fiorentino—with their circular domed roofs formed of concentric rings of stone rising and narrowing around a massive squared central pillar.[1]

But it is at Populonia that the richest concentration of early tombs is to be found, in their beautiful setting below the village, close to the silvery-black volcanic sands of Baratti Bay. Here the air is fresh and exhilarating, and the earth dark and rich, and the Bay sweeps in a great arc from the small group of buildings on Baratti Point to its long northern arm. A semicircle of gently curving hills closes in the area from behind, and the sea—at times no more than a stone's throw off—provides the seal to it.

The necropolis lies at the southward end of the Bay, close to the foot of the wooden slopes that lead up through a cleft to Populonia—its tombs dotted about the smooth open green on one side of a central track and among the shrubbed hillocks and humps of old diggings on the other. The track itself leads to a gate before an ugly post-war coastguard building, where a large map indicates the scope of the necropolis, marking the sites of other tombs in the district. There are tombs in the wooded hills, for instance, hewn direct from the rock and entered down flights of steps, both on this and on the Elba side of Populonia. And among these down here below the hills, many pit and trench tombs have been excavated with their Villanovan urns in bronze and impasto, the vestiges of a large pre-Etruscan and proto-Etruscan settlement. Then come the architecturally constructed Etruscan tombs for which Populonia has achieved, among archaeologists at least, a specially significant place—ranging from the monumental circular tumuli of the seventh and sixth centuries to the rectangular house-like gabled structures of the fifth.

Close to the gate lies a very large tumulus—the largest in fact of them all—a great circular drum-like structure built from yellowish-brown blocks of limestone reinforced at a height of 3 feet or so with a coping of flint or slate, and surmounted by a great dome of earth. It is pierced by a long narrow passage with one little chamber opening off it on each side. You have to crawl through this to get to the central chamber, which is open to the sky, its earthed and stone-stressed cupola having partly collapsed—though the mound is too high for this to be noticed from outside. Here are the compartments for the dead, walled off by slabs of dark tufo, four of them carved at the head into thick-ringed columns. And the quadrangular chamber retains part of its circular dome, the stones rising in concentric narrowing rings and interlocked in such a way as to take the stress without support. This seventh-century tomb, the *Tomb of the Goats*, takes its name from one of the many objects found inside and now to be seen in the Archaeological Museum in Florence.

To the left of the entrance there is another seventh-century circular tumulus, the *Tomb of the Funeral Beds*, of similar structure, though it is neither so large nor so complete. Again there are the ringed columns and slabs dividing narrow cubicles, and walls of skilfully fitted rectangular blocks rising to a height of four feet or so; but the chamber is fully exposed and there are no signs here of the roofing stones. But four or five dark tufo sarcophagi of varying sizes, gabled yet lidless, lie in the grass outside, the funeral beds that give the tomb its name. They lie there heavily—yet casually placed, like offerings, like symbols of the bonds of family quiet among the green beyond the endlessly curling and landwashing edge of the sea, exposed to the headland breeze and the sun.

A little way off two smaller circular tumuli stand close together, ringed with stones and protruding cornices, their cupolas gone, their mounds flattened, one of them containing four small stone-walled ash pits in its tiny chamber. Then one comes to a small rectangular tomb, the fifth-century *Tomb of the Attic Cups*, built in four diminishing layers, the first three forming a sort of base

(rounded at the corners and edges) for the larger blocks above—
solid, compact, made to last, reminding one less of a house than of
a temple, and forming a sharp contrast to the circular tumuli
around it. A few yards away, for instance, is the small seventh-
century *Tomb of the Perfume Jars*, now half in ruin, though the
stone wall of the drum is still intact. And this in turn leads to
another like that of the Funeral Beds—broken open, half collapsed, its four ringed columns echoing the common style of the
earliest and largest tombs.

And so one drifts down towards the sea, where almost at the
fence that cuts the necropolis off from the road, the superb fifth-
century *Tomb of the Bronze Offerings* is to be found. It is unlike any
of the others in form—gabled and eaved, with the remains of a
triangular pediment above the door which was probably once
decorated with coloured terracottas; built out of huge yellowish
blocks of veined limestone, like a small house. The blocks are
laid with minute precision. They seem to breathe, porous almost,
in the sun. And it is somehow not the emptiness one senses here—
the emptiness of denuded places, the emptiness and desolation of
the stripped altar—but strength and speech, an echoing of the
creative impulse of a people. We have robbed them of their
intimate possessions, it is true, but even so something the scaven-
gers have not been able to strip them of remains—something
essential and essentially unmarketable.

Inside this tomb, for instance, the proportions are geometrically
exact, miniature and intimate. The light glows reddish on the
stone, there is a curious enclosing buoyancy, the protective closeness of wall offers the intimacy of the house rather than the
claustrophobia of prison. This little place is in other words a kind
of home—built by the living for the dead to live on in, built to
give death its links with life, to conquer darkness and the nothing-
ness of the unknown.

This tomb is surrounded by tufo graves, some of them lidless,
one or two with their gabled lids still on and crowned at the apex
with little palmettes. There are also the foundations of another
house-tomb and a small tumulus of the seventh century, its earth
mound intact, in an area recently excavated.

The land on the other side of the central track, closest to the hills, is pitted and cratered like some unearthly bomb-scarred landscape. It falls away into a gulley and rises along steep quarried slopes to a high platform below Massoncello. On this platform, covered with tangled masses of blackberry and broom through which paths lead, lie three or four early tombs. The first of these, the *Tomb of the Gold Ornaments*, is small and circular, its earth mound intact above the drum of stone and its protruding cornice. It has a very low and very narrow entrance passage, just accessible, and the central chamber is small, quadrangular, enclosed, enclosing, made to contain its dead as if in the intimate quiet of the womb—earth-dark, glowing at the end of its vaginal passage, roofed with rising circles of stones, once rich with symbolic offerings of gold. Here, within this little circle, symbol of fertility, beneath the breast-like curve of the mound, the Etruscans had reconciled contradictions, returning life to the female earth as if to be re-born. They had no thought of the vandals. In the seventh century conquest was far off. And in the end it was neither the Gauls nor the Romans who broke the spell of quiet for their dead, but the vandals of the modern world, since these tombs were only discovered in the twentieth century. The ruins of the *Tomb of the Gold Coils*, stripped almost to its foundations, are one sign of this. And further down, from the high grassy platform in front of the *Tomba dei Flabelli di Bronzo*, which is at the edge of the steep dell, one can see the scars of this disrupted landscape stretching away in a chaos of earth and grass towards the wooden hill. It is a strange sight, seeming the aftermath of some violent eruption, though the green has again begun to take over. However, the tomb here compensates. It is among the most finely preserved in the whole necropolis. Again the same low ring of squared limestone blocks, the protruding cornice and the coping above that frames the mound, with two tall phallic stones outside the entrance and, close by, the shaft of a very deep well. One wonders how it can have survived in quite such virgin condition, especially in its particular context, poised on this edge of broken land.

Below on the slope are the remains of an industrial building, a vestige from the third century, when the iron trade was still flourishing. It already reflects the Romanized decadence, contrasting sharply with the lucidity of the tomb above. One is surprised, in fact, at the proximity of two such structures. It seems an odd uneasy conjunction. The sacred area above and on the other side of the dell must have been hemmed in and around by the purely functional buildings of the port—warehouses, foundries, offices and shops.

There are a few other vestiges of walls scattered about below. They offer mere hints of what went on here in the fourth and third centuries. Otherwise all one finds are the great mounds of grassed earth and silt, a stagnant pool with rushes growing around it, an occasional dark hole in the ground, the discarded diggings of the excavators. But scattered everywhere on the ground lie fragments, large and small—bits of broken bucchero and painted vase, of terracotta facing, tufo, limestone, iron, fragments of a world among the pervading vegetation. The place is a quarry— melancholy, desolate, abandoned. Or seems so—till on the edge of it, close to the track, one comes again upon a number of ruined circular tombs, among which the *Tomb of the Amber Pearls* is the best preserved—containing the characteristic walled chamber, and lacking only its roof, an intimate memorial that refers beyond chaos to the actualities of an ordered world.

Turning from the tombs, one is instantly aware of the containing actuality of this landscape, which seems to have survived the collapse of human experiment essentially unchanged—and nowhere more so than when moving up towards Populonia. The road makes its way between two hills, to the left thickly wooded, to the right (crowned by Populonia itself) glistening with olives upon drystone terraces against a background of sea and sky. Halfway up, a great umbrella pine towers by the roadside a little way on from where an ancient oak—its massive trunk inclining seaward—celebrates the hill and its sensuous quivering of light.

But the full impact of the physical immediacy of the landscape is reserved for the moment when the road flattens across an open ridge linking the two hills. For here, on both sides, the land suddenly falls away in ecstatic declaration to the sea—north along the

curve of Baratti and south to the Cala San Quirico and the low
black form of Elba lying across the water beyond it. And all at
once (if only for a moment) one has a glimpse of order and an
experience of order, a sense of equilibrium, of "unimpeded utter-
ance", of "fitness in the latent qualities and essences of things",[2]
that is beyond contradiction or question. Indeed, at moments like
this one sees not with the eyes of those who see only the commonplace in commonplace things, but with Wordsworth's "purest
passion". "Veramente il mondo canta, canta nel silenzio."

And yet what use is this, they'll say, the unenchanted literalists,
except as an intoxicant for the escapist, like music or the dance?
To which one might answer that it is of no use at all. Such recog-
nitions are not for use, practically speaking. No more than art is,
or anything else that brings us into contact with the essences of
things. We become lovers, and lovers are no use at all. They serve
their moment, they are part of the celebration of the delight of
being, even as this landscape is. And this landscape is no less real
because you cannot hold it in your hands or turn it into cash;
because you aren't surrounded by the signs of technological progress and competitive business, the "spheres of interest" that
appeal to the literalists.

So Populonia has its share of reality. Approached from the ridge
along a road that runs between old walls and cypresses above
the terraced olives, the squat tower of its castle faces on to the bare
rounded hilltop of the acropolis—which probably once covered
both heights. The village (entered through a narrow arch) is
small. A long shopless street runs the length of it to the far battle-
ments, the green-shuttered building used as the Museum taking up
one side and a row of stone houses the other. Just off this to the
left is a high-walled quadrangle dominated by the tower, that
dwarfs a tiny whitewashed chapel with a belfry standing in the
opposite corner. There is only one other street. It runs parallel to
the main (paved) one, on the opposite side, itself unpaved and
rather dilapidated. And that is all—no bar, no shops, no osteria,
nothing except the dwellings of the inhabitants and the palace-
museum inside these fortress walls, high above the sea.

The museum has five rooms in all, each filled with objects from the tombs. There are small impasto pots, cups, perfume jars, black bucchero bowls (plain and figured), kraters, amphoras, some vigorous examples of Etruscan red-figure ware, a few sixth-century Attic and Corinthian pieces, an assortment of implements and ornaments in bronze—all ranging from the eighth to the third centuries. It is not an important collection—most of the material from the tombs has gone to Florence or elsewhere—but because it is small, certain isolated choice examples tend to stand out the more. First among these is a large Villanovan cinerary urn. It is of dulled reddish-brown impasto, and stands 18 inches high, capped by a curved impasto bowl. And the intricate patterning of zig-zags and meanders scored upon the clay gives it a peculiar vibrancy and vigour that draws the attention. One may have seen many such urns elsewhere, but this one—unique in the museum—stands alone, large and compelling among the bucchero and the small pots.

Of the other pieces, even the smallest takes on a special tone from its context. One notices the tiny ointment jar from the seventh-century *Tomba del Balsamario* below—of oriental Greek workmanship, its tiny swelling bowl surmounted by a neck and lip in the form of a helmeted warrior's head. There are necklaces of semi-precious or coloured stone beads among the implements and brooches. Then in the end room, one comes upon several large fragments of tufo sculpture from the area—a fifth-century *stele* carved into a beautiful scrolled pattern, another massive piece that must once have decorated the lintel of a house or a tomb; two fan-crowned terracotta antefixes from a temple pediment, and the headless reclining body of a man in the characteristic position adopted by effigies on the lids of late Romanized sarcophagi.

This collection, then, is small and intimate. For anything more concentrated, and for the most important pieces, one has to go elsewhere. And perhaps the most notable collection in Italy is that which is housed in three rooms of the Archaeological Museum in Florence. There one can find the lovely gold filigree pins and earrings, the hammered gold leaves and gold bracelets taken from the Tomb of the Gold Ornaments and others, belonging to the early period in which Etruscan goldsmiths all over Etruria (and particu-larly at Vetulonia) were demonstrating the skills of their craft with the most exquisite workmanship and detail. These pieces, together with Villanovan, Corinthian, Attic and bucchero ware of the highest quality—with the helmets, shields, urns and orna-ments in bronze, and the iron and copper implements of everyday use—were discovered in excavations made at various periods between 1916 and the present. Of course it is in a way a pity one has to go to Florence to get a full sense of the richness of the Populonia tombs—where, lacking their context, the objects inevitably lose something of their impact. But the limitations of the little Populonia museum, one supposes, made that a necessity.

Beyond the village a track leads down into a dip and up past a farmhouse along a terraced slope, immediately above which (and almost on the line of the old wall) stand the ruins of a large Roman building in whitish-grey stone with six great sealed arches. This structure forms the base for a grassy platform on which a group of six evergreens flourishes. It lies just below the crown of the hill, choked with bramble, silently recording the persistence of the city into Roman times, and echoing the splendours it had displaced, whose idiosyncratic forms one could only guess at.

On the hilltop the sun's unwavering penetration of the atmo-sphere reveals astonishing stretches of sea and land. There below is Elba, long and black beyond a quicksilver expanse of sea broken only by the small black hump of Palmaiola. Westward the land-less water, and to the north the sensuous coastline basking in sun-light.

As one walks, one sees that the ground is literally choked with fragments half-buried in the grass. It is difficult to believe that this rubble could be all that remains of a great city. Of course, there are the stretches of massive wall to be seen at various points encircling the hill, and the occasional discarded block of squared tufo lying upturned in the grass. There is the Roman ruin, too, and the village, built on the site of the *arx* and rising perhaps out of the foundations of its ancient buildings. But surely, one asks oneself, there ought to be other more tangible signs of its existence —the foundations of temples and houses for instance, the outlines of streets and squares. But no. It is almost as if the city had never existed. What remains lies sunk under the surface of the hill, or has been taken away to lie in the dark corners of museum storerooms or encased in glass.

We can only accept that like other Etruscan cities Populonia has vanished. But the tombs remain, and the landscape remains. And this landscape has nothing of the contorted brooding quality the rust-brown tufo gorges give to places like Cerveteri, Norchia or Tuscania. Here the dark Tuscan earth and the soft contours of the hills against the sea form a different kind of setting altogether. There the tufo dominates, assuming its fantastic shapes after a series of volcanic eruptions 5,000 or 6,000 years ago. But here it is mostly hidden, so that it is only the silvery-grey colour of the sand below that betrays the volcanic nature of the land.

There are many isolated tombs or groups of tombs in the wooded hills above the necropolis. One such group I came across lies high up a wooded slope of Massoncello, reached by a path cut out of the tufo of the hillside. It is in a semicircular clearing backed by trees. The narrow passages have been cut deep into the exposed rock, one of them with a flight of fifteen steps leading down to a low rectangular doorway, the other half-buried but with an exactly similar doorway; and each contains a small roughly carved room with benches. Such fourth- and third-century tombs are to be seen at many other sites in Etruria. It is the earlier tombs that display the greater distinctions and peculiarities. Later they become more uniform, with fewer local variants.

What is of special interest about these Populonia tombs, however, is the unexpectedness of the context in which one finds them, hidden away high up in their little clearings. Here, silent among the silence of woods, confronted by the gravity of the Etruscan idea, one marvels a little at it, and at the stilled presences it hints at—images of light and movement, of delight and confidence, celebrating the gift of life in the face of death and the unknown. One senses in these things the positive creative energy of the Mediterranean spirit which has so richly nourished Europe —the spirit of the ancients rooted in the pre-Christian unities of the natural world, before the Logos, before the encroachment of the Cross. They are part of an inheritance—an inheritance passed on to us not, of course, as a father passes on his fortune to his sons, but rather as a potential to be tapped, that lies dormant, buried among the detritus of the past, waiting. Not to bring comfort but to confirm in us contact and meaning in face of the enigma of life and beyond the illusion that thought (or the denial of the sensuous actualities or the practicality of the literalists) can resolve or correct it.

THE ETRUSCAN ROOTS OF MEDIAEVAL TUSCAN CITIES

THE ETRUSCAN CIVILIZATION of Central Italy matured as a confederation of city-states out of an impulse nourished and directed by the creative spirit of the ancient Mediterranean cultures upon its Italic ("Villanovan") roots. Each city in the confederation developed its own idiosyncratic pattern of life as an independent nonconformist state linked by the common interests of race, culture and religion. In the broad sense we can talk about the nation, but that nation was not a single unified cohesive force in the sense in which every one of the great cities was within its territory. "To get any idea of the pre-Roman past," as Lawrence pointed out, "we must break up the the conception of oneness and uniformity."[1] And to find a parallel to that past we need perhaps go no further than those mediaeval and Renaissance city-states that came into being in the post-Roman past within the very same area. In fact the parallel is so striking as to suggest that "the Etruscan experiment" may have been an indispensable precondition to the development of the mediaeval city-state—or, to put it another way, that the great cities of Central Italy that we know today were a second manifestation of the same spirit and the same roots that produced the cities of Etruria.

Rome subdued and absorbed the Etruscans, as she did so many other peoples, imposing her systematic political principles upon them, and turning Etruria into a mere provincial district of the Roman state. But it is questionable whether, in conquering this people and destroying their culture, she destroyed their roots. More likely, these roots were left lying dormant while the Romans had their will of Etruria, to await the time when (with the oppression lifted) conditions would be right for them to be quickened again. The Etruscans vanished or were absorbed, but their spirit, nurtured in this soil, transformed and redirected by the impact of Rome and Christianity, remained—to reassert itself in the making of the mediaeval city-states. Even today one is tempted to identify the strange non-Roman pagan warmth and earthiness of the people of Tuscany with their Etruscan roots.

As for the cities that began to spring up all over Central Italy after the decline of Rome, a number of them can even trace their lineage directly back to the Etruscans, since they were built on the very foundations of Etruscan cities—rooted in that pre-Roman past and flowering out of it. We may say, in other words, that there are profound affinities between the vigorous spirit of the people who shaped and civilized Etruria and the people of cities such as Florence, Siena, Arezzo, Cortona and Perugia. Perhaps it is something of the essence of this spirit which gives these cities their distinction, their resilient vitality, their idiosyncratic splendour, both in the Middle Ages and in their later interpretation of Renaissance themes. It was neither Rome nor the Romans in fact who brought about the Renaissance. The Christian empire established there may have sought to make use of the opportunities for increased dominion offered by the rhetoric of the grandeur of the city's ruins and its vanished culture. But the rediscovery of ancient Rome was made for the most part by outsiders, by Tuscans and Umbrians in search of forms by which to embody their own sense of their roots; and Rome was but one infectious motive among many in an age of phenomenal creative activity. For essentially the Renaissance was a rebirth not of the spirit of ancient Rome but of the old Mediterranean spirit reasserting itself out of Christianity, with Rome as its most immediate and available image. It was a Central Italian experience; an extraordinary reawakening of roots that had lain dormant in the soil for centuries. In the ruins of Rome, the men of the Renaissance discovered a guide and an image; and inevitably because so much of it had survived, "the form and substance of this civilization were adopted with admiring gratitude", as Burckhardt puts it, so that "it became the chief part of the culture of the age".[2] But it was appropriated and transformed by that age as a means to its articulation, accepted as the symbol for a culture whose interests and aims could not have been more of a contrast to the interests and aims of Imperial Rome as the acquisitive destroyers of the ancient world. In Duccio, in Giotto, in Dante, in Ucello, in Masaccio and Piero and Signorelli and Petrarch, it is not the spirit of Rome or the form and substance of its civilization that triumphs, but the particularizing, nonconformist spirit of the Tuscan city-states emerging out of the culture of the High Middle Ages. And above all it triumphs in Michelangelo, who—for all his passionate enthusiasm for Roman forms—reshapes them into terms of his profoundly unclassical Florentine vision. If Rome, then, became the apparent symbol for this rebirth, it was not the source of it. The source of it was Italian, Tuscan, Etruscan, and Mediterranean—those roots which, far from fostering a unifying metropolitan political system, had brought about a rich variety of independent, self-assertive and proudly individualistic city-states, which even now (even with the emergence of the unified Nation of Italy) are still the key to the pattern and the character of Italian life.

Of the great mediaeval cities, none displays its roots more significantly than Orvieto, in the territory of the ancient Lucomony of Volsinii. It was once thought to have occupied the site of Volsinii itself, but excavations taking place at Bolsena on the edge of Lake Bolsena have since established that area as the setting for the capital and its shrine, the Fanum Voltumnae—where, according to Livy, the princes of Etruria were wont to meet in council on the general affairs of the Confederation or to propitiate the gods. It could, however, have been the site of Herbanum, mentioned by Pliny in his catalogue, or of Salpinum, associated with Volsinii in campaigns against Rome, as Dennis points out.[3] That it must have been a town of some significance is anyway demonstrated by the rich discoveries made at many places in the vicinity.

Orvieto rises in the midst of its wide valley closed in on three sides by heights, in a sudden sheer thrust of tufo, "like a truncated cone".[4] It is seen to great effect from these heights, its reddish cliffs affording a natural protection against attack, with its towers and houses poised above and dominated by the Cathedral. And it is surely no accident that it stands where it stands. The Christian city has grown out of roots established centuries before. And the most telling evidence of this is the sixth-century necropolis at

Crocefisso del Tufo outside the Porta Maggiore on the slopes immediately below the cliffs. For it literally seems an exposed root above which both the old and the "new" cathedrals of Orvieto rise, as if in confirmation, with the great Gothic Duomo dominating the whole town in a majestic flowering of art. Of course, the tombs of the necropolis are simple. Arranged in streets in the form of little houses, they are constructed from large blocks of lichened tufo of various sizes, with small rectangular doorways, outside which lie cylindrical or chest-like stones denoting (by size and shape) the age and sex of the dead person. Some of the lintels are carved with inscriptions, and the roofs are crowned with little flame- or breast-like cippi.

Many beautiful objects were found in these tombs—Attic and Corinthian amphorae, early thin-walled bucchero and the later Chiusian type with figures in relief, and there are two large collections of pieces, in the Museo dell'Opera del Duomo and the Museo Faina, both situated immediately opposite the great West Front of the Cathedral. Among these are a magnificent seventh-century imitation Corinthian vase which reconciles both Attic and Corinthian motives in seven decorative bands, and three or four vigorously painted Tyrrhenian amphorae with animals and human figures, warriors in battle and dancers—even a scene depicting satyrs exercising their bent for copulation in vivid phallic ritual. In addition to all those pieces that are common to any Etruscan museum, there is a beautiful small ash-chest painted with horses and men in red and black (as in fifth-century Tarquinian tomb-paintings) and a richly carved late sarcophagus. But most interesting of all is the sixth-century standing nude goddess, a Venus-image, that seems just to have emerged into lucid nakedness from out of the more angular archaic forms of the past, her body softened and given sensuous expressiveness by the curve and flow of outline, the rounding of the limbs and the subtle half-Ionian smile on the face. Such lucidity and such a smile are not to be matched by the smiles on the faces of the massive helmeted heads in nenfro (one here, one in Florence) that must once have stood as guardians outside fifth-century Orvietan tombs; but these too are impressive, the images of a mystic vision akin to that of Chiusi, if later and less compelling. Then come the superbly executed fifth-century classical figures of gods in terracotta from the pediments of temples discovered in the hills around the town at Belvedere and San Leonardo, and the late fourth-century frescoes from the two Golini tombs—which, though already rigid and too consciously posed, all the same define a further aspect of the culture of the ancient town.

Luca Signorelli, whose great masterpiece—those astonishing frescoes on the theme of the Last Judgement—is in Orvieto Cathedral, was born in Cortona, a beautiful mediaeval town high in the hills above the Val di Chiana. And Cortona was itself an important Etruscan city, said to have been one of the twelve capitals of the confederation. It still retains long stretches of its ancient walls, visible along about half of the circuit of the town, its quadrilateral blocks of sandstone being among the best-preserved and most impressive in Etruria. There are many tombs too—ancient tumuli and hypogei, or those built like the fifth-century *Tanella di Pitagora* from huge blocks of masonry with square-headed doorways, the entrance and chamber vaulted on the primitive horizontal principle with immense stones measuring ten feet in length. And the Museum of the Etruscan Academy, formed in 1727 for the pursuit of Etruscan studies in the thirteenth-century Palazzo Pretorio, is the earliest of them all, and rich in objects gathered from the district during the last two centuries. Here one finds Attic and Etruscan vases, cups and bowls, votive statuettes, a group of long-legged lightly balancing warriors and athletes in bronze, rare gems and ornaments in gold, and a varied selection of bucchero and bronze, chief among which is the great circular bronze lamp-holder, with its gorgon head surrounded by a ring of sirens and grotesque silenus-figures with parted legs, the familiar symbols of phallic worship.

Such fame and distinction did they achieve, these cities of the Middle Ages, and so dazzling were their achievements during the Renaissance, that one is apt to overlook the unsensational evidence of the Museums that speak of their roots and their antiquity, of the Etruscans and the ways in which they had enriched the soil. Cortona's lovely buildings speak for themselves and can boast

Signorelli and Pietro da Cortona among its natives. Arezzo too is
first of all a mediaeval city, the city of Petrarch and perhaps above
all of Piero della Francesca. But it yields its own evidence of an
earlier Etruscan flowering. There are the scattered remains of
walls, for instance, and the Mecenate Museum (housed in the
fifteenth-century Convento degli Olivetani overlooking the
Roman amphitheatre) contains a magnificent collection of pieces
covering the whole range of Etruscan art from its Villanovan
foundations and the early stone sculptures to late Hellenistic
temple terracottas and the famous black Aretine vases of the first
century B.C.; and these include statuettes, tools, weapons, necklaces, clasps and mirrors in bronze which would give Etruscan
Arezzo an important place among the great metal-working cities
of Etruria even without taking into account the famous Chimaera,
now in Florence, which itself was such a source of inspiration to
Renaissance sculptors.

Perugia and Siena and Volterra too have their own richly
furnished Museums to put us into contact with the underlying
roots of their culture. And both Perugia and Volterra can boast in
addition their great gateways—the Porta di Augusto at Perugia
incorporating a frieze of shields and pilasters, and the Porta dell'
Arco at Volterra its three dark thrusting heads. Volterra, site of
Velathri, one of the oldest and most northerly of Etruscan cities,
is a particularly impressive place. It stands proud and forbidding
on its towering bluff of rock, with sweeping views of the mountains and valleys for miles around. Tracts of the ancient walls
remain, apart from the great arch, along the eroded headland of
Le Balze beyond the town, and this is where the ancient tumulus
and chamber tombs once were, though all of them have now
crumbled away with the gradual creeping subsidence of these
cliffs. Its position and its atmosphere give one the sense that the
people of this Etruscan city must have been, in Lawrence's words,
"wilder, cruder" than those further south and lower down.[5] It is a
city of wind and stone, high and isolated, far from the sea, bleak
and harsh in winter, parched in summer, a place for the Stoic and
the Hermit—these are the qualities that give it its peculiar beauty,
its gaunt power, as a place. And one peculiarity of its Etruscan

past (which it shares only with Chiusi) is that from its earliest beginnings to the very end, the Volterrans burned their dead, unlike the people of other Etruscan cities, who, from the seventh century onwards, increasingly preferred to bury them. The most interesting feature of the Guarnacci Museum is therefore its large and fascinating collection of characteristically small alabaster ash-chests, from the fourth century onward carrying powerfully carved Etruscan and Greek mythological scenes and the fore-shortened stunted effigy of the dead person reclining on the lid. These are "like an open book of life" for Lawrence;[6] and as he acutely observed: "Whoever carved these chests knew very little of the fables they were handling. . . . The story was just used as a peg upon which the native Volterran hung his fancy, as the Elizabethans used Greek stories for their poems." These late carvings "hint at the Gothic which lay unborn in the future, far more than at the Hellenistic past of the Volterran Etruscan. . . . They seem much more akin to the Christian sarcophagi of the sixth century A.D." than to Roman chests—"as if Christianity really rose, in Italy, out of Etruscan soil, rather than out of Graeco-Roman".[7] By then, of course, so much of the vividness and solemnity of the great age (as exemplified in the early sixth-century *stele* of the bearded nobleman Avle Tite and so many other pieces in the Museum) has gone. But a kind of "Gothic actuality and idealism" supplants it—a pathos and anguish, a sense of suffering and defeat—that makes one think of the sculptors of mediaeval Italy, carving the peasant Christian accepting the burden of life and looking to the resolution of the future, as in the work of Nicola Pisano at Pisa and Perugia.

Throughout Tuscany, and beyond Tuscany, the Etruscan civilization has left its mark, at the roots of town after town—from Bologna to Pisa, from Florence to Viterbo, from Todi on the Tiber to Volterra, from Arezzo to Rome. And every day almost, the archaeologists unearth new proofs, to confirm the foundations of the Italianate world—that eloquent experiment expressive of the "social contract" by which, in spite of violent cleavages and upheavals, the cities of Italy have made their attempts to build upon the "blueprints of perfection".

EPILOGUE

THE ETRUSCANS HAVE survived. After the suppression and absorption of their culture by the Romans and the oblivion that was to be their fate for seventeen or eighteen centuries, proofs began to emerge that behind the great façade of the civilization of Rome there had actually existed a people as different from them in spirit as the Romans were from the Greeks. They have survived in spite of misrepresentation, the contempt of the Romans, the indifference of almost everyone from the beginning of the Christian Empire, and the almost complete absence of any literary records. It is now no longer possible to think of them as one among the shadowy forerunners of Rome, or as an inferior offshoot of the civilization of Greece. The archaeological discoveries of the last hundred years have brought us to a point at which it is beginning to be generally admitted that the Etruscans were a more important people than the painfully inadequate and dismissive references of the past have allowed them to be. And if they are to remain unacceptable to history because history and the historical process require an incontrovertible record of fact and event, then the task of giving the Etruscans their place in the world will continue to be undertaken by the archaeologists and by those who maintain that reality and fact and truth are to be discovered not only in the study of documents and recorded events, but also and perhaps as profoundly (if at a different level) through the forms of art. It may well be that archaeology and art will remain "almost the only sources for the study of the life and religion of the Etruscan civilization", as Frova asserts in *Il Rinnovamento*.[1] If this is so—if, that is, no revealing and authentic literature is ever to be made available to the historians—we shall nevertheless still be left with a wealth of evidence to work upon, even though most of it comes only from the tombs. And this has its own authenticity and eloquence—it "gets into the imagination", as Lawrence said, and will not go out again.

For with the Etruscans survives something of the essence of the spirit of the ancient world—its myths, its ritualized energy, the seriousness and awe symbolized in so many of its forms. In their funerary art, man seems to be paying homage still to the great natural powers that control. His fundamentally tragic sense of the world is represented again and again in terms of gaiety and positive acceptance and continuity. There is hardly a trace of morbidity or gloom. It is as if the tragedy did not exist, or as if this gaiety (and the gravity that goes with it) could itself conquer death in its very refusal to be anything else in the moment of awareness—to the end a celebration. In other words, it is the feeling for life, for the intangible gifts of being in face of the tragic duality of life and death, that gives this art its authenticity and power.

But if the Etruscans achieved their maturest forms upon oriental and Greek models as part of their heritage from the ancient world, it is the uses to which they put these models and the ways they transformed them that define the peculiar distinctiveness of their achievement. The influences that came their way (whether by trade or by imagination) were adapted, that is, to an essentially Italic vision. For the Etruscans were not mere imitators of the Greeks. Their standards and values were different. They had different ways of thinking, feeling and seeing. They were the product of a different environment and a different climate, a different attitude to life. The Greek spirit clarified out of the long traditions and experiments of ancient Greece, and out of the Homeric myths—myths in which the gods reflected "a race of noble and proud beings". And this was to lead to the ultimate refinements of Greek civilization—to the idealization of the human body in terms of a sophisticated logic of proportion; to the effortless ease of Praxiteles and the triumphant fluency of Hellenistic art; to philosophy and dogma and the logos. But the Etruscan vision had emerged out of a more primitive culture, a world previously undeveloped, vigorous but crude, on to which was grafted the symbolizing awareness and feeling of the archaic

Mediterranean world. And this was to produce a profoundly subjective non-Greek view of life and death, tending towards the intuitive, the intimate and the particular, the idiosyncratic and the eccentric, rather than towards idealization and abstraction. Its strange releasing vividness, the anti-classical vigour and immediacy that is in all Etruscan things before the vision of the people, and their equilibrium as a race, had begun to be disturbed, refers to values that the Greek world superseded and refined away—to the primitive archaic energies by which man celebrated his instinctive sense of being and belonging in the midst of the tragic brevity of his existence. For a short time, for perhaps no longer than three centuries, the Etruscans were able to hold their place, clear of doubt and confusion, "the terrors of transit"; and then—because they had no established intellectual traditions to strengthen or to steady them—they lost their balance, and started on that swift and bewildering fall which was to end in conquest and total oblivion.

But for that brief period of time between the end of the eighth century and the end of the fifth, the Etruscans achieved maturity and distinction, leaving an image of themselves at once unmistakable, authentic and unique. And it is on this achievement and its record that they should be judged—the record of the early tombs, the urns and ash-chests, the vases, the gold ornaments, the sculptures and the tomb paintings, from which:

> Behind the cracked façades,
> In scrupulous delight,
> Surviving dust, the bones and sherds,
> They dance the moment's truth,
> As if still just beginning,
> Caught in rapt infinity,
> Offering the gifts of youth.
> Although our rabid abstracts
> Teach us to despise their sense—
> Naïve to the mind's cold
> Triumph over singleness—
> These telling witnesses

Persist in their impulsive
Gestures to the old
Clear gift of life and light,
Homage to the essence,
To the truths of sense.[2]

NOTES

(Reference books not alluded to here may be found in the Bibliography).

Introduction

1. D. H. Lawrence: *Etruscan Places* (Penguin edition), p. 174.
2. Ibid., p. 126.
3. Mary Lovett Cameron: *Old Etruria* (Methuen 1909), Intro. xiv.
4. Lawrence: *Etruscan Places*, p. 148.
5. Thomas Hobbes: *Leviathan*. "Fear and reverence Nature no longer; she is no mystery, for she worketh by motion, and Geometry, which is the mother of the sciences, and indeed the only science God has yet vouchsafed to us, can chart these motions."
6. Donald Davie, from an article in the *New Statesman*, 1966.

Chapter One

1. D. H. Lawrence: *E.P.*, p. 147.
2. Thomas de Quincy: *Confessions of an Opium Eater*.
3. Herodotus: *The Histories*, Book I, 94.
4. Suetonius: *The Twelve Caesars—Claudius*, paragraph 42. "The city of Alexandria had the Etruscan history publicly recited from end to end once a year by relays of readers in the old wing" of the museum. (Penguin edition, translated by Robert Graves.)
5. Alluded to by Dionysus of Halicarnassus (I, 24) and by Strabo (*Geography* XVII).
6. Carlo Franzero: *Tarquin the Etruscan* (Redman 1960), p. 36.
7. Niebuhr, Helbig and Mommsen are the most important among those who have maintained that the Etruscans came to Italy from the north.

8. A. Neppi Modona: *A Guide to Etruscan Antiquities*, Chapter VI, and other sources, including Deecke, Shulze, Herbig and Lattes.

9. D. H. Lawrence: *E.P.*, p. 149.

10. Ibid., p. 146.

11. A. Neppi Modona: *Guide to E. Antiquities*, p. 78–9.

12. Aubrey de Selincourt's introduction to his translation of Livy's *History* (Penguin), p. 11.

13. Mary Cameron: *Old Etruria*, p. 23.

14. J. D. Beazley: *Etruscan Vase-Painting* (Oxford 1947).

15. The dates are those generally accepted by most authorities (Ducati, Pallottino, Modona, Richardson) based upon Polybius, Diodorus Silicus, Pliny, Livy and others.

16. F. R. Cowell: *Cicero and the Roman Republic* (Pelican 1962), p. 215.

17. Octavius is said to have sacrificed 300 of the leading men of Perugia on the altar of the Divine Julius.

18. F. R. Cowell: *Cicero and the R. Rep.*, p. 149.

19. Ibid., p. 268.

20. Ibid., p. 358.

21. Ibid., p. 65.

22. Ibid., p. 65.

23. D. H. Lawrence: *Phoenix—Introduction to Cavalleria Rusticana by Giovanni Verga*.

24. F. R. Cowell: *Cicero and the R. Rep.*, p. 66.

25. Ibid., p. 17.

26. Ibid., p. 148.

27. Mary Cameron: *Old Etruria*, p. 117.

28. Lawrence: *Phoenix—"Flowering Tuscany"*.

29. Ibid.

Chapter Two

1. Sources: Cicero—*De Divinatione* (II, 23–39), Ovid—*Metamorphoses* (XV, 553–9), Lucan—*Pharsalia* (I, 636), and others.

2. Mary Cameron: *Old Etruria*, p. 22.

3. Mario Moretti and A. Zanelli: *Tarquinia* (Rome 1964), pp. 4–5.

4. Mary Cameron, *Old Etruria*, p. 25.

5. Lawrence: *E.P.*, pp. 168–9.

6. Ibid., p. 146.

7. Stendhal: *A Roman Journal* (translated for Collier Books by Haakon Chevalier), pp. 313–14.

8. William Blake: *Marriage of Heaven and Hell* (Oxford), p. 248.

9. Sir Kenneth Clark: *The Nude* (Pelican), p. 362 (note), and p. 8.

10. Lawrence: *E.P.*, p. 165.

11. Ibid., p. 150.

12. Ibid., pp. 149–50.

13. A. Stenico: *La pittura etrusca e romana* (Mondadori), p. 17.

14. Lawrence: *E.P.*, p. 133.

15. Ibid., p. 167.

16. Ibid., p. 166.

17. Sir Kenneth Clark: *The Nude*, p. 8.

18. Ibid., p. 362.

19. Bernhard Berenson: *Italian Painters of the Renaissance* (Fontana 1960), p. 53.

20. Ibid., p. 54.

21. Ibid., p. 247.

Chapter Three

1. Lawrence: *E.P.*, p. 156.,

2. Ibid., p. 156.

3. Mario Moretti: *Tarquinia*, pp. 7–10.

4. George Dennis: *Cities and Cemeteries of Etruria* (Everyman 1907), Volume I, p. 317.

5. Mary Cameron: *Old Etruria*; p. 36, quoting Professor Milani. She calls it, alternatively, a *mundum*, as does Lawrence on pages 127 and 165 of his book.

6. Mario Moretti: *La Tomba delle Olimpiadi* (Lerici 1960).

7. Cesare Pavese: *This Business of Living—A Diary 1935–1950* (Peter Owen and Consul books 1961), p. 199.

8. See Doctor Moretti's magnificently illustrated book (Lerici 1960).

9. Dennis: *Cities and Cemeteries*, p. 330.

10. Lawrence: *E.P.*, p. 148.

11. Dennis: *Cities and Cemeteries*, p. 335.
12. Lawrence: *E.P.*, p. 148.
13. Dennis: *Cities and Cemeteries*, pp. 330–1.
14. Ibid., pp. 28–9.
15. Robert Graves: *The Greek Myths* (Pelican), I, 77.

Chapter Four
1. Bertolt Brecht: Galileo (Methuen).

Chapter Five
1. Leonida Marchese: *Il Museo di Tuscania* (Curcio 1964), p. 2.
2. See reference to *Lombard Romanesque* by David Talbot Rice in *World Architecture* (Hamlyn 1963), p. 191.
3. Dennis: *Cities and Cemeteries*, Vol. I, pp. 470–1.
4. Ibid., p. 476.
5. See illustrated catalogue by Leonida Marchese: *Il Museo di Tuscania*.

Chapter Six
1. Dennis: *Cities and Cemeteries*, Vol. I, p. 289.
2. Ibid., in a note, p. 289.
3. Ibid., p. 292.
4. Ibid., p. 298.
5. Ibid., p. 299. Referred to in a note. The epistle "mentions the *pietra ficta* without the city—most probably referring to the temple-tombs" as well as "*cava scamerata*" and "*cava caprilis*" —that is cave with rooms and cave for goats.
6. Ibid., p. 281.
7. Ibid., p. 279.
8. Ibid., p. 274.
9. Ibid., p. 280.
10. Ibid., note II, pp. 284–5.
11. Ibid., p. 275.
12. Jack Clemo: *The Map of Clay* (Methuen 1961), especially two beautiful poems—"The Excavators" and "Clay-Land Moods".

13. Cesare Pavese: *This Business of Living* (Il Mestiere di Vivere), p. 185.
14. Dennis: *Cities and Cemeteries*, p. 303.
15. Ibid., p. 304.
16. Ibid., p. 302.
17. Ibid., p. 303.
18. Ibid., p. 305.

Chapter Seven

1. Alfredo di Agostino: *La Tomba delle Anatre* (Quaderni di Villa Giulia 1964).
2. Alfredo di Agostino: *La Citta di Veio* (Nardini Booklet), p. 9.
3. Mary Cameron: *Old Etruria*, p. 27.
4. Livy: *The Early History of Rome*, Book V, 21-2.
5. Mario Torelli: An article on Veio in *Tuttitalia—Encyclopaedia of Ancient and Modern Italy*—Issue 255, Lazio II, No. 15 (Sansoni), p. 473. Dennis, p. 85.
6. Torelli: "Veio" (*Tuttitalia*), p. 474.
7. Ibid., p. 474.
8. Ibid., p. 473.
9. Mary Cameron: *Old Etruria*, p. 72.
10. Dennis: *Cities and Cemeteries*, Vol. I, pp. 118-19.
11. Torelli's article on Veio in *Tuttitalia* makes many interesting points, and is well-illustrated in black and white and colour, as is this whole edition (pp. 473-7).

Chapter Eight

1. Alfred di Agostino: *La Tomba delle Anatre* (Villa Giulia 1964).
2. Mario Torelli: "Veio" (*Tuttitalia*), p. 474.
3. Dennis: *Cities and Cemeteries*, Vol. I, pp. 121-31; Mary Cameron: *Old Etruria*, pp. 77-9; Torelli: "Veio" (*Tuttitalia*), pp. 475-6.
4. Mary Cameron: *Old Etruria*, p. 78.
5. Dennis: *Cities and Cemeteries*, pp. 122-3.
6. Mario Torelli: "Coroplastica Etrusca" (*Tuttitalia*, Issue 255, Lazio II, No. 15), pp. 464-6.

I

7. The Apollo of the Tiber is in the National Museum at the Diocletian Baths in Rome.
8. Sir Kenneth Clark: *The Nude*, pp. 37–8.
9. Friedrich Nietzsche: *The Geneology of Morals* (Doubleday Anchor edition, translated by Francis Golffing).
10. Thomas Hobbes: *Leviathan*.

Chapter Nine

1. Formed perhaps like those of Marzabotto, north of Bologna, its grid foundations still intact because, having been "captured and laid waste by the Gauls in the fourth century B.C., [it] was never rebuilt and therefore never obscured". (Pierre Grimal: *In Search of Ancient Italy*, p. 181.)
2. Mario Moretti: *Catalogue of the Villa Giulia*, p. 81.
3. Massimo Pallottino: *The Necropolis of Cerveteri* (Rome 1960), p. 6.
4. *Diodorus Silicus* (XV, 40).
5. Pallottino: *The Necropolis of Cerveteri*, p. 5.
6. Ibid., p. 6.
7. D. H. Lawrence: *Etruscan Places*, p. 109.
8. Ibid., p. 110.
9. *The Catalogue of the Villa Giulia*, p. 102.
10. Pierre Grimal: *In Search of Ancient Italy*. See also Mario Torelli's article "Le Necropoli Etrusche" in *Tuttitalia*, Issue 256, Lazio II, No. 16, pp. 514–16.

Chapter Ten

1. Pierre Grimal: *In Search of Ancient Italy*.
2. There is a large wall-map in the Gregorian Museum of the Vatican in Rome, defining the original positions of the objects.
3. Raymond Bloch: *Etruscan Art* (Pallas Library of Art, Barrie and Rockliff 1965), p. 97.
4. Mario Torelli: Article in *Tuttitalia* (256, Lazio II, No. 16), p. 503.
5. All of these objects are to be seen at the Villa Giulia and are described in the catalogue.

6. Mario Torelli: As above (see note 4), p. 503.

7. See *Catalogue of the Villa Giulia Museum*, defining the Falerii temples, p. 204.

8. In the *Catalogue of the Greek, Etruscan and Roman Paintings and Mosaics in the British Museum*, by R. P. Hinks (B.M. 1933), the dating of the two sets of slabs is discussed. Modona says they are "more or less contemporary, a little before 550". Messerschmidt places the London slabs between 600–550 and the Louvre slabs between 530–520, and Hinks is inclined to agree with Modona, while Ducati (in *Storia dell' arte etrusca*, pp. 226, 228) dates the Louvre slabs *c*. 525, later than the London. Page 5.

9. R. P. Hinks: op. cit., p. 5.

10. John Boardman: *Pre-Classical* (Pelican 1968).

11. In the Capitoline Museum, Rome.

12. From a poem by the author, called "A Former Citizen of Caere Speaks His Mind".

Chapter Eleven

1. Dennis: *Cities and Cemeteries*, Vol. I, pp. 426–7.

2. D. H. Lawrence: *E.P.*, p. 182.

3. Referred to by Mario Torelli in "Le Necropoli Etrusche" (*Tuttitalia*), p. 520. and by Renato Bartoccini in his monograph on Vulci (Rome 1960), p. 7.

4. Dennis: *Cities and Cemeteries*, p. 430.

5. *Storia d'Italia*, Issue No. 1 (Fratelli Fabri 1965), p. 19.

6. Lawrence: *E.P.*, p. 195.

7. Dennis: *Cities and Cemeteries*, pp. 434–7.

8. Renato Bartoccini: *Vulci*, p. 27—"la piu misteriosa e affascinante citta dell'Etruria". Cf. Dennis, p. 429—"Can it be that here stood one of the wealthiest and most luxurious cities of ancient Italy?"

9. See *Catalogue of the Villa Giulia*, pp. 44–6 (illustrations), and 49 (text).

10. Ibid., pp. 26–9 (text and illustrations).

11. Ibid., pp. 32–3 (illustrations) and 37 (text).

12. Ibid., pp. 62–3 (illustrations) and 64 (text).

13. Dennis: *Cities and Cemeteries*, pp. 439–44.
14. Illustrations in *Catalogue of the Villa Giulia*, pp. 22–3.
15. See Article by Mario Torelli on the plastic arts of Vulci, in *Tuttitalia*, Issue 256, Lazio II, No. 16, pp. 497–500.
16. Nietzsche: *The Birth of Tragedy*.
17. On show in the British Museum, No. 545.
18. To be seen at the Villa Giulia and Gregorian (Vatican) Museums in Rome. Illustrated in a number of books, including Bartoccini's on Vulci, plates IX–XI.

Chapter Twelve

1. Dennis: *Cities and Cemeteries*, Vol. I, p. 480.
2. Mario Bucci in an article in *Tuttitalia* (Issue 215, Toscana II, No. 27), p. 856. Sovana is "una breve sosta incantata nel marasma di questa nostra moderna follia". (See also Dennis, *C. and C.*, p. 495.)
3. Dennis: *Cities and Cemeteries*, pp. 496–7.
4. Ibid., p. 494.
5. Ibid., pp. 497–500.
6. Ibid., p. 505.
7. Nietzsche: *The Birth of Tragedy*.

Chapter Thirteen

1. Dennis: *Cities and Cemeteries*, Vol. I, p. 177.
2. Mario Torelli, in an article on Falerii in *Tuttitalia* (Issue 257, Lazio II, No. 17), pp. 541–3.
3. Dennis: *Cities and Cemeteries*, pp. 192–6. Falerii Novi is magnificently described in these pages.
4. Ibid., p. 197. "Their language was said to differ from the Etruscan." Dennis notes Strabo as the source for this (*Geography* V, p. 226).
5. See *Catalogue of the Villa Giulia Museum* for definition of the periods, and for illustrations, pp. 202–28.
6. Dennis. *Cities and Cemeteries*, p. 200. Dennis quotes Zonaras, a Greek annalist, as saying that "the ancient city situated on a steep and lofty height was destroyed and another built in a place of easy access" (*Annals* VIII, 18).

Chapter Fourteen

1. Livy: *The Early History of Rome*, Book II, 13.
2. Raymond Bloch: *Etruscan Art* (Pallas), p. 99.
3. Samuel Pepys: *Diary*.
4. Mary Cameron: *Old Etruria*, pp. 149–50.
5. Pliny (*Catalogues*—36.19.91) "was very doubtful that Varro's description could be believed". This defined "a rectangular stone base, 300 feet a side, 50 feet high and including a labyrinth, surmounted by three storeys of pyramids reaching to a height of some 550 feet and hung with bells". Quoted from p. 70 of E. Richardson's book *The Etruscans* (University of Chicago Press 1964).

Chapter Fifteen

1. Anna Talocchini in an article in *Tuttitalia* (Issue 209, Toscana II, No. 21), pp. 663–5.
2. Mary Cameron: *Old Etruria*, Intro. xvi.
3. Seton Lloyd in *World Architecture* (Hamlyn 1963), pp. 18, 39, 41, with illustrations Nos. 1, 2, 70 and 72.
4. Mary Cameron: *Old Etruria*, p. 89.
5. André Malraux: *The Voices of Silence*.
6. E. M. Forster: *Howards End*.
7. Mary Cameron: *Old Etruria*. Section on Etruscan Goldwork.
8. Ibid.
9. Ibid.
10. Nietzsche: *The Birth of Tragedy*.

Chapter Sixteen

1. See article "Le Tombe e le ville" by Giorgio Monaco in *Tuttitalia* (Issue 208, Toscana II, No. 20), p. 632, and by Giacomo Caputo in Issue 190, Toscana I, No. 2, pp. 56, 58, 59.
2. William Wordsworth: "The Prelude".

Chapter Seventeen

1. D. H. Lawrence: *Etruscan Places*, p. 135.
2. Jacob Burckhardt: *The Civilization of the Renaissance in Italy* (Phaidon Press Edition), p. 107.

3. Dennis: *Cities and Cemeteries*, Vol. I, p. 532.
4. Ibid., p. 531. Dennis thought that the Fanum Voltumnae was more likely to have been in the area of Montefiascone. The shrine is referred to by Livy in Book IV, 23, 25, 61; in Book 17; and Book VI, 2.
5. Lawrence: *Etruscan Places*, p. 211.
6. Ibid., p. 207.
7. Ibid., pp. 210–11.

Epilogue

1. Quoted in Mary Cameron's book, p. 35.
2. From a poem by the author entitled "Legacy".

BIBLIOGRAPHY

General

Livy: *The Early History of Rome.*

Tacitus: *Annals.*

George Dennis: *The Cities and Cemeteries of Etruria.* 2 volumes (Everyman 1907).

Mary Cameron: *Old Etruria* (Methuen 1909).

P. Ducati: *Etruria Antica.* 2 volumes (Turin 1927).

M. Pallottino: *The Etruscans* (Penguin A310).

D. H. Lawrence: *Etruscan Places* (Penguin 1513).

L. Banti: *Il Mondo degli Etruschi* (Rome 1960).

A. Neppi Modona: *A Guide to Etruscan Antiquities* (Florence 1963).

E. Richardson: *The Etruscans* (University of Chicago Press 1964).

Renato Bartoccini: *Vulci* (Rome 1960).

Art

P. Ducati: *Storia dell'arte etrusca.* 2 volumes (Florence 1927).

G. Giglioli: *L'arte etrusca* (Milan 1935).

P. J. Riis: *An Introduction to Etruscan Art* (Copenhagen 1953).

V. Antonioli: *L'arte degli etruschi* (Mondadori 1955).

R. Bloch: *Etruscan Art* (Barrie and Rockliff 1965).

M. Moretti: *Catalogue of the Villa Giulia Museum* (Rome 1963).

Sculpture, Painting, etc.

L. Goldschieder: *Etruscan Sculpture* (London 1942).

M. Pallottino: *Etruscan Painting* (Skira 1952).

A. Stenico: *La pittura etrusca e romana* (Mondadori 1963).

M. Moretti: *La Tomba della Nave* (Lerici 1960).

M. Moretti: *La Tomba delle Olimpiadi* (Lerici 1960).

A. di Agostino: *La Tomba delle Anatre* (Quaderni di Villa Giulia 1964).

J. D. Beazley: *Etruscan Vase Painting* (Oxford 1947).

INDEX